BEYOND THE KAKOTOPIAS
— OF THE —
LIBERAL STATE
AND ITS NEMESES

AMERICA FREE WORKERS PARTY

IVAN MUÑIZ BROWN

AFWP Press

Paperback ISBN: 979-8-218-97870-9
eBook ISBN: 979-8-218-98566-0

Library of Congress Control Number: 2024912716

Illustrations by Richa Kinra © 2025 Ivan Muñiz-Brown. All rights reserved - used with permission.

PRINTED IN THE UNITED STATES OF AMERICA

Publication date of paperback edition: November 8th, 2024

AFWP Press
1337 N. Gardner St., Unit 5
Los Angeles, CA 90046

www.AmericaFreeWorkersParty.org
www.AFWPPress.org

ACKNOWLEDGMENTS

To the will, that most divine spark in us and the very quiddity of the Self; ergo the alfa and omega of actual and potential human life. As the rubric of God deep within, to you be all the glory.

DEDICATION

This founding work is inscribed to those who, the smiting beast notwithstanding, suffer the flickering embers of justice, liberty and truth to abide deep inside.

DISCLAIMER

I herein declare that I am not advocating overthrow of government; that I am not supporting seditious conspiracy; and that I am not inciting, assisting, engaging, or giving aid or comfort to any rebellion or insurrection by force against the authority of the United States or the laws thereof.

◆———————◆

Contents

PART I

AFWP: POLITICAL PHILOSOPHY; FOUNDING PRINCIPLES; ETHICS AND LOGIC; WHAT WE STAND FOR AND WHAT WE STAND AGAINST; THE WILL, THE BLOOD AND OUR HERO ARCHETYPE, THE ULTIMATE SUPRA-MAN.

———◆———

1. Introduction

Compatriots and compeers:

Truth has always been at the core of any successful human endeavor worthy of that name. And truth, like its most concomitant property, love, always ripples and grows outward, from the source itself to its periphery. The Stoics' cosmopolitanism certainly comes to mind when talking about ripples and ethical concentric circles. Hence the worthy enterprise unavoidably draws its first and most primordial impulse from the realm of personal experience, whether the knowledge derived thereof is intellectual or emotional in nature.

It is for this reason that I set out to create this work. Because I want to speak truth for the sake of the truth itself but also for my own sake, lest I end up in the belly of the dreaded Leviathan to suffer the indelible torture of remorse for inaction, as the ancient story goes. I intend to be as concise and clear as possible, leaving the tilting at windmills for another less pressing occasion. And if further clarifications need to be expounded upon whatever subject I am touching on, I am afraid that will have to be tackled in a later work. I truly do not want to leave any fellow worker twisting in the wind, struggling with this or that issue; but for the sake of reasonable pithiness which I am very much fond of, I have to focus on what I deem the most important fronts in this battle.

This founding treatise is intended as an infrastructure of axiomatic ideas and principles upon which the people in the future organic state must fill in the blanks, through the institutions of the America Free Workers State (AFWS), so the actualization of the party ideary (the set of ideas and principles identified with our philosophy) takes place through the workers' drives; i.e., a bottom-up proposition. All these concepts will be clarified in due time. Furthermore, my style and composition are precisely that: mine. They are, in my opinion, appropriate and adequate for the goal I intend to accomplish. Natheless this is not only an intellectual and political exercise, but also an artistic creation insofar as it is an original work. It is for this reason that I decided to remain faithful to my own idiosyncrasies and tastes; thereby the writing appears and feels as I want it to, as a reflection of who I am. As an example thereof, I can highlight my usage of both archaisms as well as neologisms of my own creation. Either way, a dictionary or the context itself will suffice to unlock the intended meaning, when a paren-thesized annotation is not present. Excursuses also abound throughout the text, for truth-seeking often requires an undaunted spirit similar to that of a terrier, always willing and eager to ferret out its prey from the promising rabbit hole. And what is an excursus, but the courageous plunge into the proverbial rabbit holes that life challenges us with from the moment consciousness bursts forth into the stage of our self-awareness? With respect to punctuation, I have opted for what is generally known as "logical punctuation", as I have just evinced. I had no choice, since the so-called "American style" of punctuation is offensive to English as a metalanguage in logic; and the overriding character of this consideration will become clearer to the reader with ev-ery passing page. Moreover, I have been forced to use the word "state" hundreds of times, because its synonyms do not quite represent the same reification of the underlying idea or they emphasize different aspects of the idea—hence I reckoned the substitution inadequate. Anyway, I am con-fident many compeers will appreciate these artistic licenses and stylistic decisions, but if they do not, at least I hope that this language does not subtract from the main purpose of conveying concepts and feelings, which is the basis of communication.

This work is also a creation at the crossroads of conscious-ness and will, so not for a second have I been tempted to disrupt the magic flow with the inappropriate and unwise chaptering of this book. Chapters represent a very old struc-ture which was invented as a means to facilitate the con-veyance of information and knowledge in an orderly and systematic fashion. I am sure they did, for the most part, succeed in that purpose; but what I have done, however, is still conducive to effective communication without hindering the organic stream. This is a stream of consciousness made whole by the unconscious contents of the Self, for I regard myself as a happy man inching ever-closer to that most desired state of individuation. I have created a table of contents so every fundamental concept preceding and following the AFWP principles are directly referenced there. I believe a book, as a partial representation of the logos as our consciousness interprets it, must be a continuum. Life itself is a continuum in the sense that no matter how small the units of time considered, there is another smaller unit above zero in which life exists. I do believe as a fundamental truth of reality within and without, that there are three golden principles ever-present everywhere: hierarchy, movement and continuity. These principles are embedded in the political philosophy of the AFWP and they will be herein fleshed out. Particularly, the principle of continuity manifests itself in my life as a modus operandi, so to speak; as the way I personally take on tasks and life itself, always being aware of whence I come, paying attention moment by moment to what I am doing, thinking, and saying as I move along. It is akin to what many people call "living here and now".

Another important concept paramount to the political philosophy that I am about to explicate is the power of symbolism. Thus I pay a lot of attention to the design of our party badge. Later in this book it will be minutely described and its symbolic meaning explained. But for now suffer me to say that symbols are the conduit used by the conscious in its hierarchic journey toward the transcendent; toward the ultimate ideal; toward the judge. They are also the means whereby the unconscious communicates with the conscious (the Jungian archetypes), and their importance to develop a balanced and integrated man cannot be overstated. Deism and its most ambitious cousin, theism, are also a potential logical conclusion for those who pay close heed to the archetypes, and on this subject matter there will be more later on.

◆———————◆

2. The source of the pathos

And I would like also to say for the record that I am well aware indeed of the uphill character of the aforementioned enterprise. It derives this peculiarity from the fact that many social constructs, in some cases long established and ingrained in the ethos of the state since its founding, will have to be utterly upended and rejected. For there is nothing more daunting for a warrior, or a philosopher for that matter, than the task of confronting and overcoming a social construct when it has become canonical over the centuries. And I do not pretend to be as naive as to believe this existential revolution, carried out through the means of this party with the goal of becoming enshrined into a new state, will happen any time soon. Or maybe even in our lifetime. But I am truly convinced it will happen nevertheless, through this party or some future version of it. Because life always finds a way to overcome, and this struggle is a matter of life and death. This sword, or work if you would rather call it that, is two-edged. On the one hand it is a treatise on political philosophy and the ensuing founding manifesto. On the other hand it is a denunciation of the dystopia we live in, whose multifaceted nature is so deeply rooted in our collective psyche that the field of its true and sound opponents has been bare for two hundred and fifty years. And allow me to say that the truth (and the love) that I intend to spread is by no means just the product of a worker's good heart seeking to prop up and feed other hungry souls, but rather the painful realization that self-preservation is also, however meekly I state it, a powerful motivational force. Indeed, I was a neurotic for a long time and my condition did nothing but worsen over the course of many years, as I suffered from crippling bouts of depression and anxiety which made me career down the very maws of self-destruction. Then happened a fateful day when by lot or should I say providence, I came across with a video about a college lecture on Carl Jung, and as the cliché goes, the rest is history. Noteworthy in the brief account of my recovery, was the rediscovery of the classics of literature and philosophy, which sadly through the rough jumbles and tumbles of my existence I had unwisely left by the wayside.

And of course a paramount element to that recovery has been my unwavering attention to my own dreams and a world of archetypes which I always paid heed to, even before I delved into Jung's works, at least in an intuitive fashion. Because indeed, I am very aware of the truths revealed by my own unconscious, which makes me wander on in this life with the inner sense of peace that we all desperately covet since the moment (and the timelines of the process are specific and personal to each of us) we behold, nay! rather stare at the bottomless pit of despair, which we proverbially start to fall into as soon as the realizations of aging, death, and a perchance purposeless life set in. But the true nature of my neuroticism was multifaceted. And it took lots of reading and studying the subject matter before I was able to pinpoint the root causes and hence its nature. I came to the painful realization that much of my neurotically experienced pathos was stemming from a deep-seated sense of imprisonment. A feeling of not belonging, not being heard, not mattering; a feeling of poignant irrelevancy and even worse, the conviction that the hemming in was so definitive that there was no way out of it. I was a number, and all the fallacies, injustice, oppressions and else that I was witnessing and experiencing were something beyond my reach, perverse lies i could do nothing about. I was coming to understand that my suffering was due to the weird nature of society itself. And it is, in sooth, this most magical triad of the world without, the world within, and the mystic will always on the move to bring those two impostors together that Friedrich Nietzsche best encapsulated when he wrote: "Whoever, at any time, has undertaken to build a new heaven has found the strength for it in his own hell."

And the more I thought about it, the stronger my belief that I was not alone in that hell. And it seemed that the loneliness and absurd emptiness of the social dimension of existence was so pervasive and ever-present because the relations that we have with "strangers" (and even with family and friends on occasion) are essentially economic; in other words, based ultimately on hard, cold "money". I began to suspect that the perennial pandemics of ennui and suicide that grip the people are just the symptoms of a body politic that is sick, nay! even worse; already dead and in the process of putrefaction. Methought the gigantic structure of the state was not synergistically matching the shallowness of the inter-relations between the cells of the body politic, and I found that quite odd. In my mind, I fancied a massive, clammy blob, perhaps the body of some huge baleen whale, slowly dying (and maybe even pointlessly) alone on some distant shore at the end of the world. I never thought of that situation as inevitable or normal, for the natural state of a body cannot be sickness and decay. These ugly fellows are always caus-ally induced, and it occurred to me that a parasite might be feeding upon our body politic. But concomitantly this bale-ful Leviathan is thriving (although superficially), building itself ever larger on the carcass of our people. It seems a foregone conclusion who the parasite is in this grim picture.

Yes, in sooth, long ago it appeared to me obvious that this administrative state expanded to enormous dimensions by bureaucrats and grifters for their own sake, was not what we workers deserved on any level of analysis. The liberal state is in fact the superstructure that veils a de facto plutocracy operating through a partitocracy with a rotating selected king at the helm, and a complex network of bureaucratized agencies propping up the entire edifice without the realm of the law. This entire setup is antidemocratic and illegitimate. It is, however, legal, because of the inductive continuity of any legal system once the state is founded (in our case in the late 18th century). In this inductive sense, all states in human history are inherently legal once established, thereby in the-ory, the constraints imposed by the law should not ever be considered in the struggle to topple an illegitimate regime (however this statement will be adequately predicated in the last section of this work). In other words, the illegitimacy of the state can be consistent with the legitimacy of the law.

The former is epistemologically an ethical concept; the latter a logical concept, namely the practical application of the principle of induction. It is for this reason that I will devote a considerable amount of time and effort to lay out the basis of legitimacy as it pertains to the realm of the state.

---

3. The paradigm

But while I struggled trying to explain to myself by what means and when we had slipped (since the very beginning of my intellectual journey, I weened that slippage very gradual), I started to delve deeper into the origins of this republic itself and the political philosophies which it was founded upon. I keenly and unrelentingly cross-referenced those aspects to the values, structures, and operations of a hypothetical state founded and developed by philosophers single-mindedly bent on protecting and nurturing the freedom, justice, respect, and prosperity of workers. Soon enough it became evident to me that the problem of what this state is not, but ought to be, was larger than once I reckoned. Indeed, this political system, in its purest and most philosophically uncorrupted form, let alone in the current state of grotesque depravation, is wholly inadequate and even more, contrary, to the ideals of a truth-based, fallacy-free, pro-worker state; to the ideals of a state set up by moral philosophers, by thinkers unabashedly basking in the bliss of knowledge, and practice of ethics and logic, both philosophical and mathematical.

For I want to establish here, loud and clear, without any further ado, the ultimate purpose of the revolution which will by and by happen and succeed if we are not all to perish in this ill-begotten, hopelessly fallacious (in the literal sense as I will prove later on), anti-worker to a ravaging degree, warped political reality. This purpose is real, practical, based on logic and ethics. This purpose is the cause of liberty, justice, respect and prosperity (material and more importantly spiritual and intellectual). This purpose is the establishment of a true democratic state with the worker at its center, for work is value and value is work. And there is no legitimate work without value, or vice versa. And money is the ultimate repository of work, and the most ready means of exchange for it. Whence the concepts of wage, debt and credit will need to be redefined as we comprehend the true nature of the one-to-one relation money-work. I will discuss all the syllogistic inferences necessary for the above conclusions and the fallacies which make the paradigm of the "liberal democracy" so pernicious to a free and just society. And I will look deeper into the sophistic equation "democracy=liberal state", which in turn has stifled the lives of so many for the sake of so few. As a result of venal picaroons ineluctably in charge of a system which is not what it purports to be, we find ourselves in the predicament of our lifetime: a state without the ethics to march forward into justice and righteousness, and without the adherence to logic and truth to look backward and critically understand the wickedness of the intellectual seed whence the tree of the present state sprang forth. Indeed, without this understanding we cannot hope to take on this most transcendental task.

4. Of words and numbers

And now I would like to take a short detour. The reason is to explain why I will take my words very seriously and consequently why I will strive to be precise in their use throughout this work. Perceived reality is expressed in our minds by symbols, among which words and numbers are very prominent. Propositional and predicate logic, for example, utilize other symbols which constitute its own particular language. But for the most part, words and numbers are the backbone of our interpretation of reality as we empirically make it out to be. A world of space, time, quality and quantity, although these concepts themselves are very problematic as to the objectivity of their understanding. However, I would say that the word is the epitome of reality because it is the apex of human comprehension and the capacity to communicate it to others; i.e., the word is superior to the number. Indeed, every number is the value of a functional relation between the empirical world and our consciousness. On the other hand, the word is the value of a functional relation between the empirical world and our psyche. This is explained by the fact that there are countless sets and subsets of numbers inductively created that are infinite; however every imaginable set of words is very much finite. Without going into endless details, by the compactness theorem every word should be able to be expressed by a number or a set of numbers, finite or infinite. However, such an operation is totally impossible to be performed. It logically follows that the quiddity of number and word must be totally different as per the sources of their origins. Because the number is evidently conscious in nature, in other words, can only be generated by a conscious function, the source of each and every word must have at least partially, an unconscious origin.

The theory that I have just sketched out is consistent with another fact: the success of Gödel-numbering and the failure of Leibniz's characteristica universalis within the framework of a universal logical calculation also called calculus ratiocinator. Indeed, Gödel was able to create a system to potentially codify through numbers every single true formula in the standard model of arithmetic. Conversely, Leibniz's pipe dream of creating a universal and formal language beyond the confines of arithmetic never came to fruition. Hence the complexity of life is unquestionably, when we strive to understand it to the fullest of our capabilities, a matter to be elucidated with words, and not with numbers.

This would explain a rather curious linguistic phenomenon: I have noticed that highly educated people are able to perceive differences in meaning between a set of synonyms whose definitions very often enter a circular pattern, invoking one another in the process. Interestingly enough, these individuals are able to discern minuscule differences in meaning and opt for the same choices within predetermined contexts. When asked why they use a word over another, the reason is elusive; they do not know why. Nevertheless, the choice is still common to all. The only explanation for this is that the origin or development of words, or at any rate of many words, is at least partly unconscious in nature;

and through the collective unconscious (using Jung's terminology and idea), we are able to interpret the nuances of
those words the same way, as an interactive organism. This
theory will be rejected by many academics stuck in their old
ways, but that is no concern of mine. I do have faith in my
ideas. Yes, faith! For after all, and contrary to the opinions of
so many educated and not, the belief in induction is indeed
the ultimate act of pure faith, for it will never be conclusively
demonstrated, empirically and otherwise. And yet, induction
is the little nasty secret shrouded in priestly hubris at the core
of the language for formal number theory, upon which arithmetic and the rest of mathematics are founded.

And going down another rabbit hole within the previous
rabbit hole, I am sure that nobody will be surprised when I
state my firm belief that this world, whatever that may mean,
is logical and not necessarily mathematical. I believe logic,
both mathematical and philosophical, has been discovered,
and that mathematics has been created. Mathematics thus,
is synthetic and not analytic, as shown by Kurt Gödel, much
to the chagrin of Bertrand Russell and Gottlob Frege. It is, in
fact, the offspring of logic plus set theory. This is tantamount
to asserting that if there is a God, or perhaps should I say
demigod, He is a logician and not a mathematician. These
statements need a massive amount of predication which is
outside the purview of this book. I will deal with these subjects and many more in a subsequent work on natural theology, logic and epistemology.

5. The Enlightenment

From the outset, this "constitutional republic", as some commentators and lawyers call it, was a regime based on property, not on work. The revolution of 1776 itself was mainly a reaction of proprietors against what was deemed at the time abusive and untoward taxation on commerce and property by the British king, which was obviously the case. But a new state, stemming from an armed insurrection, cannot be properly established unless it is founded upon a broad and coherent (albeit wrong) political philosophy of sorts. Since the Framers, whose wits and knowledge cannot be doubted in most cases, were nonetheless not particularly prone to philosophy of their own, they decided to draw their inspiration for the legal and political framework of the new state—or rather a confederation of states—from the philosophies of Francis Bacon and John Locke, with the unavoidable accommodations for the multinational character of the new enterprise. Locke was the gentleman literally acknowledged to be the intellectual creator of what we call today "liberal democracy" or "liberal representative republic". The fact that America is neither a democracy nor a republic is irrelevant compared to the fact that if it were to be, the American worker would not be better off anyway.

But before I address this most important issue, I shall delve a little further into what the Framers seemed to have in mind. Undoubtedly, to them liberty was property and property liberty, and any other considerations, rights or duties inexorably revolved around that notion. That was a revolution of the capital, of ownership and of a generation which was utterly invested in the teachings of a particular school of philosophical thought. The Enlightenment, as it is generally referred to, literally identified freedom with some sort of representative political system. They equated one term with the other. From the fallacy of referring to one as the definition of the other, even though they are concepts which do not even belong to the same genus, let alone species, all kinds of inferences were deduced and acted upon. The enthymematic conclusions deduced from that mistaken identity are the source of many discomposures, confusions and pains we are going through today, including but not limited to the prevalent theory of money; the righteous role of the state; the social and economic upheavals of our time; and the arrant misunderstanding by most of the true nature of debt, credit, work and wage.

As a Bachelor of Economics and someone who has studied for years all the differing macroeconomic models and the microeconomic theories underlying the former, I can unequivocally state that Adam Smith is probably the father of many confusions as to the quiddity of work itself, which is at the heart of a stream of other misunderstandings whose final outcome has been dozens of trillions of dollars in public and private debt, dozens of millions of homeless and "working poor" (an oxymoron accepted canonically as not a contradiction), massive levels of violence, crime and self-destruction in numberless ways, and a body of people suffering from an overwhelming malaise of spiritual, psychological and intellectual emptiness, an existential emptiness.

6. Laissez-faire

Adam Smith published his most renowned work, *An Inquiry into the Nature and Causes of the Wealth of Nations*, interestingly enough, when the American Revolution solemnly embraced a declaration which was both a battle cry and an attempt at a national ethos, Anno Domini 1776. In his book, Smith regurgitated many ideas which were already prevalent in the zeitgeist of the age, but he gave them a more formal, definitive form. In that treatise, he assertively treated the subject of work or labor in a way that has influenced countless schools of economics after him, leading so many thinkers to so many mistakes. Smith, and the rest of the laissez-faire school (Jacques de Gournay, François Quesnay, David Ricardo, etc.) for that matter, thought a worker is a commodity, i.e., the quiddity of the barber is the same as that of the haircut, and thus if the value of the latter can be determined by a price in the open market, the value of the former can also be determined by a price (wage) in another market, the labor market. But of course the fallacy in that syllogism consists in mistaking nature (what a barber is) with action (what the barber does) and hence cause with effect, thereby mixing together propositional terms that do not belong to the same genus, let alone the same class. As a result of this confusion, which has been canonically passed off as incontrovertible truth ever since, all schools of economics for over two hundred years have built in their models that grotesque concept, namely that the value of work is accurately and justly measured by the corresponding wage as established in the labor market. Evidently (even without any understanding of propositional, predicate, or modal logic), anyone should be able to spot the inherent sine qua non that

Logical labor: A new paradigm of integrative cooperation for a new state.

lies at the bottom of that idea; and that is the readily perfect substitute for every worker who does not accept the market wage as is. By equating workers to commodities, the substitution of one worker for another in the labor market can proceed on, since there is supposedly nothing immanently different between them. They are reduced to a raw material. That way the race to the bottom, or the competitive equilibrium, rages unimpeded. So ultimately as I reinstate truth to its proper place, I will conclude that the real value of work is the sum of the market value, i.e., the competitive wage, plus the marginal value as determined by the marginal utility that the employer receives from that worker in the absence of an alternative.

In other words, if we are to figure out the just worker compensation in any given situation, we ought to ensure employer and worker negotiate under the assumption that the latter cannot be readily substituted by the former for another worker willing to work for less. In practical terms, this concept is tantamount to the idea of an all-inclusive unionization of both workers and employers where the contracts are laid out so the worker receives the maximum compensation beyond which the employer would not be interested in continuing operations. At that point, the employer still achieves a level of profit whose marginal utility is big enough as to make the ceasing of operations undesirable.

Through this political mechanism, which is the social enactment of a construct by legal means first until it becomes a fixture in the ethos of the people (I will herein expatiate on this concept from different perspectives), we are transmuting a competition on prices of labor power (wages) into a competition on quality and intensity of work. Thereby we are metamorphosing productivity into what righteously ought to be: not a race to the bottom, but rather an endeavor to the top. And this rebirth will be infused, through doctrine and law, with the intensional or organic quality of the National Liberextremist State. I will further define, explain, and elaborate on these concepts by and by, but for now the most relevant idea is that of transforming a search for the lowest possible salary that a worker would accept in exchange for his labor power, into a search for the highest salary that an entrepreneur would pay for labor power above which he would not want to stay in business.

Therefore, if something must be comprehended after reading these initial pages is the following: liberalism is an ideology wherewith the economic construct of wage labor is passed off as the necessary feature—and not a contingent accident—of a mode of production called laissez-faire capitalism. By virtue of this function alone, liberalism is sophistry. Thus its ideological offspring, the liberal state, is immanently a fallacious enterprise, contaminated from its very genesis.

But as a side note, from where did Smith and other proponents of laissez-faire capitalism draw their ideas? At the time these theories were taking shape all across Europe, the depraved institution of slavery was being challenged and progressively eradicated, in some countries earlier and in other countries later on. This reality had the potential of a huge disruption to the interests of the ruling castes at the time. If serfdom and slavery were done away with, the production and transportation costs of raw materials could potentially spiral out of control. Additionally, the incipient bourgeois industrial class saw themselves ultimately unable to reap the benefits of that wicked institution, as land owners and merchants had done historically. What a convenient coincidence that just when slavery was about to die away, these gentlemen came up with the idea of laissez-faire! Undoubtedly, a quite perfect substitute for the slave of old is the slave of the new world order, where his essence is reduced to a commodity, and hence subjected to a type of slavery particularly pernicious, as now the worker cannot even stand on a higher moral ground and decry his state of enslavement—because after all, everything is perpetrated "voluntarily". How devious and grotesque are those shackles, when the tormented cannot even claim that the chains even exist!

Laissez-faire capitalism in regard to work is predatory within, whereas economic systems based on colonialism and mercantilism are predatory without, regardless of the mode of production. In other words, prior to laissez-faire some workers were kidnapped, carried across oceans and finally exploited by force in a state of slavery. When the "enlightened" understood that that state of affairs would irrevocably break down, they came up with a suitable alternative. So when nowadays we mention "modern day slavery", that reference is actually rooted in moral and economic philosophy and history, much more so than most even suspect! The "Enlightenment" and its concomitant economic system, liberal capitalism, effectively gave philosophical cover and institutionalized the proverbial "homo homini lupus est". It has been an intellectual disservice that I qualify as the most disastrous set of ideas put forth in centuries, and we workers and the whole of the nation are suffering their consequences as we speak.

So, as I already pointed out, the American Revolution, like the laissez-faire revolution on the philosophical and ideological side, were entirely revolutions of the proprietor and therefore the end result, both politically and intellectually, laid squarely their foundations on the backs of workers—whose very quiddity was stamped out and distorted by devious ideas poorly cobbled together. In fact, the moral bankruptcy of those who have hitherto espoused the economic conclusions of the Enlightenment and laissez-faire capitalism, or liberal capitalism, know no bounds or shame. For Adam Smith, in his foregoing book, literally equates workers to working beasts such as cattle, from an economic perspective. Drudges or working stiffs, as some call us, are deemed not above brutes in a substantial way and their quiddity thus, a shared reality. This individual has been the lauded hero or at least inspiration of political economists of all persuasions to this day, with the notable exception of Karl Marx. It does convey a wealth of information about the depravity and absurdity of liberal economists and apologists generally when even Marx (I will hereinafter engage in an epistemological and economic deconstruction of this gentleman's political economy) seems to make more sense!

---

7. Strikes

I feel compelled now to briefly touch upon a subject which I think is both revealing and particularly poignant, and I will herein broach it again in a different context. This is the matter of the so-called "labor movement" and one of its more concomitant tactics, namely the strike. For centuries now, ever since the advent of the "industrial revolution", the strike has been the last resort of a desperate working population confronting a ruling caste and a state that exists only to serve the interests of that power caste. In sooth, I can assert that strikes have always been and still are the squirms and squiggles of a community struggling helplessly to realize the AFWP ideals within the liberal kakotopia. As I already intimated, those ideals can be only materialized within the AFWS (this statement will be amply explained and proven throughout this work), because the liberal paradigm is incompatible with the notion of logical capitalism (a concept expounded upon later in this document), or an economic system where the dynamic set of wage equilibriums is a reflection of a meeting of marginal utilities and marginal labor values. The wage labor theory, or "wagslave labor" as is my wont to call it, upon which classical capitalism and its modern liberal versions (corporate creditism, state-sponsored capitalism, etc.) are predicated, will evermore render any and all labor struggles ineffective (with the exception of a nationwide general strike under circumstances which will be treated in the last section of this book). For it is impossible to reach a state of justice and grace by ameliorating a state of depravity and injustice. The former state will never be born out of the latter, for their very nature is contrary to one another. It will take a revolution, not an evolution. And it is in this most important topic where the instruments of this mammoth state to quell workers' opposition manifest themselves glaringly to say the least. Indeed, back in the day, at the onset of the labor movement and for many decades thereafter, the state and the proprietor caste tried to crush union activity (including strikes), by a combination of legislation and violence carried out by police forces and hired goons. Over the long haul, however, it became increasingly obvious that the ruling caste could not forestall the ever-increasing demands of unionized workers. These unions were able to move the needle toward an equilibrium which, albeit within the constraints of the liberal paradigm, and therefore qualitatively of the same nature, nonetheless in quantitative terms is substantially above the rock bottom the elites had grown accustomed to enjoy for so long.

So the tactics, or should I say the strategies, of the upper echelons of the laissez-faire state's managerial caste dramatically evolved. Instead of repression through antidemocratic laws and brute force, the system almost in such an organic way as to call it homeostasis-driven, pivoted to a much more slick, encompassing and comprehensive approach. It involved a number of interrelated elements: indoctrination in schools, propaganda through corporate media (traditional media at first and also social media in the last decades), and ultimately infiltration of the political and labor organizations themselves. The main instrument of indoctrination and propaganda is the constant dwelling on a barrage of tangential issues along circumstantial lines, namely gender and sexual identity, sexuality, race, religion, national origin, immigration status and others. This reticulation (an exhaustive and mutually exclusive division) of the phalanxes of American workers allows for a total disintegration of the revolutionary drive behind each and every worker, which hinges ultimately in his identity, precisely, as a worker. But the ultimate tool of the state and the power elite which manages it for its own profit and that of the usufructuary caste, or donor caste, is massive and systemic shilling and deception through infiltration. There can be no mistake about this: by their deeds you will know them. This self-explanatory biblical reference should serve us as a lodestar when we navigate the muddled and treacherous sea of politics in the liberal Leviathan. Indeed, a swath of politicians claim to be "leftists", "socialists", or "progressives". And yet, instead of advancing the cause of liberty, justice, respect and prosperity for workers, they reticulate our phalanxes into a cancellate mass, ruthlessly practicing what we call these days "identity politics", thereby dynamiting our revolutionary strength by obliterating our shared quiddity.

How patently and painfully obvious this con job on workers is! And nevertheless how effective, perchance due to the befuddled condition that the indoctrination and propaganda arms of the state have shoved masses of workers into. And I am sure the lobotomizing effect of mass entertainment (cinema, music, professional sports, social media platforms, etc.) plays also a critical role in this scheme. It is so insulting to hear these "leftists" espouse the same policies that the Chamber of Commerce relies on to make its members and the biggest multinational corporations ever richer: cheap labor at home through open borders and slave labor abroad through open trade and offshoring. And when an upheaval looms in the horizon in the form of a strike, its extent and force is conveniently limited and weakened by the omnipresent lack of acknowledgment and support from those same "leftist" politicians ... until the revolt fizzles out into oblivion. Those "socialists" are in effect serving the regime as the intellectual and operational scabs they are, getting rich and holding onto power in the process; all for their own selfish sakes and those of their families. These shills are unabashedly wicked, and they will be the first ones to be held accountable retroactively by the AFWS. I place the union bosses across the country in the same category, for their activities as paid actors and assets for this caste system could not be any more evident. They are effectually acting as slick temperers of the workers' goals and actions, and their paid-for gaslighting is nothing short of criminal.

Therefore, it is our will that:

◆————————◆

8. First founding principle: logical labor

"All workers and employers will be integrated in an all-encompassing union at a company or sector level wherewith free negotiations will occur as if the total labor supply were limited to that contained in the union itself, so as to procure a connection between the employer's marginal utility from labor taken and the worker's marginal value of labor given. This mechanism ensures an equilibrium, local and general, where the employees receive the maximum compensation for their work beyond which the employers would be better off ceasing operations."

This first principle is especially endearing to me, because it is not only the conclusion of an intellectual exercise, but also the result of the acumen developed through personal experiences and the emotions attached to them.

---

9. Worker above citizen

For indeed, my most esteemed badge of honor is not to be a citizen, but a worker. Citizenship is exogenous, a contingent circumstance; an accident for those who were born in the land, and the culmination of a legal process for those who naturalized, whereby the state granted you that legal status. But to become and remain a worker is up to you, to your own ethics and effort. It is the result of your personal actions and behavior; it is not awarded or bequeathed to you. Nobody gave it to you so nobody can take it away. Its merits are not judged by a higher authority, but born out of the ethical action of work itself. It is an absolute value, and therefore one of the safest guides in life, in this perennial struggle toward the ideal. Therefore, to be a worker is to position and orient yourself in life. Then you become a revolutionary (which is an inevitable conclusion if you are an honest philosopher); this is my second most precious title. That energy within you propels the movement toward our perennial ideal judge; our lodestar. The perilous pilgrimage is a struggling slog, constantly wading through the muddy waters of the liberal dystopia. The journey might be tiring and long, possibly yielding a life of sacrifices and sufferings of all sorts. In the end, the practical manifestation of the worker/revolutionary reaching the ideal is the becoming of a citizen in the new AFWS. And I am not only a worker, but a poor worker, a drudge. This is yet another advantage in the struggle. Why? Because this condition compels me to delve into the issues not only logically, but also emotionally, since I feel the subject matters personally. And in the hierarchy of truth, the knowledge we derive from the output of the entire psyche is superior to that derived only from consciousness and its concomitant process, rationality. For life is way too convoluted to cut off a huge part of our psyche in the quest for truth. For this reason, when I feel the issues personally, I am evermore able to transcend our cause and turn it into the necessary political actions through the unquenchable fire of passion. Not to mistake this mechanism with any kind of aversion to my own condition; to the contrary, I have come to embrace it and I quite enjoy this journey.

⟶———⟵

10. A logical revolution; a clean break

I hope it is by now patent that we are not right, left or center. We are not conservative or liberal. We do not hew at all to the revolutions of old, namely socialism, marxism, communism, fascism or national socialism. And even though we are philosophically repulsed by the liberal abomination, we do not set goals or policies as a reaction to it. We do not come into existence out of the sins of the present regime or its counterparts. We are up and forward; we are the revolution of the judge, the eternal ideal toward which we orient ourselves in life, ethically, psychologically, spiritually and politically. We do not operate within the confines of the liberal paradigm, neither within the bounds of its antitheses. We are a revolution of virtue and truth. We are not born out of negations of old vices but out of the affirmation of newly found dreams and aspirations. Yes, indeed! We are the revolution of the new, and not the revolution of the contrary. And we are the sons and daughters of our time. Let the old rot die and let us fearlessly build upon the righteous new. Besides, let us not ever forget that philosophy is revolution, and not history. In the course of this book I will instantiate the meaning of this over and over again in many different ways, so as to make perfectly clear the practical and logical conclusions of our movement.

We are also the revolution of logic, unlike the failures of the past. Pray, pay now close attention to the following propositional argument:

Let us say formula A stands for "To live in a liberal state". Let us say now formula B stands for "To live in toxicity". Let us consider the truth-functional connective "implication" as termed in English as a metalanguage, as well as the truth-functional connective "negation". Let us now ponder the compound formula "A then B". And let us remember:

1. The revolutionary nemeses of the liberal state, namely socialism, fascism, national socialism, and the rest, were born out of the fundamental negation of anything liberal. They were effectively the philosophical contrary of the liberal fraud, i.e., political entities whose quiddity was its diametrical negation.

2. Any revolution is predicated on a promise, not on a contingency. Not one single time in human history has a revolution been born out of the puny motto "Trust us because perhaps we are right", but always out of the forceful declaration "Trust us because we are indisputably right".

Now, by running the truth table of "A then B" and the truth table of the negation, we come to the corollary "If A then B, then if no B then no A". However, the formula "If A then B, then if no A then no B", as a simple check of the truth tables shows, is fallacious.

The anti-liberal revolutions of the 20th century were predicated on the aforementioned fallacy and therefore their validity was not a necessity, only contingent or accidental. No wonder, by draw of the proverbial empirical lot, that they ended up in disaster since they were never syllogistically sound in the first place. In other words, our initial premise "A then B" with modus ponens incorrectly applied, cannot yield necessarily "No B", and thus the calamity can be anticipated in a sound and complete fashion. However, the AFWP revolution is predicated on formula number two, which is a statement of fact and yields necessarily "No A" through modus ponens and "A then B". Consequently, we are starting our quest for the righteous state by rejecting all which is immanently objectionable, ethically and deontologically ("No B"). Proceeding thus, the organic state is a logical consequence, and not a conditional premise. In other words, our revolution is logically sound and its veracity will be proven once it is empirically completed—unlike the revolutions of yore, which were formally invalid to begin with, and hence condemned to failure.

So let us now march on, together ....

———————————

11. Indoctrination, virtue ethics, and the deontological state

Education is intrinsically indoctrination. It follows that good education must be the indoctrination of good values plus the useful knowledge necessary for a complete development of the individual, both as a free man and as a productive member of the community; of that tribe of tribes that is the nation, one day articulated and protected by the AFWS.

But what are good values? The answer to that question is and has always been found in the realm of ethics, which along with aesthetics, politics, epistemology and logic are the branches of what I call true philosophy. I consider metaphysics (with the exception of my beloved natural theology) to be related to philosophy in the same fashion that theoretical physics relates to classical mechanics, where the less useful and more pretentious sister wallows in her own shortcomings as a never-ending stream of fictional works impossible to prove on any level and bound to never become canonical, always falling by the wayside as a new school of thought erupts into the scene. So I regard those metaphysical treatises as wonderful works of fiction deserving of the brightest and most imaginative minds and worth reading as entertainment, but certainly never to be   considered serious philosophy. Ethics, on the other hand, contends with the very essence of what I deem a worthy way of living, thinking and altogether being human. It is an enterprise of the utmost importance and one which lies at the core of what our state should be all about. Men cannot live without ethics. We cannot have any kind of society, organized or even in state of transitional con-fusion, without a set of norms, principles and conventions, or canonical beliefs, wherewith we orient ourselves in terms of behavior, both personal and social.

A life rooted in spirituality backed by a track record of per-manency in literary and oral tradition is the best antidote to despondency, ennui, and ultimately neurosis. For, as Carl Jung rightly indicated, "atheism is an urban neurosis". I will take it a step further by saying urban life itself is a neurosis. Hence, the Free Workers State will indoctrinate its people into a life of communion with nature through horticulture and forestry, outdoor activities, small farming and generally rural private property itself. The state will develop policies to divvy up the land into as many proprietors as possible, and to maximize the number and quality of small farm owners, seeking to bolster the domestic production of organic, sustainable food sources. Educational programs will be implemented so as to ensure as many workers as possible are able to directly procure for themselves a certain measure, no matter how small, of their food consumption—the ultimate goal being the establish-ment of a vital relationship of the worker with the land.

Pertaining to this most important subject matter, although

not necessarily obviously so, I would like to briefly comment on my own personal habits. I am indeed what some call a lacto-ovo vegetarian February through mid-October. However, from mid-October through late January, during my chosen open season, I eat the meat that I harvest during my hunting outings. That translates into the consumption of meat just about six to twelve days a year, for ultimately I do not want others to kill on my behalf. This arrangement allows me to remain directly connected to the land not only in principle through my conscious thoughts, but through the flesh itself. Very often, during my hunting excursions, I bend down and inhale deeply while keeping my mouth and nose really close to the ground. This exercise is what I can qualify as exhilarating. I feel a savory stream of life rushing down my throat and lungs and the sensation is so intense and positive, truly like no other. I wish all my brethren the same communion I have been enjoying myself for so long.

On the spiritual front, the state will invest the youth with the armor best suited to minimize the anxiety, fear and despair inevitably spewed forth from the bottomless pit of existential doubt. Doubtless, that armor is and has been proved for millennia, what in scholastic tradition was called the heavenly virtues (cardinal and theological) and the capital virtues. Those lists partly overlap and not all the virtues are equally fitting into a 21st-century vision of our Free Workers State. Thus, the virtues which will be indoctrinated into the youth are those that will most effectively inculcate all the character traits considered most adequate to instill a sense of liberty, justice, respect and dignity among each and every person regardless of family background, profession and financial status, relationships or any endogenous or exogenous consideration.

Those virtues are: prudence, temperance, justice, fortitude, diligence, patience, and kindness. The development of these virtues will be at the core of the educational system, and they will be honed up through a myriad of theoretical and practical instruments including but not limited to classroom learning, hypnopedia, clubs (focused on sports, communion with nature through contemplation and work, charitable activities and any other active engagement deemed worthy by the people), and state-sponsored mandatory service. Both the conjoining with nature and the development of the virtuous armor will be the core of the spiritual and psychological revolution.

The aforementioned seven virtues constitute the perfect ethical infrastructure for the people to live by and the perfect bases for organic complement to the deontological state. This is just the first integrative step. Eventually, the state's ethical and political goal is the Jungian individuation of the entire body politic, and the actualization of the most divine and supra-intellectual power within, or the individual will. All of these matters and much more will be extensively treated in a prospective work on the logical and epistemological bases of natural theology and ethics, as I understand these matters in my framework, the outrage that some might feel at the reading of my words notwithstanding.

In our state, the duties of men to one another are organically materialized and aided by the economic and political structure of the state itself. And the duties themselves are causally generated by the state through its principles and institutions, rendering the Kantian categorical imperative weak and unnecessary. This runs parallel to the indoctrination of virtue ethics so as to eliminate any source of internecine strife within the body politic, because it stands to reason that the deontological orientation of an organic state must facilitate and be harmonious with the ethics of its people. Otherwise we would be witnessing an internal schizophrenic struggle yielding malcontent, confrontation, hatred, and a pervasive feeling of ennui and impotence. That is the liberal paradigm, where the state represses and castigates large swaths if not most of its people casting damning aspersions on them because their ethics are in contradiction with the state's policies, interests and priorities.

Some schools of philosophy over the last 2,500 years have come up with worthy ethical systems, cohesively defined and integrated. However, I never understood many moral philosophers' obsession with axioms, categorizations and properties to the exclusion of practical matters. I argue the only two essential characteristics of an ethical system are teachability and functionality. Any moral philosophy that does not revolve around these two concepts fails its innate purposes, which are to give guidance and inject order and justice into the body politic; and to enhance the subjective attributes of the individual to successfully undergo a process of individuation and the maximization of the creative and literally transcendental powers of the will. Therefore, the most important part of any treatise on ethics should be related to how effectively it can be taught and to its teleological value (this last statement will be predicated later on).

Indeed, I will affirm that ethics or moral philosophy should be considered a branch of political philosophy. Ethics are a subject of consequential reflection within a body politic, or at least that is the implicit assumption that historically has been made. When we talk about ethics we are really talking about not only thoughts, but more importantly actions, behaviors and habits that generally involve others more than ourselves or God. It is the most quintessentially practical branch of philosophy, and it is social in nature. However, to my dismay, many giants of philosophy throughout history, in their dissertations about ethics, have hopelessly created traceried narratives interjecting metaphysics into the subject matter, and the result has been a muddled confusion, very much to the chagrin of just about everybody, contemporaneous or not.

Case in point is what they call nominative and meta-ethical moral relativism, the ill-begotten offspring of postmodernism, a philosophy nowadays very influential in decaying academic circles and one that has bled off deep into the ethos of some subcultures, introducing chaos and purposeless anxiety and despair galore. Postmodernism itself is an extreme case of solipsism and ultimately its roots date back to the most prominent of the rationalists in the 17th century, namely René Descartes. No matter how some want to sever his connection to the genesis of that disintegration of thought or postmodernism, I believe that the grandfather of that school is Descartes. Taken to its logical conclusion, his philosophy of mind renders postmodernism. More generally, I have always found Cartesian metaphysics catastrophically absurd, very much worthy of a Frenchman. Nevertheless, his genius as a mathematician amply offsets any philosophical shortcomings.

And moving on to the purely intellectual side, special emphasis will be placed on the trivium (logic, grammar and oratory), aesthetics, political philosophy and of course natural theology; for I regard it as the true and most solid of all branches of metaphysics, and the worthiest of study. Ours will be a state of informed, critically thinking, moral and healthy workers, physically and psychologically. And it is worthy of noting that one of the most important deontological duties of the AFWS will be the well-researched and informed counseling of the youth as to what studies or courses to pursue given their temperament and natural abilities and disposition, on a case-by-case basis. Thereupon the youth will choose at the fork between college or vocational schools, or even perhaps other alternatives, once their mandatory militia service is completed at age 21 (more about this service later). This optimal matching is partly the duty of the state because it benefits immensely from the work of people when they are making a living out of their calling and passions, maximizing their productivity in the process. In consequence, the state must contribute to the actuality of that individual potentiality so as to become the causal agent of that whence it profits, making it thus a partner with the people and not a mere passive and even worse, parasitic beneficiary.

We do not believe in a state religion, but we acknowledge that spirituality comes in many forms, with or without dogma, and these decisions are appropriate to be made within the nuclear family. In the end, everybody is religious; unfortunately many saunter through life unaware of their secular god or gods, calling themselves "enlightened", "atheists", and all the rest.

12. The grandest narrative: the purest spring of functional ethics

However there is a caveat to what I just stated. At this juncture it is paramount to take a brief but necessary detour.

Human life is and has always been, as interpreted in our consciousness through the logos, a narrative. Ethics are and always have been the comprehensive sets of corollaries to narratives. And the grandest narrative in human history is, by its very definition, revelation. For if God exists, what could possibly be grander than His word? Therefore religious dogma, which is the corollary to the grandest narrative that ever existed, is the basis for the strongest and most enduring and effective of all ethics. If we reject that foundation we are in essence removing the safest possible bulwark between man's deeds and his natural proclivity to wickedness, since the natural state of man is not individuation; in other words, the massive subconscious contents of his mind have not been harmonically integrated into his ego. Tearing down theist beliefs without a sufficiently strong alternative is psychopathic, and there is not a proven alternative for the time being. Which leads me to another question that I will address in due time, namely the role of psychopaths and their catastrophic actions throughout the upper echelons in the state's apparatus, both as an accident and by design. Furthermore, the patent animadversion that many atheists feel for Carl Jung is anything but unjustified. For in my opinion, or my philosophical interpretation of his work, the Swiss psychologist and philosopher went beyond the debate about the existence of God and instead proved another thesis: irrespective of His existence, we as a species need Him.

⬥————————⬥

13. Beyond His existence, God as a biological and hence necessary function

I think Jung's thesis is much more powerful from a practical standpoint, because within it we find the logical reasons for a deist, or even a theist ethics. Jung proved that the unconscious communicates with the conscious mind through what he termed the archetypes, symbolic figures we can picture in dreams and which also have been profusely represented in art throughout history. The grandest of those archetypes is the archetype of the Self, a divine archetype in nature, representative of our God-like quiddity once we have gone through the process of individuation, using Jung's terminology. The archetype of the Self is the God within. It is the ideal man, who lies dormant in us only to spring forth into existence once we have harmonically integrated our initially fractured psyche. That is the man, using modern verbiage, who has become enlightened or awakened. But if we as a species, since time immemorial (even before recorded history, going as far back as the onset of our collective unconscious itself), have this image-concept of God himself, the utmost ideal judge, even before we could consciously develop the idea of God; it stands to reason that this idea represented by the archetype of the Self is something innate, inherent to our very biological nature. In other words, it goes far beyond an idea or concept engendered or imagined by our conscious mind. And since what we are biologically is by definition necessary to be what we are, it automatically follows that we need God; or at least we need the concept of Him. And with this I will put an end to my logical rather than metaphysical reasoning. Certainly a detour from our journey, but a necessary one in order to clarify the drive behind our ethics. Much more about these transcendental issues will be offered in a subsequent tome.

And as a complementary note to what I just expounded upon, I would like to bring up now one of my favorite poems of all time, at least in the English language: "If—" by Rudyard Kipling. In this poem, Kipling describes the potentiality of a man which corresponds with what Jung termed a few decades later a man who has undergone successfully the process of individuation. The ultimate goal of the education system within the AFWS is to facilitate such process of individuation for all workers, and it is my firm belief that a life lived by the standards of our virtue ethics will be very much conducive to that goal. Implicit within that ethical framework is the rejection of blind empiricism and materialism. And I will state categorically that that rejection will have as a byproduct in the long run the development of awakened, individuated, spiritual and centered men. Sometimes people have difficulties in undergoing an individuation process because the magnitude of the endeavor is too daunting and the psychological labor too taxing, without going any deeper into this matter. But the development of an ethical behavior that results in a rejection of materialism and mindless empiricism is something which can be easily achieved through training and indoctrination, after which we are in a state much more receptive to the changes we need to implement that individuation process. So here we can see immediately a very positive synergy between the end goal and the mechanisms of the state.

---

14. The youth militia

But it stands to reason that if all of the above is a collective effort for the benefit of the community, of the tribe of tribes that constitutes the nation, it follows that the state should guarantee the happy completion of that effort by taking direct command and responsibility in the whole affair. And that responsibility has to reassert itself unequivocally through the means of a state monopoly in the education/indoctrination of the youth in those teachings and philosophical principles, all the way through college and vocational schools. For what benefit is to be found in a competition which is to drain valuable resources from the ultimate goal, and without yielding the same levels of ethical and educational standards?

The process of sociopolitical integration of the youth should be completed by the establishment and proper management of a three-year compulsory program for ages 18–21

The National Liberextremist Youth: The crucible of brotherhood through the intensional dimension of the AFWS.

whereby a properly attired, regimented and regulated militia of active members should engage in productive labor and learning, including the subjects and activities already mentioned: forestry, farming and gardening, crafts, road works and other public works, altruistic endeavors, the study of the classics of philosophy and literature, more formal and mathematical logic, endurance and strength sports, and of course marksmanship. For it is the ultimate Platonic goal to turn citizens into warrior-like philosophers with an unwavering and steely work ethic, the most virtuous of all possible functions of the state; workers with an uncompromising and overwhelming passion for love of others and truth, for justice as commonly defined in the sense of virtue, and for freedom (to think and act as your reason and conscience prompts you). Marksmanship is certainly an ability to be taught, systematically practiced and encouraged in order to create a nation of party members who can effectively have plenipotentiary powers to keep tabs on their government, so it never drifts off the course mapped out by the revolution. To this end gun ownership will be promoted. Additionally, a nation of armed and able workers is the most powerful deterrent to unwanted foreign interventions. National defense should be a true national cause, not entrusted to the few, but ensured by all, or at least by many. More about this most important topic later.

In that regimented militia, people from all walks of life will serve shoulder to shoulder as true brethren. Economic status, ethnicity, religion, and any other possible tribal factor will be rendered irrelevant in the service of one another and the whole of the people, through the Free Workers State. Those years of intense camaraderie will forge friendships and loyalties across the board which will further our ultimate goal of development of a true national community, where each one of us will become truly our brother's keeper. Our brotherhood will not be based on religion, economic or social status, ethnic background, sexuality, or any other circumstantial factor. Our allegiance will be founded on a shared ethos, political ideary and love for the country that makes it possible. Our communion will endure; it will be all-pervasive and ever-purposeful. We will forever share the conviction that we are not a body, but rather that we are spiritual beings inhabiting one, in deep communion with one another in the body politic. We embrace our transcendental nature to the fullest; hence we know our body is an outpost even more than a fane. It will not be only about the logos, but about the world of action too. In sum, the goal of this militia is the development of a youth physically indefatigable, emotionally unconquerable, politically fanatical, and ethically unshakable. We are looking forward to it.

And without more preambles, it is our will that:

---

15. Second founding principle: comprehensive indoctrination

"The education of the youth will be carried out by the state on a monopoly basis, and through the appropriate courses and curricula the ultimate goals of love for virtue, freedom, truth and justice will be perennially branded in their minds consciously as well as on a deeper unconscious level. A state-sponsored and partially self-sustained militia ages 18–21 will precede college and vocational training, whereby a conscientious worker, ever-questioning philosopher and virtuous man will merge harmonically into one, ready to spring forth into the world for his own sake and that of his brethren."

---

16. Money's genesis and essence: the tool to barter work

I would argue that one of the topics most brazenly jumbled and distorted over the last centuries is the concept of money. The reasons for that canonical intellectual tergiversation were always—surprised?—spurious. To put it simply, they have been for the benefit of the few at the expense of the many. It has been always accepted that money itself, whether backed by actual gold reserves or other commodities, or printed ex nihilo, is issued by the government on behalf of the people and hence the physical notes are public property (I will hereinafter predicate this statement in the context of central banking), but the value they supposedly represent is private property belonging to the actual possessor of those moneys. Countless treatises on this subject matter have been published over the centuries, and it is a most important issue in any college of economics. The concept of money, in its current form, is so convoluted as to allow for any government to print it at will so they can cover expenditures they could not fund otherwise. It goes without saying that deficit spending is always paid off through higher inflation or less employment due to misallocation of assets, bigger debt and consequently higher taxes and untoward expansion of the credit market, or through a combination of all of the above.

Obviously, workers are the first and foremost victims of such spending. An additional and very pernicious policy, which further debases the currency and makes workers even poorer, is the practice by the central bank of buying up government debt thereby increasing the monetary supply. After all, inflation is the expansion of the monetary supply, and an increase in prices its concomitant effect. Massive government contracts for the profit of the donor caste and all sorts of calamitous policies are bankrolled by workers who get crushed by the policies I listed above. Corporate media, complicit in the scheme (since their owners are the same Wall Street characters who own everything else), refuse to denounce the practices or to explain to the people the mechanisms wherewith they are being fleeced. Meanwhile, the politicians get even richer while in office by means of insider trading, asset revaluation due to convenient "public investments" and, once they finally leave office, absurdly lucrative book deals (in most cases being mathematically impossible for the publisher to recoup the investment), speaking engagements and grotesque media gigs in which they get paid absurd amounts of money for lying, equivocating, or simply reading fiction off a teleprompter. The books, public appearances and media deals are overt kickback schemes that cannot be fought by a political system fraught with corruption and lacking the tools and the will to do the right thing.

But all this immoral framework is wrought by money. Or more specifically, by the modern meaning and utilizing of money. By today's ethos, money is a repository of wealth. And why is that? Because it is a repository of value, whose accumulation creates wealth. And why is money a repository of value? Of course, you ignoramus, because it is a repository of wealth! And so on and so forth ad infinitum. Evidently, we cannot establish a formally valid enthymeme on the basis of terms which are ill-defined. The only way to break this fallacious arguing in a circle is to go back to the original and true meaning of money. Before it was considered God. Before it was considered a depository of wealth. Before it was considered a depository of value. Before it was considered the means for trade and commerce. Even before it was considered the means to pay for labor.

Before all of that, money was, and still is in truth, an efficient way to barter work. For I do not believe money is the root of all evil, but our misunderstanding of its quiddity is. (A misunderstanding, might I add, gleefully abiding in certain minds and one which has caused so much pain to so many for so long.) Let us remember that in antiquity it was not altogether uncommon to have your wages paid in raw materials or, as we call them today, commodities. Some historians believe the etymological roots of the word "salary", which proceeds from the Latin "salarium", comes from the alleged fact that some Roman soldiers were paid their emoluments in salt. Regardless, diverse commodities have been used throughout history as money. The reason is twofold: on the one hand it was due to their psychical properties but on the other hand because their value was intrinsically linked up to the work performed to obtain them. Once this going back to the future is established, I wonder how wicked or ill-conceived practices like lending at a profit (let alone exorbitantly high interests) could possibly happen. For if you understand that money is a repository of work and the means to conscientiously barter it and measure it, and if you understand legitimate work itself properly carried out is the cardinal virtue of diligence (and not all activities that generate money ought to exist since many of those are not legitimate work), it follows that follies involving money or work will be avoided by any worker or generally a person of any integrity; and by a state which calls itself legitimate. (However, unethical behavior involving money and all its implications will be regarded as a weapon in the struggle against the illegitimate kakistocracy, later in this work.)

17. Usury

Indeed, for millennia and in some cases well into the 20th century, many countries, especially of the Catholic tradition, had the crime of "usury" in their penal codes. The philosophical roots of that crime are to be found in the original concept of money which I just laid out. For if money is work, lending at an interest is akin to enslaving others, since the lender obtains fruits which are not the result of any work added by him to the total social product, beyond the work already traded. It was considered quite literally an illegitimate activity with an additional negative effect, insofar as it encourages the debtor's impulse to live beyond his work (or means), which is the rejection of prudence. So in sum, it is this true quiddity of money that prompts me to consider the expression "work money" far superior, literal and more descriptive than the expressions "make money" or "earn money".

Here I find pertinent to bring up a biblical verse, Matthew 19:24, which too many philosophers and even theologians fall very short of understanding in connection with the true meaning of money itself. It reads: "And again I say unto you, It is easier for a camel to go through the eye of a needle, than for a rich man to enter into the kingdom of God." Indeed, the farther back we go into history and away from the Enlightenment, the greater the comprehension of money. It is precisely that understanding which compelled the disgust and even hatred for many people involved in money-lending. That frowning upon the accumulation of money by way of interests did not spare traders and merchants either, although those were viewed with more sympathy, since they were providing an invaluable service by making goods accessible which otherwise could not be enjoyed. In other words, they were viewed as workers. The royals and noblemen were not workers, but their riches were often attributed to their very status, a blood right, so to speak; an entitlement endowed by God himself and therefore worthy of exception. But those who accumulated money without working or without a blood exception were considered leeches feeding off the healthy body of a people. Not until the Enlightenment came about were bankers and lenders accepted by many at last as productive members of society.

But of course those 18th-century intellectuals told us all this was sheer nonsense, for paraphrasing Adam Smith, "What is the difference between a barber and a haircut? ... None!" As I already mentioned earlier, this propositional fallacy is the cause of innumerable and devastating developments which, even though they were already brooding and manifesting in countless ways prior to the Enlightenment, burst forth totally unbridled ever since. The "enlightened" crowd, those who inspired the notorious absolutist motto, "Everything for the people, nothing by the people", effectually created the liberal monster. A stultified and totally ossified version of it, the managerial state, is America presently; and the second proposition in that maxim is the tragic inheritance by which this state lives, and even kills, today.

18. Legitimate, prior to legal

But if I have clearly stated what money is and its proper function, it follows that I accordingly delineate the activities that ought to be regarded as legitimate. I hope it has been already made clear, perhaps even painfully, how absurd is to believe that anything that "generates" money is legitimate, just because it happens to be legal. To the contrary, nothing that stems from anything but work is legitimate, irrespective of its present legal status. And only those activities that are conducive to the well-being of the people are work, for who would freely exchange his own work for that of another if it is not truly beneficial to him personally, or to his family and community more generally? So right here and right now, I will unequivocally declare that nothing that is not legitimate should be legal, and everything that is illegal should be illegitimate. And thus in this revolutionary fashion, the Free Workers State will link up, conceptually and practically, work with money, money with legitimacy, legitimacy with legality, and legality with the virtues that we hold dear and are at the foundation of the state itself.

Notice that the heart of this soritical sequence (for indeed work is condensed virtue) is legitimacy. By making legitimacy a prerequisite to legality, we slash corruption by majority at the knees, making the state and the people ever closer. Corruption by majority or multilevel systemic corruption in the administration of the state is one of the most stifling and habitual onslaughts that workers in "liberal democracies" are forced to endure. The laissez-faire state itself does not have any meaningful mechanisms to fend off that kind of corruption, and the matter stands so by design. In fact, the zeitgeist of the time (roughly early to mid-18th century) was one of profound spiritual corruption, or what they called liberation from the old Christian dogmatic shackles. The ruling bureaucratic caste felt entitled to undue compensation for all their work to advance the welfare of the "lower classes" and they proceeded to engage in corruption schemes of all sorts without the nagging conviction that "He" was watching.

That moral vacuum, that cataclysmic devolving into the belief that there is not a judge anymore, which mounts to believing that there is not an absolute ideal we should all strive for, is the crux of the rot within the liberal state. That neurotic ethos was embraced by subsequent political ideologies and movements that emerged all across Europe in the 19th and early 20th centuries, namely socialism first, and later on Marxism, communism, fascism and national socialism. All of them were ill-begotten attempts to overcome the rotten laissez-faire paradigm. As they took hold of different countries in the continent, they eventually collided with one another in a futile pursuit of total political, economic and territorial hegemony. Some of those countries were financially aided by international banksters interested in the obliteration of states outside the purview of fractional reserve banking, the sham whereby that clique of lazy usurers manage to bleed the workers in liberal states dry. But at the very core of all those movements there was an irreconcilable enmity against the political system born out of the philosophical decay of the Enlightenment. Those anti-liberal philosophies were doomed to fail, for no successful revolution can be anchored solely on a negative ethos, or the negation of a prevalent culture (as I already exposed from the standpoint of propositional logic). It has to be born and grow out of the minds and hearts of workers able and willing to soar up way above the predominant political reality and envision something entirely new, not as a negation of the old, but as a totally original spring that flows forth untainted by rancor of any kind. Thenceforth an organic state becomes a possibility.

No legitimate revolutionary movement can lay out and structure a new state on the basis of the negation of old ideas, for that is a recipe for unsatisfactory results. On the contrary, first we must envision what we want according to virtue, and then that vision must confront the current state. The intellectual path of this process is the inverse course of that taken by those frustrated revolutions of yore. They were unoriginal, and at their onset was already planted deep within the rotten seed of injustice and tyranny. For the opposite of injustice and tyranny is not justice and freedom, but only another type of injustice and tyranny. It is an old philosophical idea that good is not the opposite of bad, but rather its absence. And without question, that idea has been proven sound by the disastrous consequences that the mentioned anti-liberal revolutions brought about.

But as I just stated, at the heart of the syllogistic connection between work and law is legitimacy. So what is it exactly? And how can it be brought into existence? Legitimacy is the quality of created action according to the canonical virtues we already talked about. In other words, legitimacy is the quiddity of anything created if it is virtuous. Sometimes the immanent legitimacy of an activity is transparent. Other times it must be ascertained by more conscious means and an intellectually honest debate on the subject would be appropriate. Ultimately, if we cannot attain a formally valid conclusion by means of philosophical logic, it is the duty of the people, the educated workers themselves, to establish the validity and morality, i.e., legitimacy of any hypothetical endeavor or already functioning enterprise. And this means direct vote on the question at hand. This is the tool and I would argue the litmus test of a true direct democracy: the referendum. And we will make sure the worker-voter has been already established beyond any doubt as a moral philosopher by means of the educational system, for what good can be derived from the vote of unethical or uneducated individuals? So on matters of the utmost importance for the state and hence the people, and when logic is not conclusive, it is the worker himself who will judge upon legitimacy through the gavel of the vote. And so we have harmonically blended together in a logical sequence work with money, legitimacy, virtue and ultimately law.

Many passages will be dedicated to evaluate the legitimacy of this or that policy in many different fields, but it is my obligation now to give some explanatory examples of how certain activities and enterprises are illegitimate and therefore impossible to be legal in the Free Workers State.

One glaring example is the mass media. Hellbent on spreading lies, made-up stories, and hatred for one another on the basis of group identity (whether that group be political, racial, sexual, etc.), corporate media, also called state media, is an illegitimate business and so it will not exist in the AFWS. The definition of intellectual dishonesty is the deliberate engagement in sophistry, and that activity will be eradicated from the public discourse without hesitation. It stands to reason that the nefariousness of that activity is enhanced by the purpose thereof, namely keeping our workers' minds distracted by tangential issues and divided along circumstantial lines so the current status quo can be maintained. Divide et impera from within will not be tolerated because it is essentially an anti-virtue criminal activity which adds nothing to the national output of work. The people engaged in these unproductive, illegitimate, anti-worker activities will be given the opportunity to put their talents to virtuous efforts and be retrained into other fields.

Another related activity, even more destructive and illegitimate than corporate propaganda, is corporate censorship. Any organization that engages in the suffocating of the voices of the people in the public sphere, by any means, technological or otherwise, will be seized, properly dismantled, and liquidated through the budgetary process for the benefit of the people. And those involved in that repression will be accordingly retrained so they can do something productive with their lives; in other words, they will be retrained so they can finally work.

I hope by now it is made sufficiently clear the seriousness wherewith the AFWS will adhere practically and conceptually to the logical sequence connecting work, money, legitimacy, virtue and law. It is the ultimate triumph of reason and goodness; the ultimate blend of justice and liberty; the ultimate fusion of respect and prosperity for workers.

And I am certain that it is abundantly clear by now how boundless my abhorrence of the liberal paradigm is. That 18th-century concoction of limitless hubris, moral decay, intellectual narcissism and shortsighted empiricism, is the source of this state of confusion, stagnation and ennuis that we find ourselves bogged down into. Yes, and a thousand times yes! or a million or a trillion! It is beyond any reasonable doubt that the 18th century gave us the horrors and chaos of the 20th, and the desperation, unsatisfaction, and emptiness of the 21st. We are stuck in a paradigm which in its current form will stop at nothing to keep the workers divided, stupefied and utterly addled with tangential issues (very often artificially created), uncalled-for wars, and a never-ending stream of trickery and manipulation so the usufructuary caste keeps on illegitimately profiting from us, the workers. The kabuki dance played out in corporate and social media, Washington, D.C., and academia; this absurd omelette of inconsequential debates about the old and new tropes of deception, is tragically working out as intended. We workers are being spiritually asphyxiated so the will to power and to a new national order is forever kept stunted. This oppression forestalls the awakening and yearning for more freedom, justice, prosperity (intellectual as much as material) and respect which inevitably would arise without the walls of this liberal paradigm; this godless ruse, this empty scam, this lie ....

Wherefore we declare our will that:

19. Third founding principle: the logical chain of work-money-legitimacy-legality-virtue

"In the AFWS, legitimacy and legality will be inextricably united so all legitimate work is legal and all legal work is legitimate, according to virtue, ethics, logic, and ultimately according to direct democracy through referendum. Money will recover its true original meaning, as work in essence and its measure in practice; and all the policies of the state will be reoriented in order to reinforce that meaning. We will live by the aphorism that work is money; work has to be legitimate; legitimacy is law; and law must be infused with virtue."

I will make a pause to summarize the two basic points which reflect perhaps better than anything else how dystopian the laissez-faire state is, unwilling and incapable of probing deep within in self-reflection, lest it uncovers its baleful nature to the world. The first point is this: when an activity is not legitimate, it is by definition economically unproductive for the whole of the people, although it might yield a short-term or even a long-term profit for those engaged in it. Regardless, the state is uninterested in protecting the people from such activities, as long as they redound to the profit of the donor caste. The second point is this: the economic hallmark of an illegitimate state is the generation of deficit spending funded by an expansion of the monetary base through debt. When that happens, money becomes an illusion as it is not a reflection of actual work anymore, and it is issued at interest to boot. The inevitable result is inflation, debasement of the currency and societal decay.

20. The hopeless (and corrupted) mathematization of economics

It is at this point where I find myself compelled to delve deeper into the economic implications of the definition of work over the centuries. I must do this for the sake of both clarity and proof of validity. Economics was considered a branch of political philosophy before the 19th century. But at that time, the subject was increasingly mathematized and thus economics started to be regarded as a social science. Precisely due to this, I always found especially alluring the methodology adopted by the Austrian school of economists, who were from the start very resistant to the use of mathematics and more precisely, differential equations, in their macroeconomic models. Unfortunately, their theories and conclusions were ill-advised and nonsensical. I know because I studied macroeconomics and well-nigh all schools and models extensively when at college. I had to become very proficient at mathematics generally and differential analysis particularly. And although I found the subject really interesting, and even fun to learn and utilize, I really never took its forecast capabilities very seriously. There are two reasons for this, one empirical and one theoretical.

The empirical reason is quite obvious. Indeed, no matter the macroeconomic model we are using, the historic record of its foretelling powers is really dismal. The theoretical reason is purely mathematical, and it is the irrefutable fact that all the models are implicitly ideological in nature, thus subjective and prone to self-delusion. The mechanism for this trap is pretty straightforward: the differential equations used in the models utilize a great deal of constants, i.e., values predetermined before the model is put into motion through the equation. The values assigned to the constant are such that the equation can do nothing but guarantee the result whose ideological implications line up with the inclinations of the modeler. As a telling example, we can mention the Keynesian multiplier effect. That effect is mathematized in the form of a constant in the equations, and given a value randomly higher than one, thus reaching the conclusion, once the differential model is developed, that government spending has a more than proportional effect on national output, which in reality is predicated upon the productivity of the spending itself. Keynes was a socialist; therefore his bias needed to be reinforced by an assumption which was altogether hypothetical.

It is a case of self-fulfilling prophesy by manipulating the numbers, or better yet a case of circular reasoning where the conclusion is reached because it has already been factored into the preliminary proposition or hypothesis. It is a form of fallacious syllogism. All the mathematical models that I have studied in the field of economics (whether "right-wing" leaning or "left-wing" leaning) are riddled with these ideological, empirically unproved presuppositions substantiated either through random values assigned to constants, or through convenient restriction of domains.

Now, at the foundation of macroeconomics is the micro-economic theory of prices determined in markets by demands and supplies that are functions separately drawn up, nowadays, on the basis of utilities in the former case, and business theory in the latter case. In other words, prices and quantities in the equilibrium are the result of the mathematization of personal behavior (whether producer or consumer) and the aggregation thereof into entire economies. There is a huge number of assumptions and statistical probabilities built into the models. In the final analysis, the individual agent is simply regarded as a number in an aggregate. Not for a second did I ever think those graphs representing functions explicative of aggregate behaviors had any validity, let alone accuracy, whatsoever. Neither has ever proven that mathematization to represent reality as it stands. The questionable predictions rendered by all those models uneath ever come to pass, and when they do, a great deal of the explanation can be squarely placed at the feet of pure chance.

The truth of the matter is that economics is unlike, let us say, classical mechanics. The infinite combinations of possible behaviors by individual agents makes the mathematization and standardization an exercise of sheer faith of the wrong kind, even if we consider the matter in the aggregate and over the long haul. When it comes to people, we must consider consciousness and free will (I will address this most important topic and many more, as I already mentioned, in a comprehensive work on natural theology, epistemology and logic that I am already working on, where the axioms, theories, demonstrations and conclusions will shock many). Those two factors alone render economics and physics impossible to be lumped together in any way. However, that is what we are implicitly doing by mathematizing the former. So there is no question in my mind that that treatment of economics as a social science rather than a branch of philosophy, has advanced neither the cause of truth nor progress. But if we go back to the philosophical roots of this discipline, we can apply both logic and ethics to explain reality as it is, as well as to predict future events to a certain degree. It is for this reason that the system that I am putting forth is rooted in both logic and ethics, and in incontrovertible historical facts.

21. Logical capitalism: an integrative model

On a side note, and even though it is not necessary for the purpose of this political work, I would like to expose as clearly as possible the connection between work and price of goods (commodities and others) and services from the standpoint of our ethical and logical economy.

As I stated earlier, money is immanently a repository of work as well as a measure of it. The value of something is a function of its usefulness relative to its scarcity. The price of it is the amount of money, i.e., work, that we are willing to pay based upon the two variables it depends upon. Therefore scarcity is a measure of the work that we are willing to sacrifice to obtain a good. Scarcity or the lack thereof is a quantitive measure of work insofar as anything that is scarce requires more work to be obtained and vice versa. Conversely, usefulness is the qualitative measure of work inasmuch as the person ascribes a value to something according to his want. Usefulness relates to the utility subjectively attached by every individual agent. I already talked about the employer's marginal utility extracted from labor in relation to the worker's labor marginal value within a self-contained negotiation unit. And hence I have theoretically and practically connected physical reality with price, money and work. This systematic relation works and will always work, even in the interesting cases of goods which are infinitely valuable but whose price do not exist due to a lack of property rights and a market for it. Case in point would be air. The price would be a function of its scarcity, i.e., zero, and its usefulness, i.e., infinite. Zero divided by infinite is an indeterminate form, so we do not really know the amount of work that good is worth, i.e., there is not a price for it. Consequently, that good has no market.

And before we extend this analysis any further, I would like to address the doubts that might arise in keen minds trained in the orthodoxies of economic theory. It is at this point that I would like to explain the inner works of a system which on the one hand still approves of competition in the retail and wholesale markets, but on the other hand advocates for a vertically structured, all-inclusive and self-contained negotiating process between employer and worker, so the aggregates that are implicit in all the labor market models are rendered a nonfactor. In this scenario, it is obviously the employer who will have to bear the brunt of the new equilibrium and that is to be effected only through eating into his own profits. It is here when I remind the sagacious reader about the core of what this revolution is all about: indoctrination and a radically new, purposefully engineered ethos. I said it before and I will repeat it again: education is indoctrination. And we will inculcate into every child's mind that the entrepreneurial personal goal is profit, no competitiveness and opportunity costs. And that the measure of the acceptable profit will be up to the individual entrepreneur and not to standardized methods of analysis based on market expectations and old conventions. Profit linked up to individual marginal utility must be the basis for this logical capitalism, and not competitiveness or efficiency. The individual employer will be taught, from an early age, that it is based on his own marginal utilities that his decisions in negotiating with workers are to be made, and not on conventional and theoretical cookie-cutter criteria, which are the ways of the old models. His drive must be his own utility, and from it an acceptable profit margin will arise spontaneously. A standardized or average behavior based on an aggregate of individual behaviors turned into a mathematical function makes no sense, since every man is different and ultimately it is all up to his own will, which is a divine power not subject to any algorithm whatsoever.

In our revolution, which is a movement that reverts back to the freedom in each individual heart, no decision will be made based upon charts and statistics and equations which only show bondage and artificially imposed universality. The employer's decisions will be made directly with the worker, at a negotiating table and without any kind of intellectual shackles based upon expectations of margins, market shares, competitiveness and a myriad of other nonsensical factors. We will revert, through education, the relevant economic decisions to the realm of personal utility and morality, to the realm of consciousness, independence and the peculiarities of the individual—a man who is not a number in a function or equation, who is not a pawn in an absurd game of aggregates, but a free and virtuous man. Yes! Undoubtedly the end, practical result of this process will be much better paid workers and smaller profits and margins, but nevertheless more than satisfactory to the employer because otherwise they would not even exist according to the mechanism of negotiation already discussed.

I will now briefly depict how this new dynamic model of successive equilibriums works. To deduce that many employers currently operating would rather quit than continue operations under this new negotiating framework would be certainly a reasonable inference. As that happens, the available workers increase correspondingly, so their expectations fall off concomitantly to their new situation. As a result, they will meet the marginal utility of their new employer more easily; and this constant tug of war will logically yield a succession of equilibriums which is indeed a dynamic model. However, ceteris paribus, all the equilibriums will be higher than those reached under the old laissez-faire model. So ultimately the wages of workers in different companies and industries will keep on going up and down, but the baseline will always be higher than that of the old predatory model. There are still market forces that make the equilibrium dynamic, but now value and utility will always meet every step of the way. Justice therefore reigns supreme.

I have mentioned that economics was once a branch of philosophy, before it was hopelessly mathematized during the 19th century. And in fact, something that has puzzled philosophers of all schools has been free will. As I have just suggested in the foregoing commentary, that is exactly the decisive force behind any economic decision. The quiddity of it is not easy to be determined and much of this subject is often dealt with metaphysically, which I do not altogether approve of. But nevertheless, behind every single economic decision, lies at its heart an issue of free will. So it is only appropriate to emphasize that connection within the context of our new approach to employer-employee relations. Notice that free will has nothing to do with aggregates or expectations of any kind, but rather with the individual and his own drives and idiosyncrasies. We need to revert the economy of the people to the individual man, so we can break free from the chains of the "expert" and his one-size-fits-all recipes. Only through this individual approach we will be able to realize something akin to a collective individuation (in Jung's jargon), a total integration of our unconscious contents into the conscious so as to develop a full personality.

When this most desirable state happens not to a singular person, but individually to the whole body politic, then we have not only the Jungian collective unconscious, but also the collective conscious take center stage in the life of the nation. And the outcome of this, from the point of view of the employer-employee relationship, will be a very complex equilibrium, differing from case to case depending upon the peculiarities of the people involved. It will not be possible to aggregate the individual equilibriums into one collective equilibrium through mathematics, but the collective conscious will be realized nonetheless. And that state is something to strive for. That state is the definition of fulfillment, both individual and tribal, as a community, as a nation. That will be, in brief, the ultimate goal of the AFWS.

Delving into these notions even deeper, I marvel at the absurdity of that dichotomy between the liberal idea of individual rights and the old totalitarian states' idea of collectivism. For only an ill-conceived political philosophy and the corresponding revolutionary countermovements can fixedly stare at one side of the coin and utterly ignore the other. All decisions are in fact made at an individual level, and it is the individual alone who ultimately exists. But to think that a nation like ours, a tribe of tribes, a compound of very diverse communities, is just the aggregate of its people is downright fatuous. That would be tantamount to asserting that a living organism is the sum of its cells. But in reality an organism is the cells plus all the complex relationships and communications between them. We plan to transform an illegitimate organization like this political mastodon into an organism where individuals choose their path for self-realization and that in return is part of everybody else's self-realization. We are designing a state where finally the collective unconscious and what I have termed the collective conscious are brought forth and the individual undergoes his own process of individuation, all at once.

It is easier than it appears, because it is the natural aspiration of man. We are destined for self-fulfillment and all the barriers to it will be removed without hesitation. Much profound damage has been inflicted upon the worker in America by this emptied-out state. Most people live their lives without even daring to dream any dream, let alone those contents that burst forth from our unconscious in the language of the archetypes. We have become a dreamless herd, very doubtful of our own capabilities and energies, barely hoping to get by and not sticking out lest some ominous force stamps us out. Everything is decided for us, our prospects are really limited; our function is just to keep running the rat race so the puppeteer gets to amass more power and pelf. The masses are manipulated into believing that money is God, the judge, hence the ultimate goal to strive for. And the laissez-faire state calls that "freedom", and the "American dream". Grotesque, empty words if I ever heard any. They also mention "capitalism", and they bring up the threat of "socialism", as if a mode of production can be propositionally related to an ill-defined political philosophy. It does not matter, because the masses do not study logic anymore. The idiot box and the rest of the propaganda industry keeps blaring their hubbub; the entertainment industry keeps the people dazed with cheap products; the education system keeps the youth on the right track, namely away from knowledge and critical thinking; the politicians unrelentingly hammer the focus group-tested, well studied shibboleths and the show goes on. The bad news is that this all-pervasive, overwhelmingly stifling show of force will have to be met with an even greater display of force, in some version, if we are to overcome it (this will be addressed and predicated afterward). But unlike so many times in the course of history, this time around the sacrifice will not be in vain.

To finish off this most important point, I have to come clean and reveal my true feelings and thoughts about the base of the particracy. Its fanatical commitment to empty causes or worse, and its unwavering, zombie-like support for the corresponding faction, were to me painful realizations of how destructive and effective mass media, academia and the entertainment industries can be. But over the years a spirit of optimism has taken root in my heart. I have come to the conclusion that this army of politically involved people, with no critical thinking and a lack of coherent philosophy, could become potentially a spearhead of a revolution which must happen before the organic state is born. For with some straightforward training and knowledge, and since the enthusiasm is already deep within, who is better positioned to lead the first stages of the struggle? If a man gets all worked up over tangential issues, concocted for political expediency, is not it reasonable to expect him to be really excited about something infinitely more radical, just, and meaningful? The human raw component is there, we just need to tap into it and turn it finally into a force for good.

◆————————◆

22. Karl Marx: the good, the bad, and the ugly

I could have inserted a commentary on Marx anywhere in this work, but I just find this point particularly suited. I will start out by declaring that Aristotle and Marx had a lot in common. Aristotle believed lending money and charging interest was by definition money out of money, so that out of all modes of making a living, it was the most contrary to nature; and that is because the conversion of money into capital is illegitimate since it is unproductive, due to the fact that no surplus value has been added to any commodity exchanged. The scholastics predicated their concept of lending money at an interest on Aristotelian tradition and they called that activity usury, a very regrettable sin. Marx believed that money turns into capital when surplus value is created and the capitalist appropriates it by seizing the difference between the value of labor power and the wage-value; a predatory and exploitative activity to begin with.

I want to acknowledge something very important that Marx, surprisingly enough, got right. As opposed to liberal economists (both classical and modern, of all proclivities), Marx understood that political economy is philosophy, and not sociology. His theory of value, wages, capital and business cycle is indeed on point insofar as he strives to understand the nature and epistemological dimension of those concepts. On the other hand, orthodox economists obsess with turning out predictive models based on behavior, i.e., they are effectively reducing the scope and interest of economics to a mere sociological interpretation of economic transactions. This is misguided and pointless. Out of all the massive criticisms that I will shower Marx with, unoriginality or stupidity will not be among them. Marx was an excellent political economist but a disastrous political philosopher; hence *Capital* and *The Communist Manifesto* were shockingly written by the same person.

Karl Marx's definition of the value of necessary work is

approximately that amount of labor necessary to produce laboring power, or the cost of keeping the worker alive and in a condition such that he is able to sustain a family and himself in order to repeat the cycle of wagslave labor, in a successive series ad infinitum (or at any rate, until death). Unfortunately, Marx's conceptualization falls prey, inter alia, to the trap of infinite regression and circular reasoning, and that is problematic if you are striving to present a system that is logically sound. He failed to understand wages as a function of cost and laissez-faire profit, rather than the innate value of work. Work is indeed money in essence, but the amount of it in every instantiation is a social construct, not an intrinsic value. That social construct is altered exogenously through different mechanisms, like force, a national crisis or a paradigm shift. An example of force is a strike; an example of a national crisis is a currency crisis with accompanying hyperinflation; an example of a paradigm shift is a revolutionary instrument such as our enclosed negotiation process contemplated by the AFWP in the context of logical labor. The value of labor is not innate or fixed but predicated upon the ethos of the people permeating the legal infrastructure of the state. In other words, wage-value is contingent and not necessary.

In this sense, wagslave labor is a social construct, actuated through the political institutions and the legal mechanisms of the liberal state. It is not, contrary to what Marx deeply believed, an inevitable and concomitant property of a functioning capitalism. It is an invention concocted for the benefit of the usufructuary caste and in praxis a case of game theory where the initial premises are laid out in such a way that the foregone conclusion is a wage representing the minimum value whereat the worker will labor; whereas the equilibrium within the framework of logical labor is a wage-value that represents the maximum value above which the producer will cease operations, because it renders his marginal utility null. This is the linchpin of logical labor which will be institutionalized in the National Liberextremist State (AFWS). This nomenclature will soon enough be explained.

Through the device of logical labor the Marxist surplus value is retained by the worker to the maximum proportion as will allow the employer to extract enough utility from the labor applied to the business activity in order to not discontinue operations. Mathematically speaking, for those inclined to think that way, the Marxist surplus value will asymptotically approach the function of our logical wages above it, and the gap between the two will equate to the marginal utility necessary for the employer to continue operations. That gap will fluctuate in a series of dynamic equilibriums but it will always be measurable, since otherwise no employer will be incentivized to keep his business open. Correspondingly, the wag-slave function will at every step be far below both the Marxist asymptote and the logical wage function (more on this conceptualization at the end of this commentary on Marx). And in this logical fashion our AFWS averts the catastrophic aberration of socialism and communism, and their counterpart and reason for being, the infamous liberal dystopia.

Why render those ideologies and associated regimes in such harsh terms? Firstly, the Marxist concept of communism is at best very fuzzy and I ponder that it has never come into existence, so I would rather focus on Marxist socialism. Even though I am tempted to trow the German philosopher's diagnosis of the problem of capital and labor to be fundamentally right in principle, his propounded solution is downright ill-devised and frightening. Under no circumstances should the solution to any problem be the creation of a bigger or stronger caste to watch over the people and their economic and political interactions, and that is precisely what a socialist state entails. Even worse, in the Marxist kakotopia the bureaucracy of the state itself becomes a master caste under which the people are subservient and any possibility of individuation is nipped in the bud. His idea of a solution to the wagslave labor is a substitution of a plutocracy for another caste of anointed people, willing to do anything in order to preserve their tyranny over the body politic. Evidently Marx did not think through his alternative, peradventure due to the fact that he himself always had a relatively easy life compared with those for whom he purported to advocate, although still harsh compared to the lives of many of his contemporaries in the intelligentsia.

I have always been of the belief that, as I already alluded to, personal experience expands your cognition beyond the realm of the conscious, and ultimately furnishes your imagination with the sparks necessary to put forth ideas that are more complete and concordant with the reality of the problems you set out to address. In consequence, ever since I can remember, I have been very leery of so called professional experts and academic philosophers, whose lack of common sense in their fancies comes across as dilettantish to me. This realization is particularly present when I study the theories of certain political philosophers (like Marx himself), metaphysicians, epistemologists, and philosophers of the mind and of language; but this is a topic for a prospective work. The above reasoning notwithstanding, I have misgivings about attributing to Marx shortsightedness in his analysis. Irrespective of the validity of the alternative he propounded, his diagnosis and description of the problems that laissez-faire capitalism is steeped in are not without merit.

However, a certain odd incoherence is blatantly revealed in his *Capital*. On the one hand, he describes all the nefarious instruments that the classical Leviathan uses to enhance the worst exploitative tendencies of the capitalist caste, ensuring an ample, cheap and desperate supply of workers; and on the other hand he lets the state off the hook by placing all the blame on the beneficiary. This perpetrator would be rendered harmless had not the enabler paved the way. The actions that this caste-driven state has been carrying out against the workers, in order to keep them divided, poor, willing and submissive heretofore, were profusely discussed by Marx in his opus and very well documented. They were the same techniques in his century as they are nowadays: taxation to keep the workers poor and dependent; free trade and offshoring to cheapen labor costs and diminish domestic labor demand; immigration and displacement of workers to increase the labor supply and thus decrease the wages in the macroeconomic equilibrium; cultural terrorism by contributing to an ethos of acceptance of menial work as not worthy of certain living standards; or in other words, deliberate and systematic destruction of expectations and its concomitant creation of submission (through overt and covert propaganda, indoctrination, entertaining industry, diverting schemes, etc.) and the list of ruses goes on. So considering the intelligence and ratiocinative powers of Marx, I confess myself utterly puzzled when he seems to draw the conclusion that the state is more a bystander rather than the vital spring of the crime against the heartiest part of our body politic, committed by the beastly caste for which the state itself exists.

I would like now to focus my critique on Marx by highlighting the apparent internal contradictions between his method and his conclusions. Let us thus concentrate on chapters 19 and 25 in his *Capital*, and on his notion of free trade as intimated just about everywhere in his work.

To begin with, Marx struggles throughout to explain the difference between market price of labor (wage) and value of necessary labor. But of course a value of any kind is immanently bound to be expressed as an amount of something else, namely money. In this case, value without a monetary quantification is a non-functional concept. And this is because the value of something is by definition a quantity. Hence we can state that the quiddity of value itself is quantity. Consequently, use value is, in an economic context, an expression of money both as an object and as a subject. Thus use value of a commodity will always be a function of personal income and wealth and personal utility. Therefore it will always be expressed as an amount of money. When that amount matches the price of the commodity, an instantiation of an exchange in the market place will occur. A very lucid example of this is the rental market. In it, rental properties are auctioned off to whoever wants to apply to secure them. A rather convoluted and even in some cases random selection process takes place, wherewith different applicants are whittled out until it is narrowed down to the bare minimum and finally a decision is made. All the applicants have something in common: all of them believed the use value of that commodity was meeting or exceeding its market price;

otherwise they would not have applied. Therefore they all agree upon the judgment "this property is worth that price for me". Otherwise, the statement agreed upon would be of the type "this property is overpriced for me", and the instantiation of an exchange would not have occurred.

And here is where the first glaring contradiction arises. In chapter 19 of *Capital*, Marx intuitively stumbles upon the explanatory and functional, and therefore true, conceptualization of wage, beyond his mere quantitive expression of the market value of necessary labor. For indeed, a wage is the instantiation of a social construct (partly carried out through the Jungian collective unconscious), through the power of wills agreeing on a decision: the capitalist offering a laissez-faire wage and a worker accepting the underpayment. Nothing is immanent or innate about that price, as he propounds everywhere else ad infinitum, but to the contrary: it is the outcome of individual wills seeped in culture and ethos.

Let us elaborate further. Marx generally argued that the market price of labor (wage) could equate or oscillate around the "value" of labor power as necessary labor, to just a certain extent. In other words, he did not believe possible the instantiation of a collective political will through a social construct, capable of absorbing the greater portion of surplus labor into necessary labor. Thus I deduce that Marx considered the liberal state the only possible state compatible with the capitalistic mode of production. I would further predicate his dictum by proclaiming that liberal capitalism (laissez-faire, corporate creditism, crony capitalism, etc.) is only possible within the liberal state; certain versions of capitalism developed around national syndicalism were only possible in fascist states (these strains of capitalism sprung out of political revolutions in the early 20th century, long after Marx had passed away); and logical capitalism will only be possible within our organic state. At the core of his belief lies dormant the serpent of ennui and pessimism—the conviction that the laissez-faire form of capitalism is the only possible form and that the state is born causally out of that rapacious version. As I already remarked, had Marx witnessed the power of the revolutionary states mentioned herein (and how some of them shifted the tenets of their respective capitalistic economic systems by brute force, although nevertheless quite superficially), I seriously doubt he would have maintained the notion of the liberal state as a natural offspring of liberal capitalism, for it is obvious that the causation is exactly the reverse.

23. The liberal state: overt racism in its formation of surplus population

Another clear example of Marx nonchalantly dismissing the liberal hegemon as the sine qua non of predatory capitalism, very much in contradiction of his own reasoning, is found in chapter 25 of the aforementioned *Capital*. In this chapter, titled "General Law of Capitalistic Accumulation", he lays out very systematically the causes and functions wherewith liberal capitalism is dependent upon a surplus population, a large section of it necessarily kept unemployed or underemployed.

Marx puzzlingly fails to understand that without the conniv-ance of the illegitimate state, a surplus population could not materialize and hence the conditions for expansion and con-centration of capital could not be possible. I can unequivo-cally declaim that Marx rejects the logical conclusion that his well rationalized propositional framework led him to, in a stunning display of both ratiocinative powers and sheer stub-bornness. (I surmise it is a Prussian trait.)

And how does the laissez-faire state go about the creation of that surplus population, including an obscene and tragic layer of pauperism? The answer is through the obliteration of its own borders and the creation of tax incentives for the be-getting of as many future wagslave workers as possible; and both policies arise irrespective of the lack of merits, means or acumen whatsoever, or rather because of this lack. Indeed, this illegitimate state's function as the political and ultimate guarantor of liberal capitalism and its most grueling feature, that of wagslave labor, requires from it the ruthless imple-mentation of all and any policies aimed at the creation of a surplus population. But not any population; only that which needs to approach the market as a commodity bearer, totally dependent upon the underselling of its social labor power to procure its subsistence. It stands to reason that such a generic man needs to be, a fortiori, lacking developed multi-faceted skills which could render him an independent opera-tor, capable of making a living without entering a wagslave labor contract with a capitalist/employer. For reasons I hope will appear to most readers unmistakable, this man cannot be of above-average intelligence or endowed with a will and a conviction incompatible with the acceptance of a state of liberal serfdom and a meager living.

It is thus paramount for this predatory state to produce a surplus population considered "unskilled" or "low-skilled", docile and obedient, weak of will, intellectually limited and without aspiring expectations. It is therefore a foregone conclusion that this putrid state is among the most racist organizations that ever existed in human history, for it equates the aforementioned mongrel population with the peoples hailing from so-called "underdeveloped countries", where colored races are prevalent; and conversely, this state considers natives of developed countries (mostly white races) to be of a superior breed and consequently unfit to join the ranks of the surplus population. Thus the assumption of the ruling, political and functionary castes in this laissez-faire swindle is that colored peoples are racially inferior to white peoples. And this is the basis for an immigration policy that criminally obliterates our own southern border while contemporaneously placing significant restrictions on people trying to immigrate from Europe. That such a blatantly racist state is never called out by the "American left" is yet again, another indisputable proof that there are no leftists in America, but rather a clique of bought-and-paid-for impostors.

◁▭▭▭▭▭▷

24. The supra-race in the America Free Workers State

The AFWS will reject, on the other hand, any racist proclivity or policy. To that end, we will unabashedly engage in the creation of the state's supra-race, or the social aggregate of the state's supra-man—supra-race composed of the most virtuous, brightest and strongest men derived from the interbreeding among the pinnacles of moral, intellectual and physical excellence from each and every race and ethnicity within the organic state, in an intergenerational effort. Our supra-race will soar to heights of achievement never before reached or even dreamed of, an absolute peak of glory towering over local peaks within each and every ethnic subset. We will unceremoniously toss aside the unadventurous and dull follies of the racist states (the liberal state and some of its old nemeses) and we will start from scratch, Anno Domini 1 in this new world of our own creation! More about this will be discussed in the context of tax credits, as well as the immigration exception for foreign supra-men.

◆——————◆

25. More deconstruction of Marx from the standpoint of logical labor and logical capital

Another example of Marx's obnoxious refusal to accept the logical conclusions of his own arguments is his critique of free trade. His arguments against it are spread out all over his work, so no specific chapter linked to this issue is worth mentioning. It is in no way controversial to affirm that trade of any kind is impossible in modern times without the permission of the state, for legal and logistical reasons. The preferred trade arrangement for the liberal state is, unsurprisingly, the so-called "free trade". As Marx would put it in his quaint par-lance, free trade is the ultimate weapon against the worker for it maximizes the creation and appropriation of surplus value through the exploitation of foreign surplus labor, as it depresses the price of domestic labor power well below the market value of necessary labor. Suffice to say, on this ac-count he was exactly right. It did not make any difference in Marx's mind though, since he still was unwilling or incapable to place the blame where it belongs.

Another critique of Marx beyond his absurd notion of ac-cepting the reducibility of uniqueness to a measure of quan-tity, is his problematic use of the terms "exchange value" and "use value". He uses them preceding any conceptual-ization of money and utility (although he equivocates when he claims exchange value is "related" to the price of the commodity); thereby in my estimation he makes them non-functional concepts. In fact, I doubt any human being ever since Marx burst into the philosophical scene could explain those concepts without resorting, implicitly or explicitly, to the economic concepts of price or cost (money) and function or desire (utility). But in Marx's philosophy exchange value and use value are concepts designed to stand on their own, and I do not understand how concepts that only one person agrees upon can form the basis for an economic or political philosophy.

Closely related to this problem is the conundrum of in-finite regression and circular reasoning, and that of lack of induction.

Indeed, it is my view, that nothing true or functional, or

useful to communication or knowledge generally, can have an infinite or just unbounded number of definitions. But according to Marx, the use value of a commodity is tantamount, conceptually, to an unbounded number of exchange values, namely those of every possible commodity in existence, and all of it independently of the concepts of money and utility. And vice versa, the use value of any of the commodities employed to define the use value of any other commodity, is in turn the exchange value of any of the latter. This scheme is an example of circular reasoning when we define the use value of any one commodity as the exchange value of another and vice versa; and an example of infinite regression when we define the use value of any one commodity as the exchange value of an unbounded number of other commodities ad infinitum. I would call it an infinite regression of circular reasonings, and it is very much prone to collapsing unto itself in terms of propositional or predicate logic, only to be quasi-saved by the crutches of metaphysics, which are notorious for being finicky and unreliable.

The problem of induction or rather lack thereof is yet another problem I observe in Marx's philosophy. For his edifice of thought to stand, the number of commodities in existence must be always larger than one, since its use value requires the exchange value of another commodity to be established. But the class of natural numbers is, according to the standard model of arithmetic, also known as the intended interpretation, inductively generated from zero and the successor function, and thus his theory should, a fortiori, uphold the principle of induction if it is to be considered internally coherent. According to Marx, in a hypothetical economy with only one commodity, its use value is impossible to be determined in terms of exchange value, and yet the use value of such commodity is labor power "congealed" which cannot in this case be ascertained or measured. However, it stands to reason that the foregoing congealed work is real, and under any circumstances, no matter the number of commodities in the economy, we should be able to measure it. In other words, the theory does not uphold the principle of induction. Every time this occurs we will encounter contradictions and paradoxes and generally we will be forced to reject some or all of the premises, in this case Marx's conceptualization of use value and exchange value.

If instead of work as use value of a certain commodity in terms of the exchange value of another, I define work as a function of the price of the commodity, we are introducing demand into the conceptualization. In this manner we ultimately assign value based on personal wants or utilities, which in the aggregate will always be the reflection of social constructs. This way, we avoid Marx's pitfall of an unbounded regression of circular reasonings. Work is qualitatively money and vice versa. And the quantification of work as an amount of money is a pure exercise of assigned value based on social constructs, or in other words, the mere upshot of a shared culture and social conventions, also known as the ethos of a people.

Therefore I can say money is not work as a universal quantification of value, as Marx would say, but rather the quantification of the work we are willing to sacrifice in order to obtain something we want through exchange, which varies from individual to individual, and it is bounded by a common ethos. So money is a social construct that acquires meaning in an actual or potential exchange and not in the production of the commodity itself. In any event, we can affirm "work is money", and not only "money is work". They are one and the same to such an extent that either one is defined as a phase in the process of the other's materialization.

Furthermore, the fact that we are able to bargain and haggle until we reach a meeting of the minds, in other words, an exchange through that instrument, is irrefutable proof that exchange value is not inherent to the commodity itself. It is an instantiation of legitimate money being agreed upon as legitimate work that we are willing to give up to procure something else which is also the product of legitimate work. But different parties will reach different deals through the instrument of bartering, for example. This makes impossible the notion that work is the equivalent of use value of a commodity expressed as the exchange value of another, because use value as defined by Marx seems to be innate to the commodity and should not have different quantifications depending upon who is quantifying.

At this point, I would like to approach Marx's deconstruction or critique from a very different perspective. Although Marx was a lousy and unimaginative political philosopher, he was also one of the greatest and most original political economists of all time, and therefore somebody very difficult to contend with for those who do not fully grasp the issues. It is quite comical to behold the histrionics and rhetoric of the liberal apologists, who shamelessly heap all kinds of insults and opprobrium upon Marx, but quite often fail to put forth serious economic and philosophical counterarguments, because they just cannot. The fear of that man is palpable; they are always experiencing misgivings about his overall message catching up among the masses and eventually burning through the entire system like a raging wildfire. And that fear is somehow justified, for in fact a corrupt and illegitimate state cannot wall itself off from the malaise of a philosophy which feeds off people's misery. In truth, the laissez-faire ideology and Marxism in its various strains unequivocally deserve each other in their relentless march down to hell.

Notwithstanding the aforesaid, I dare to surmise that, had Marx ever envisioned what money would become one hundred years after he wrote *Capital*, he would not have propounded his theory in the first place. Indeed, for Marx and in truth any political philosopher or economist before him and for a long while after him, money was an equivalent commodity or a universal measure of value. I doubt he ever thought it possible to consider money as a mere political instrument to facilitate deficit spending without taxation, without any connection whatever to the output or labor power of the country, literally being printed physically or digitally at will, and without any connection at all to any known commodity subject to monetization or not.

Today's money has nothing to do with what has been called money for millennia because a banknote within the modern understanding of central banking is not money. Nowadays, money has become the archetype of the social construct—the ultimate example of a collective belief sustained only by the faith and the will, and also the fear, of those who choose to fall under its spell. Indeed, the U.S. is a country formally bankrupt, in the sense that its national debt has reached such an amount that the state is not and will never be able to pay it off, and on the brink of becoming incapable of even reducing it, or barely contain the rate of its growth. It is the definition of a failed state, monetarily speaking; a state very close to resorting to new debt in order to service the old one, which is the definition of a death spiral springing from debt. All dollar-denominated assets, such as stocks, bonds and cash itself, are liable to become worthless overnight in the case of a catastrophic event or perhaps through a dragged-out, painful and tragic crisis. The value of the US dollar is predicated on beliefs that are quite illogical and a matter of sheer faith, but they could be summed up as the conviction that the creditors will never come banging at the door at the same time and that panic will never set in. In reality, of course, this sea change will in fact take place unless this illegitimate Leviathan is finished and substituted by the organic state before the calamity materializes. How the AFWS will resolve this debt and currency conundrum will be hereinafter amply discussed.

Beyond Marx's critique of classical capitalism, and especially the capitalist or proprietor caste, there is another troubling aspect to this very issue. The "enlightened" believed the conceptualization of workers as commodities was a matter of empirical observation, an objective reality. In this context, the word "commodity" is a matter-of-fact definition, and therefore there is no room left to regard it as a social construct or the outcome of convention; or the offspring of an ethos, potentially subjected to a historical dialectical rejection for the better (or even for the worse). Smith and the rest of his ilk thus closed the door to any development of the fundamental status of workers as members of a body politic, effectively slashing any hope of a transcendental movement to the any ideal. It is therefore a foregone conclusion that the forefathers of the liberal kakotopia never contemplated, either politically, economically, ethically or even metaphysically, a worker as anything but a conduit to advance the interests of the caste they themselves belonged to.

Elaborating further on this topic, Marx and the classical economists and political philosophers of the Enlightenment had something very peculiar in common, which would have been to the chagrin of the former had he been aware of it. Neither camp considered a worker for what he really is: the constitutive cell of the state, whose only reason to be is the maximization of the material and moral well-being of those workers and their freedom, at all and any cost without any further predication. Marx considered a worker the potentiality of a "congealed" commodity, equating work to the use value of commodities. Smith considered a worker himself a commodity, equating the quiddity of a man to a social function. Either way, both saw a worker as a potentiality of work, which is the ultimate ontological obliteration of "who I am" by "what I do". Smith was unwilling or incapable of understanding the difference between "a barber" and "a haircut" as I already explained. He therefore rejected the divine quality of the human condition. Marx was analogously stupefied by the idea that "this worker" is not "that worker". He implicitly rejected the miracle of uniqueness present in each and every human being, which has been scientifically proven (not that this was necessary at all to be true) after Marx's time. But of course in reality and morality this worker is not that worker at all and neither one is solely his work but infinitely more. Both Marx and Smith's implications are prima facie wrong, in a moral sense, but they are also logically unattainable.

Let us call this proof the "Rembrandt counterexample", and let us imagine a legitimate Rembrandt painting and a fake, so perfectly made that there is no appreciable difference whatsoever between the two. The perfection of the copy notwithstanding, it is still a fact that nobody will pay the same price for both, unless he is not aware that one of them is a knockoff. Let us examine this situation closely. If Smith was right, and a worker is fundamentally his work, and both paintings look the same, then why should not both painters receive the same compensation? The answer is that Rembrandt is more than his art; he has become a quality unto himself by virtue of a social contract, and therefore Smith was wrong. And if Marx was right, why are not two identical works that have congealed the same amount of labor paid the same once the fake is identified? The answer to this is obviously that there is not such a thing as two identical works of art, and that is why the copy was identified as such in the first place. Even if we must resort to microscopic proof and other advanced techniques, eventually the fake and the original will be told apart. In consequence, Rembrandt is unique; therefore Marx was wrong.

I shall now draw the attention to two very interesting aspects of Marx's doctrine, which I hinted at when I denounced the contradiction between his condemnation of the paramount role of the state in capitalism, and yet his surprising consideration of that same laissez-faire state as a mere bystander in the plight of the working man. Implicit in his philosophy is the presupposition that the liberal state proceeds causally from capitalism, but for irrefutable reasons it seems obvious to me that the logical and empirical causation is the reverse. Indeed, unless we prove ourselves to be unaware of historical facts, we should notice that a large number of non-liberal states by the classic definition have had capitalism as a mode of production ever since Marx put forth his theory. But every time a liberal state is reflected upon, we encounter some version of capitalism. And this reasoning, although neither first-order nor propositional, it is certainly modal. Furthermore, it stands to reason that since capitalism is predicated, inter alia, on property rights and these in turn are the core of the Lockean contract, which is the basis for the liberal state as is currently understood; it follows both logically and empirically that the relation of causation between capitalism and the liberal ideology starts with the latter and ends with the former. Therefore, any substantial reform, including the most radical, the revolution, must start at the fountainhead of the problem or its cause, namely the state itself, and from it the redefinition of the effect or mode of production should logically ensue. So unlike the Marxist deterministic explanation of economic conditions as causally generating political regimes, I believe life is a conglomerate of reinforcing causal relations between the economic and political in concatenated cycles.

The liberal state is thus the causal force behind laissez-faire capitalism, but also the effect, in the subsequent historical period, of the aforementioned instantiation of a toxic mode of production, characterized by a spurious ratiocinative exercise which renders a vice and a capital sin—greed—a constructive vital drive in the entire system. Life is indeed infinitely messier and more nuanced than any ideological theory, and therefore we strive to be first and foremost logical instead, in an attempt to solve the inherent pitfalls of the socio-political dimension of reality. The tandem logic-will is the sacrosanct mechanism wherewith the party will always interpret the world and modify it, so as to make the people maximally integrated within the body politic and through its intension, the organic state. The AFWS will have for its extension, as any other state, the body politic. But only an organic state, our august National Liberextremist State, is the intension of the people; in other words, two entities functionally interrelated sharing the same quiddity.

The second curious aspect of his theory is that of the subterfuges of the system to keep the workers in line and away from revolutionary ideas and intentions. He identified religion as the "opium of the people", a dictum which strangely enough resonates among modern day liberal elites, as always wrestling with phantasms that no longer exist but ignoring the monsters that ravage the masses of workers in the body politic they profit from to no end. The lack of awareness of that power caste is sheer stupidity in some cases and an interested pretense in others. Either way, a shame. For in fact the state, and not its rotten economic system, utilizes plenty of devices to keep the workers numb and entertained; a cornucopia of subterfuges to reticulate the phalanxes of those who truly endure taxation without any representation whatsoever. The pseudo-religions of the modern Leviathan (government, climate, trans activism, scientism, materialistic hedonism, multiculturalism, globalism, etc.) and the "entertaming" industry are the stupefacients and ruses of this state, reinforced by the onslaught of propaganda and indoctrination at the core of the programming scheme. These instruments are thus an existential necessity for this state to endure in its continuous march away from the judge, or the supreme moral ideal. It goes without saying that the AFWS will do away with all of them, and will restore or rather institute the path, as illumined as we can possible conceive of, toward the aforesaid ideal.

There is another troubling aspect of Marx's philosophy that I must bring up. I am referring to his concept of surplus labor. He seems to not recognize the work of the capitalist in the production of the commodity, and that work is as legitimate and paramount to the productive enterprise as everyone else's. Consequently, that contribution needs to be assessed and valued accordingly. In fact, using Marx's own conceptualization and nomenclature, we can assert that there is plenty of work or use value which would go uninstantiated without the legitimate work of the capitalist as a worker, but not as a reaper of surplus value. In other words, many legitimate activities, which could potentially induce necessary labor in the process of creation of use value, would never come to fruition without the labor of the capitalist himself acting in the process of production, not as a recipient of worker's surplus labor but rather as a generator of surplus value himself.

In this regard, a proprietor or capitalist is two-dimensional and those dimensions need to be appropriately identified; as a capitalist proper is exploiting the worker by seizing his surplus labor without paying for it, in an all-consuming push for expansion of capital. But the capitalist is also a creator of the conditions necessary for production, and in that role he is legitimately working, i.e., adding social use value to the body politic by making possible the necessary labor of others. Anybody who performs legitimate work is a worker, and therefore a capitalist or proprietor is a worker while in the process of production, and his work is part of the price of the commodity itself.

Marx's solution to all these problems, the creation of a socialist state run by an all-powerful caste of bureaucrats, will not yield a just and functional equilibrium. This can only be achieved not through centrally planned transfers of resources, but rather through an upending of the wagslave labor as a social construct, and its substitution for another social construct instilled in the body politic by the party and the state through propaganda, indoctrination and law; I have called it the institution of logical labor. Our revolution will integrate legitimate proprietors into the phalanxes of workers through the mechanisms of the party and the organic state. We do not seek to turn the tables so the castes of old reverse positions; we seek the obliteration of castes altogether. We seek all the compatriots and compeers to break bread together at the table, in justice and respect, through an organic, multifaceted and comprehensive co-dependance promoted and protected by the state.

In Marx's theory, the economic and even ethical concept of illegitimate for the AFWP would have an analogous expression, which would be propositionally logical if we accept Marx's conceptualization of use value and surplus value as ideas capable of standing on their own without predication relative to other universally accepted concepts such as money, price and utility. In Marxian parlance, our concept of illegitimate economic activity would be that which ultimately renders an exchange of commodities proper or services, where the use value generated for a party is equal to a negative use value of the same magnitude for its counterpart, yielding in the process an illegitimate appropriation of the latter's surplus labor without the creation of social surplus value. Paradigmatic cases of illegitimate activities would be those perpetrated by shylocks, shysters and bureaucrats, although by no means is this conceptualization restricted to them.

I will finish up this stint on Marx's theories by tying up the concepts of price and wage within the context of the institution of logical labor. After all the critique and deconstruction I have subjected Marx to, fairly I hope, it would be almost mean and uncalled for to mathematize the fundamental conclusion of this analysis, which is a base and classless act in most circumstances; but because it is Marx after all, I feel the urge to kick him even further no matter how down he is. For I do not wish any reader to conclude that I do not fully exercise due contempt for philosophers who engage in caste-generating fancies, irrespective of how gifted they might or might not be. So I talked at the beginning of this section about the logical labor function growing and approaching the limit or asymptote represented by the Marxist wage, being the gap between those two functions the quantification of the capitalist marginal utility. Since over the long haul, ceteris paribus, income is a very strong prediction of wealth (and vice versa), we can assert the following: logical capitalism will yield a merging of the functions of wealth for all the people in an intertribal fashion across so-called "socioeconomic classes" (by the nomenclature favored in this state). Mathematically, those functions will converge asymptotically with one another in such a way that over time the gap between them will narrow down to a point where all the functions will have the same limit equal to that asymptotic value. Or in plain parlance, the "wealth gap" will narrow down to the lowest level below which economic activity based on choices and contracts as instantiation of free will would cease. I reckon that the aforesaid level will be surprisingly low!

I am going to expound on this further, but from a different angle and conceptualization. The quantification of work as money in wage-form is determined through the operation of a social construct; and the quantification of work as a price of labor is an equilibrium of economic functions (supply and demand) based upon wants, costs (including wage-form itself) and expectations, some of which could be interpreted as universal objective phenomenology (specifically most kinds of operational costs), and others as mere localized or generalized social constructs. The sequence of dynamic equilibriums brought about by the instrument of logical labor is such that its limit superior is the asymptotic sequence of prices implying a wage with no profit, or a surplus value equal to zero; and the lower bound the wagslave wage. The instantiation of any social contract can be interpreted as an act of collective will; and it is the will of the AFWS that this sequence of dynamic equilibriums infinitely approaches its limit superior, or the asymptote of the Marxist wage, granted, without ever reaching it. In other words, the mechanism of logical labor is an economic instrument based on negotiations with a limited set of alternatives as I have already explained, put in motion upon the instantiation of a social construct as a mechanism derived from the expression of collective will through the law. Or said in another way: logical labor is the harmonic union of logic and will, the two basic components at the core of the organic state and all its principles and actions.

If I am to conclude this deconstruction on Marx, I ought to do it in a spirit of creation and with a problem-solving attitude, because ours is the revolution of the extreme, positive, and yet pragmatic. So let us briefly highlight the solutions that Marx could not discern even though his analysis of the problems was to a degree satisfactory, from the perspective of political economy. Indeed Aristotle, much to Marx's skepticism, was right when he declared man a political animal. And it is for this reason that the social constructs designed and actuated by the state through the law are instantiations of collective will which surpasses the force and social influence of all and any mode of production, as those who survived, for example, the Bolshevik and national syndicalist revolutions all across Europe very well know. In fact, when a mode of production exists, it does because the state has thus decided.

As Marx constantly exposed, albeit inadvertently or so it seems, at every step of the way in the development of capitalism, the liberal behemoth was there to make sure such a mode of production endured. In most instances the interests of the masses of workers at large were brutally trampled. Hence, it appears a matter of historical record that without the political force and even crazed violence of the state, that construct of wagslave labor could not have survived. Consequently I can proclaim that traditional capitalism as an economic system and mode of production has been begotten by the liberal state or at the very least nurtured, protected and given a canonical status. In addition, the outcries of Marx about the alienation of the worker from the final product as a commodity (very much a matter of fact) as a consequence of capitalistic division of labor, will not happen in the AFWS. The reason is clear: the instrument of logical capital will organically obliterate that alienation through the transformation of the worker into a partner of the capitalist in the enterprise. We will be effectively turning capitalists into workers and workers into capitalists, in an ever-reinforcing cycle of organic brotherhood. We will be overcoming Marx's quandaries not by destroying or reversing roles, but by elevating the whole structure to a new level of conceptualization actuated through a social construct; as a matter of fact the organic state will instantiate socially every example of that construct through the materialization of the power of its collective will, or what is commonly known as law. I will herein develop the theory of logical capital in the leading up to the founding principle number five.

In this manner the AFWS, as an ideal projection of the AFWP and its philosophy and platform, and through the social construct that we call logical capital, reduces to rubble the alienation of the worker with his social contribution to the body politic, which is ultimately only possible with the cooperation of the illegitimate state. We have in this way linked the state with Marx's alienation and solved the transcendental problem through the liberating force of the political organism. Marx was, or so it seems to me, utterly preoccupied with combating the drought by rationing the water in contrary ways so to speak; we, on the other hand, intend to combat that very same drought by flooding the fields with the water that abounds underneath, hidden away under the cover of rotten constructs.

And in this fashion I draw the commentary on Marx to a

close. His was a power, as evinced by the political economy that he put forth, fundamentally deductive and ratiocinative or analytical. His power was, therefore, a deconstructive power. But construction requires an antithetical power, which should be imaginative or creative, and inductive. Unfortunately Marx lacked the constructive power, thus his recipes for the overcoming of the socioeconomic problems caused by the capitalistic mode of production were de facto the outlines of yet another nightmare. Aristotle was right, and man is indeed a political animal. Hence, the instantiation of the collective will of the people through the absolutist will of the state is metaphorically miraculous, for it renders mountains movable if necessary; and socioeconomic quagmires crushed by its unequalled force. Of course I am talking about a righteous state, a responsible state, a deontological state, a democratic state, a state of the worker, an organic state—the future National Liberextremist State (this concept is forthcoming). And I now humbly declare that, much to the benefit of my compatriots and compeers, and to the party itself, I am abundantly endowed with both powers and I intend to exercise them to my last breath on this Earth.

And thus let us shed for good the stale and broken, because the journey forth is so arduous that no dead weight shall be carried along.

26. Inflation, debasement of the currency, and debt

A very important subject on the topic of work, i.e., money, is inflation. It will be henceforth addressed and analyzed from many different perspectives, but for now it is the most apparent symptom of a sick economic system where illegitimate money is created and flows throughout the economy; money that does not reflect actual legitimate work or output. I would like to go back and expound on it a bit further. Inflation is an absolute concept, objectively expressed by a number which quantifies the growth of the money supply as a function of the monetary base. And it is precisely because of this that the central bank cannot allow any independent audit least its follies be unearthed. Consequently, the stewards and apologists of this kakistocracy declare the Consumer Price Index (CPI) the measure of inflation, nay, even worse, its very definition! And anyway the CPI does not reflect the variation of prices in the economy, but rather an agreed-upon convention; a dubious correlation explained on the basis of a random methodology, cunningly devised so as to minimize the fluctuation in the first place. Furthermore, the increase in prices of goods and services throughout the economy is only a symptom and not the cause or a definition of inflation. Another symptom is the massive increase in the price of assets in so-called "financial bubbles", irrespective of the general weakness of the real economy and the almost permanent impoverishment of the masses of workers regardless of the phase in the business cycle. We can thus conceptualize inflation as opposed to liberal inflation: the former is the monetary cancer spread out into the body politic for the benefit of the usufructuary caste; whereas the latter is the social construct wherewith this state—through its agents and propping castes—sows the seeds of confusion and misconception, in order to cover its involvement in the creation of yet another catastrophic bane for the phalanxes of workers.

This phenomenon is the culprit of innumerable societal collapses over the centuries. Nowadays, workers are always the victims of this disease concocted by the power elite. Inflation is and has always been a monetary dysfunction created by the ruling caste for the benefit of the illegitimate caste. Inflation appears when money does not reflect a measure of work in a society. As I already mentioned, inflation is the increase of the monetary base and its most glaring effect is an increment in the price of assets, goods and services. In other words, bubbles in the financial markets and poverty in the streets. We always live in a permanent state of inflation. The government just changes the methodology to measure it so in appearance it does not exist or it is very low, most of the time.

This is another clear example of how the mathematization of economics is in the ultimate analysis, just a ploy for the benefit of the power caste. Paper money issued by central banks at an interest always yields inflation. Once the banksters are left free to control the monetary supply, they will always do so with the only objective of propping up its own caste at the expense of workers, who will pay for this scheme through the most regressive of taxes: inflation. This most ruinous malaise is brought about by creating interest-bearing notes out of nothing, irrespective of the actual output or work present in the nation at any time. Any monetary system which is not grounded on the reality of present work is a scam on the productive caste. For that reason, money issued by central bankers is a scheme to separate workers from the fruit of their labor and funnel it upward for the lucre of the power and propping castes, and into a financial system that thrives on inflation and debt. Money is work, so the relative abundance of the former should be the reflection of the relative abundance of the latter. Anything that deviates from this golden rule will impoverish the country at large, and the ruling caste and everybody who lives off "investments" will become richer, therefore increasing the measure of injustice and through wicked means to boot.

And that measure of injustice is particularly flagrant in countries that are war-oriented, disease-oriented (wicked and unproductive "health care" systems paired with the production and importation of toxic or unhealthy food and prescription drugs), vice-oriented (drug industries, consumerism running amuck, and the denial of the transcendent) and deceit-oriented (corporate and social media as the propaganda arm of the liberal kakotopia, manipulation and dumbing down in the realm of academia, the "entertaming" industry, criminal psychological operations carried out by the security state, etc.). Those are the four horsemen always trampling upon workers, feeding on them with the connivance of the laissez-faire Goliath for the benefit of the caste for which that travesty of a political system exists.

Indeed, every time something is destroyed, an amount of work is destroyed with it. In order to build it back up, another amount of work must be employed. At that point, no matter how many individuals have benefited from the process of destruction and rebuilding along the path of circulating capital, the community as a whole is worse off because much work has been employed to end up where we started off. If all the work employed in the building up would have been employed somewhere else, the people would be way ahead. Of course this is the true sense of opportunity cost of work, which is immediately understood once we comprehend the real nature of money. (However, the classical understanding of opportunity cost is always in reference to an economy frozen in a particular moment in time, rather than an analysis projecting into the future, comparing different alternatives at different moments in time: a dynamic model.)

One of the many practical reasons why current economic theory, irrespective of the model considered, fails to understand these concepts, is the econometrically insurmountable difficulties of evaluating the opportunity costs of the unintended consequences. As I already discussed, the macroeconomic models developed through differential analysis are hopelessly limited in their predictive powers by both the methodology of the analysis and the ideological contamination. In the case of the opportunity costs of the unintended consequences caused by illegitimate activities, the models are literally unworkable, due to the massive number of variables involved. Under this pretext, the study of the economic devastation of illegitimate work has been avoided and swept under the rug.

The conclusion is unavoidable: an industry developed on growing toxic food; or the destroying through military spending and wars; or the middle unproductive layer between the people and their heath care providers; or a sector whose collective business model is the propagation of fiction, hatred for one another and toxic self-loathing ideas; or this other industry providing an endless deluge of cheap and numbing entertainment—all of it is considered "productive" because many make a great living off of it and it adds to the GDP, even though this metric was never intended to measure anything relative to the public weal of a nation when it was first conceived. Make no mistake: a nation with a set of workers and a set of people who do not work is infinitely more productive and prosperous than a nation with a set of workers who are forced to clean up after a set of destructive people involved in illegitimate businesses. The opportunity costs of all the work employed to cauterize the existential damage caused by those destructive activities is impossible to calculate, and the unintended consequences of such activities so far-reaching and devastating that terror and disgust both strike me as I think about it.

Illegitimate (in the destructive or nonproductive sense) government decisions, businesses or whole industries, will have the effect of increasing national and personal debt, inflation and generally the impoverishment of workers while the ruling caste, the managerial caste, and particularly the master or usufructuary caste will benefit. The end result will be a bigger measure of injustice as the welfare chasm between workers and the privileged elites grows ever larger and the country as a whole ever poorer. And it is with the intent to achieve this unholy outcome, and within the moral turpitude of the laissez-faire state, that war is quite often used as an instrument to overcome depressions by increasing government spending way beyond its means, thereby expanding the monetary supply through new interest-bearing debt; as a result money pulls even further from its original meaning as a repository of work and its measure. The result is that a few get rich or richer, and some find work in the war industry; while the vast majority of workers get poorer by means of inflation and personal debt. The war industry is an anti-worker industry. It causes destruction of work and the waste of more work to build back up, while the opportunity costs are incalculable. Therefore the AFWS will be extraordinarily careful as to matters of peace and war.

From a mere chronological standpoint, this very issue of war is the startling beacon that straightforwardly sheds light on the degenerate nature of the liberal state in the journey from its very inception to the present calamitous phase. Indeed, in European tradition—and in most others—monarchs and large sections of the ruling castes, used to lead their armies into battle, and to such an extent this is a documented record that we can unequivocally affirm that countless battlefields have been soaked in royal blood throughout history. As the liberal states progressively took hold of Europe and beyond, the sovereigns and their administrative and political castes grew wary of the personal dangers of war, albeit their appetite for power and riches at the expense of the workers' blood remained unquenched. Nowadays this liberal state is under the stewardship of a clique of wretched warmongers and psychopaths operating at the behest of the usufructuary caste—an inevitable situation given the quiddity of the laissez-faire state. They send the workers' children to kill and die in absurd wars of aggression, thereby becoming richer in the process—and contemporaneously their own children are sent to expensive colleges, universities, and military academies to perpetuate the cycle of exploitation in the liberal caste system. In fact, at this stage in the liberal decomposition, the master and ruling castes do not even pretend that they are not benefiting from the common man's blood, for the ownership of massive holdings in the arms industry among that throng of rogues is rife and overt.

Consequently it is our will that:

<hr />

27. Fourth founding principle: the AFWS as a pacific state, stringent tenets of just war, and legitimacy in its execution and goals

"When it comes to war, it will never be a war of choice of any kind. If a defensive war for survival becomes unavoidable, the state will decide upon any military action beyond our borders by a two-thirds majority in the Council, and a two-thirds majority of the people consulted in a referendum of mandatory participation. Conscription will be enacted and the whole of the people will bear the brunt of war, democratically. It will be paid for by an increase in taxes and an interest-free expansion of the monetary supply to reflect the increase in national output (if such contingency materializes), but never interest-bearing, liberal debt; and special vigilance will be exercised so as to bar anybody from profiting directly or indirectly from it. The only just war is that unequivocally defensive, overly pledging disproportionality and of total annihilation of any foreign aggressor in order to avoid conflict in the first place. This is tantamount to the extension of the nuclear doctrine to the scenario of a conventional war so as to prevent it by increasing its cost to unacceptable levels. But if war breaks out after all, the deontological goal is always to bring the conflict to a victorious end as soon as possible, minimizing the loss of life and wealth among our workers, and discourage future wars of aggression on our people, by making the costs associated to that enterprise not only unbearable but irreversible and final."

I have included in the above principle terms which pertain to the structure of the state and the government themselves and I will expound on them later on.

I am sure it is by now totally apparent how immanently different our philosophy is from those inspired by mere opposition to the liberal anti-utopia and laissez-faire capitalism. However, I am not as naive as to believe that what we actually are or are not will be properly understood. For example, I doubt most of people who called themselves "leftists" have any idea of what a leftist really is. But I do know what that philosophy, or rather that state of mind, truly is. My grandfather Cesar, a truly terrific man whom I to this day miss dearly, volunteered and fought as a lieutenant in an infantry unit on the leftist, pro-Bolshevik side in the Spanish Civil War. The opposite faction was a loose coalition of conservatives, traditional Catholics and falangists (Spanish fascists). Before the war ended he became prisoner of war and did forced labor for a German regiment. After the war was lost, he spent several months in a prisoner camp until his ultimate release, when he was allowed to return home— only to move abroad a few years later. He was a socialist.

A true believer. The only possible way, the European way. For not in vain did they invent socialism and all its variants afterward. And as much as I despise socialism, for its roots are putrid as a philosophy of the negative, of a reaction, and therefore stained with the sins of its alter ego; yet, I know very well what a true leftist believer is, what he sounds like, and all the topics and matters that make him tick, as the idiom goes.

And my dear compeers, let me state here categorically that we do not have leftists in America, or progressives, as they are wont to call themselves for propaganda purposes. What we certainly have is a medley of postmodernists on the one hand and ruling-caste stooges or paid actors on the other. Without wasting time and effort going into the details of postmodernism, I would like to point out that it is a philosophy of negation and destruction, of moral and epistemological relativism, and rejection of objective identity and hierarchy. In the final analysis, postmodernists render their own philosophy and everyone else's a futile exercise, since ultimately nothing matters. They come very close to reducing their entire philosophy to a circular fallacy. It is a self-devouring way of thinking. No wonder it is a philosophy born out of academia, engendered and more importantly spread and endorsed by college professors, but not true philosophers. For make no mistake—a philosopher is not an intellectual. An intellectual is the peddler of others' ideas, whereas the philosopher is the inventor of the ideas. And since most ideas are cacodaemons rather than eudaemons, it follows that I admire the latter and despise the former. That is because to make a mistake or even a few is quite reasonable, but to teach them and promote them out of stupidity and narcissism, that is intolerable. It is for this reason that Marx, for example, was a mediocre political philosopher but nonetheless not an intellectual, and therefore, and despite all his shortcomings and misguided fancies, I still respect him.

---

28. Logical capitalism versus laissez-faire capitalism

It is at this juncture when I find the ineluctable necessity of defining what is the economic system postulated by the AFWP and what is not. Ours will be a state born out of the revolution of logic. And the primary battle that logic ought to fight is the battle for exposing what capitalism has been and was never meant to be. Laissez-faire capitalism, as I already pointed out, is a leftover from the times of slavery and serfdom carried over into the industrial era, brought about by a political and economic philosophy riddled with fallacies and hubris. It was also an epoch of unmitigated moral turpitude and projection. For there is no other explanation as to how could they possibly have considered themselves so enlightened or awakened while philosophizing about turning workers into mere commodities. The intellectuals involved in this movement were reminiscent of the liberal ruling caste of today: conceited, hypocritical, philosophically incoherent, and godless, although many pretended this was not the case since back then atheism was frowned upon by the whole of the people, and hence the credibility of those self-declared atheists greatly diminished.

This last point is especially significant, for only someone who believes that no judge is watching over could come up with such arrogantly insensitive degradation of the human condition to a number in a game of aggregates. Laissez-faire capitalism in any of its manifestations is at its core predatory. It pitches man against man, and it forces him down a never-ending spiral of constant competition to the bottom of the barrel. It is predicated on the assumption that if a worker demands that his work be measured by its true value, i.e., by the marginal utility that he creates for the employer, then he will be undercut by someone else with a less lofty self-image; namely by somebody willing and able to race down to the bottom of the pit and meet there his competitive wage. This system thus defined is therefore based upon the condition that plenty of spiritually broken-down workers are available for any single job.

Ergo the liberal anti-utopia motto, as I have already mentioned, is and always will be, "Cheap labor at home through open borders and slave labor abroad through open trade and offshoring". Ultimately, the dystopian colossus is dependent upon an almost unlimited army of workers who accept the classical theory of work as a irrefutable social construct, never to be even debated, let alone opposed or denounced. In order to guarantee that docile behavior, philosophy at large and particularly ethics, politics and logic have been systematically removed from our educational system, or at least deliberately contaminated. Young people are these days only taught to perform efficiently a set of tasks, simple or convoluted, in a standardized, noncritical approach. To this end, special emphasis is being placed on technology and other practical matters that make the future worker productive, and anything but inquisitive, rebellious or quite frankly, logical. The administrative needs of the state are also met by training a relatively large section of the population in all kinds of managerial matters, rewarding these people accordingly so they become happy drivers and overseers of the larger mass of workers. Along these lines we can appreciate the huge chasm between the managerial caste and the workers themselves. The managers are the gatekeepers of an order which is illogical in its very premise. Whether it is in government or in the private sector, the elites and those workers who can afford it send their children to the institutions where "titles" are awarded to those willing to not ask many questions. And the consequent guerdons will be reaped in a lifetime of intellectually accommodating groveling.

29. Liberal apologists without any functional skill

Let us take right here a detour which is nevertheless important to take, for its very clarificatory nature. Most people nowadays have barely any survival or even practical skills. They cannot hunt, fish or field dress their prey; they do not know how to sow, tend or reap any crop; most do not even know how to protect themselves from anything at all. They do not have much knowledge about plumbing, electricity or anything else for that matter. Most people rely on somebody else to do everything for them, in exchange for "money". But what if workers stop offering their services for money? What if they decided to form their own communities, their own private clubs where only certain types of people were allowed in? And what if the prospective members were to take a litmus test? Maybe a test based on practical skills, or an examination about their ethical philosophy, their past earnings, their education, etc. What if only the admitted members were able to trade work within the community? The truth of the matter is, money as a means of exchange is a social construct. As we saw previously, money is work. That is its quiddity. As a means of commerce, it is a mere social construct in the context of a central banking system that issues interest-bearing banknotes creating a monetary supply disconnected from actual economic output.

It is utterly baffling to observe all these proponents of the enlightened version of capitalism, most of whom have no practical skill whatsoever, propound that a "competitive" wage is the measure of a worker, and that nobody does anything against his will. These people would be the first ones to starve to death if money as a social construct were to disappear. That can happen, and has already befallen countless societies throughout history in the form of revolutions, scorched-earth invasions or inflationary collapses. So it takes a special type of gall to advocate for predatory capitalism and call It freedom when you have no skills worth anything once banknotes are not considered a repository of value or a medium of exchange anymore. Therefore how illogical the "rational self-interest" crowd is when they treat their fellow men in that fashion; just as a stranger you can buy with money, with a competitive wage based on the assumption that an enlightened worker (this would be a much worthy context to use such a hackneyed word) can be supplanted by a benighted one, if the latter is desperate enough? These are the thoughts that spring to mind when I witness customers at all kinds of commercial establishments being served by clerks, attendants and waiters without even deigning to look the workers in the eye so as to show some measure of acknowledgment, kindness and respect. I am aware that this behavior is mainly urban (and I already said that urban life is a neurosis), therefore my expectations should be curtailed thereunder. Nevertheless, I always found that behavior predatory—or, at the very least, ill-mannered and uncharitable. Such approach to life is indeed rather risky, for it is based upon the assumption that nothing will ever happen, and society will remain stable at least as long as the predator is alive. Sometimes that is the case, sometimes it is not. In any event it seems to me that if ethics and logical capitalism are not your lodestar, at least a certain aversion to risk should be. Or maybe they have pondered the odds and they have drawn the conclusion that it is all worth it. I only can surmise.

So in conclusion, laissez-faire capitalism is illogical in a literal sense because it is founded on a philosophical falsehood and all the deductions implicit in its corpus are either formally invalid or empirically wrong, or both.

On the other hand, we advocate for logical capitalism. That is capitalism with many of its concomitant attributes, including: private ownership of most means of production operated for profit; competitive markets; a self-regulating price system; property rights and private property; capital investment and voluntary exchange. Logical capitalism rejects, however, wagslave labor and private banking since this is predicated upon a theory of money which is invalid and false. On the former I have expounded extensively. On the latter, suffice it to say that if the state issues the currency as a true reflection of the work value in the body politic, it stands to reason that any activity involving borrowing and lending of any kind and through any instrument must be done without the perpetration of work destruction or misappropriation, which would ineluctably occur either by the unvirtuous character of the activity funded or by the generation of profit in the form of interest (which has already been explained and exposed as theft, being the appropriation of social work not created by the lender himself).

So the state should have complete monopoly of the banking system (with a notable exception that I will analyze when I talk about logical capital). In that way all activity to be funded by debt can be evaluated virtuously and economically. Eventually, one of the benefits brought about by this arrangement is the total substitution of debt for capital in publicly traded companies and big corporations in general. That way, the success of a few ripples out into the success of the many, even many millions: whoever decides to invest his money/work in a public company. In this fashion the investor-worker does not become a lender, but an owner. And that is a model that in large corporations as well as in the realm of LLCs and other small companies, the proprietorship becomes rife, furthering social cohesion for the benefit of all the people, and protected by the state itself.

And it is without any qualms that we proclaim our

unequivocal intention to turn debt into property and invest-ment, a nation of overconsumption into a nation of virtuous production, and a nation of overspending into a nation of sensible spending not funded by debt. And a nation struc-tured by a state that leads by example. A state that lives within its means, without splurging or wasting or living on credit; always demanding from the people exactly what it demands from itself, without exceptions (this point will be the focus of the section dedicated to the explication of the sources of a state's legitimacy and thus its right to exist).

Whence it is our will that:

◆————————◆

30. Fifth founding principle: logical capitalism

"The AFWS is a state with a logical capitalist system, where wagslave labor is rejected and substituted by logical labor, and the banking system is the monopoly of the state for the preservation of work, the stability of money, the virtuous as well as productive evaluation of debt, and the elimination of interest; as well as the radical transformation of private debt into private investment in the capital markets as a means to democratize the wealth and strengthen the internal cohesion of the nation. Money will always be a perfect reflection of the output of work, and so the state and the people will live in truth, and not in debt and inflation. Money will be finally sound in the utmost sense, and virtuous, as is the work it represents."

31. Autarky

This is the ideal economy as it pertains to the interconnection of production and trade. Since times immemorial, nations have strived to achieve this most natural state, namely that of a community able (and willing) to be self-sustaining, self-reliant, free and independent. Autarky represents the collective realization of a national conglomerate of tribes which ultimately aspire to become the masters of their own present and of a destiny not tied down by foreign entanglements, or even worse, submissions. It is the state of a people capable of producing all the necessary goods and services to meet their domestic consumption. It is the noblest desire to become a self-sufficient organism, with the resources and the will to prevent itself from fighting wars over raw materials and from careening down the path of self-destructive consumerism.

In fact, over millennia the longing for autarky has been so overwhelming that countless nations poured forth all their energies to expand into empires, which through mercantilist policies could replicate that state of affairs. At its core, imperialism and colonialism on the political front, and mercantilism on the commerce front, are the two ever-present historical manifestations of the yearning for autarky. When nation-states were incapable of meeting their demand with domestic production, they embarked on expansionist policies so trade with foreign nations out of that self-contained economic unit could be kept at a minimum. The reason is evidently the desire for independence and strength. It is also the realization that a healthy body politic is able both to create the institutions that structure the state as a conduit of the people themselves, and to perform the work necessary for the maintenance of those institutions and of the state itself. For only in this way can an organized society eventually turn into an organism. And this is ultimately the goal of any high-achieving people, as we recognize that a human body is and will always be superior to any machine. That is the superiority of the organism over the organization.

The most virtuous economic system, in the strictest sense, is the logical capitalist autarky. Its antithesis, which is what liberalism represents and promotes explicitly, and needs implicitly for its survival, is the open trade/globalist/offshoring laissez-faire capitalism—an immoral swindle which is founded upon the backs of the workers, for the sole benefit of the political and financial ruling castes and their peripheral and subordinate caste, i.e., the managerial conglomerate.

But America has such a vast population, landmass and natural resources that the economy could be close to self-contained if the state and the people chose to go down the path of freedom. In a logical capitalistic autarky, most of the domestic production is used to meet the internal consumption, exporting the rest in exchange for the commodities we cannot produce domestically. Specific, bilateral trade agreements are made with those nations that can provide the raw materials we lack either altogether or in adequate quantities. The trade can be carried out through the conventional means of currency (but not gold reserves for reasons I will hereinafter explain), or if those nations are more predisposed to it, through the exchange of goods at a predetermined, negotiated rate. This last mechanism of trade was extensively used by many nations in Europe back in WWII when, for example, Germany could not or did not want to pay in gold and their counterparts did not accept Reichsmarks.

The equilibriums reached domestically in an autarkic economy versus the current model of globalist open trade would be massively different, but before going deeper into it I need to clarify some points. Firstly, an autarky requires the one-to-one relation of money-work to be enforced very strictly. In other words, the monetary policy must be constantly based on truth, based on the actual output of work in the country. On the other hand, the state must scrupulously adhere to a philosophy of permanent balanced budgets. The reason for all of this is straightforward: in an autarky, the state cannot meet an excess of domestic demand by additional imports in exchange for banknotes or in the AFWS case, state notes or treasury notes. The reason why this kakotopian behemoth has managed to run massive and permanent trade deficits is because the USD remains the reserve currency of the world. So we print money ex nihilo, this money bleeds off into the economy through credit and debt, and subsequently the American consumer spends it on imported goods, as the trade deficits grow ever larger and inflation pays for the expansion in the monetary base.

Or better phrased, inflation is in and of itself the expansion of that base, whereas the increase in consumer prices is one of its many side effects. So the sham is based on consuming what we do not produce through the creation of money that should not exist because it does not reflect the real size of our economy, i.e., our total social work, our output. As the national debt balloons due to the state not living in truth, we are fast approaching a point where dollar-denominated debt will spiral down in valuation as our capacity to pay down that debt will be deemed mathematically and practically impossible. Whenever all our creditors try to liquidate that debt, if it happens all at once, in the wake of a panic or a crash or conversely in the lead-up to it, the USD will inevitably enter a debt-driven death spiral. Once nobody accepts the Fed's banknotes as payment, it will become apparent how poor we have become. We will be a country without the industrial base to meet our own domestic consumption and without the resources to import it.

It will be a rude awakening for the American worker, but not for the financial/master caste. Most of their assets will be in the form of foreign currencies, gold and other precious metals, cryptocurrencies and investments held overseas. In fact, as of right now, most American corporations are multinational enterprises which produce most of their goods using slave labor in China and elsewhere, and it is over there where they keep their money and physical capital to a large extent. In this wicked scheme, the American worker is only left to toil for cheap wages doing whatever work the elites cannot offshore, and to buy the subpar goods that we import, whether they are foreign products or the result of offshoring.

Only what we produce at home, employing American workers, investing in productive capital domestically, and paying taxes to our state, will result in an advancement of the justice, prosperity and respect we are striving for. The legal residency of corporations and the nationality of their owners are irrelevant to the prosperity and welfare of our nation. But for decades now, the political-industrial complex and their propaganda branch, corporate media, have been selling this absurd modus operandi in the economy by arguing that on the one hand American workers are able to pay less for products, and on the other hand the corporations themselves have countless investors who are in many cases workers. This is a flagrant case of ignoratio elenchi, for it is true that goods are cheaper when they are made by slave labor and anybody who invests in companies that offshore their production will benefit correspondingly, but the nation as a whole will be worse off: fewer jobs and hence lesser output; worse-paying jobs; more dependency on foreign countries, both economic and strategic; more debt; generally more inflation over the long haul; and ultimately a bigger chasm between the upper castes and workers, leading to a much flimsier social fabric and political cohesion.

Interestingly enough, the mouthpieces for the liberal state's policies of open trade and offshoring are (inadvertently, I presume) validating Marx's analysis of the capitalist mode of production. He believed that the capitalist caste, in order to increase the ratio surplus labor/necessary labor and therefore expand capital further and faster, would engage in a constant pursuit of productivity increases of variable capital by means of technological improvements, or resort to new sources of labor immanently more productive; the ultimate goal being the ability to sell commodities in the open markets at ever lower prices. This interesting dynamic was looked into by Marx and his approach is not easily refuted from the strict point of view of political economy. And as a matter of fact, the obsession with free trade and offshoring by liberal apologists and the propagandized defense thereof, makes the rebuttal to that part of Marxist theory even more challenging.

It is abundantly clear by now that the laissez-faire Leviathan exists to protect and further the interests of the capitalist master caste. To that end, all relevant agencies of government strive cohesively within their own realms of action: the intelligence and law enforcement agencies cooperate to eliminate any possible threat, foreign or domestic; the IRS harasses those who are seen as not sufficiently orthodox; the Department of Justice turns the law into a political weapon against those not welcome into power. Meanwhile, corporate media engage in a massive and constant campaign of delusion and hatred to keep workers divided, and academia is happy to do the power caste's bidding because of ideological conviction or financial dependency, or both.

Is it not beyond dispute that this state is not legitimate? It exists only to advance the interests of those who control the political and bureaucratic castes; the ones who wield the powers of the state through the various branches of government, agencies and departments. The laissez-faire state is not only illegitimate in the sense already discussed. It is also the antithesis of democracy. For what power do the workers have at their disposal? The vote? Even if we are as naive as to presume that elections are conducted fairly and the votes adequately counted, what is a vote? And an election? Unquestionably we should be talking about selections instead.

All the candidates in the kabuki dance we call presidential elections have to jump through massive financial and political hoops and be vetted by the only caste that matters in America: the donor caste. If the candidates are willing to play ball and prove themselves useful, they will be funded. Otherwise they will be politically neutered through various plots, most of which involve massive amounts of propaganda, money, and legal persecution. We can rest assured that if anybody is allowed to run a campaign at that level without hindrance, he is a dirty politician. How can we call a regime that only allows rich people and those who woo them to run for office and hold power, a "democracy"? Workers are only permitted to vote for their masters, never to run. This is a system purposefully designed to make political power too expensive to achieve. How is that "democratic"? How is it democratic for a bunch of bought-and-paid-for professional politicians to make fundamental decisions that will affect every single American worker for generations to come, without ever asking for the people's opinions on the subject matter directly, via referendum? And how can a "professional politician" with a decades-long "political career" be called a "public servant"? This kind of oxymorons are the currency in the liberal hegemon, where truth can only be discussed under the table, lest its effulgent face shames everybody partaking in the maze of lies.

The fact is the worker is only an insignificant pawn in a scheme devised to make a particular caste of people ever richer and more powerful through the misdeeds of another caste, that of scoundrels and picaroons, willing to carry the proverbial water either for pelf or raw power. To this end, workers are constantly programmed to hate one another on genetic and environmental bases so they remain in a permanent state of division and delusion. They are also bombarded with constant propaganda perpetrated by state media, and cheaply accessible, attention-span-shuttering mass entertainment. Of course there are plenty of exceptions to the rule, but generally a classless society is the perfect match for a talentless caste of corporate shills. The tastes and wits of the people have been perniciously degraded by a corrosive "education system", which has dumbed down vast swaths of workers to levels difficult to believe possible if it were not in full display before our very eyes.

We virulently oppose the incoherent concept "liberal democracy" and we embrace the organic democracy, or that instantiated in the body politic through the organic state, and it implies:

1. The categorical destruction of all castes through the mechanisms discussed in this work.

2. The abolition of all parties and the articulation of the state through the AFWP, for political parties are anathema to democracy.

3. The absolute adherence to the founding principles of the party, or in other words, the constitutive principles of the organic state.

The final objective is the realization of a sociopolitical ideal, a composite of justice, liberty, prosperity (moral as well as material) and respect. An ideal which stands as a judge at the end of an onerous and demanding collective travail and which involves the creation of a new ethos and its corresponding social constructs.

In the ultimate analysis, this particracy is a toxic conspiracy perpetrated on the American worker for the financial benefit of a few and at the expense of the nation as a whole, as a people.

Their means of exploitation is what some define as corporate creditism, made possible by the infamous collusion between government and business. It is a scheme which runs on banknotes passed off as real money in order to pump the financial bubbles; inflation to pay for deficit spending; slave labor abroad through open trade and offshoring; cheap labor or wage labor or competitive labor or what I term wagslave labor (no pun necessarily intended but I admit it is debatable) at home through open borders and a construct; a nation of debtors, progressively impoverished in that interest trap; savings only in the vocabulary of privileged castes, and a massive number of individuals engaged in illegitimate, destructive activities whose unintended consequences will require massive amounts of future work to counteract and an opportunity cost of present uninstantiated work impossible to evaluate.

An autarkic state and an ethos derived from our political principles are a binomial function that yields the organic state. In an autarkic state, workers' incomes increase and so do the production costs. The macroeconomic aggregated equilibrium might be less consumption at higher or lower prices or more consumption at higher or lower prices, depending on the sector and the development of sound saving and investing habits in the legitimate caste. In any event, the margins fall off and the workers increase proportionately their share in the national output. It is a much more cohesive society, where the incomes and wealth grow closer together, savings and investments among the people at large increase as the nation transitions from a culture of overconsumption to self-sustenance, from debt to savings and investments.

In the transformation of this ethos, which will indeed usher in an even more successful autarky, the national education system will play a crucial role. For it is a fact that this fundamental transformation is utterly dependent upon the acceptance of a virtuous life by the whole of the people. At the heart of the autarkic state, there is a virtuous people, educated in love for prudence, diligence and temperance—a people who love values more than things, and who well know they own their bodies, but they are not bodies. All of this is education, doctrine and ultimately culture. All of this will represent the zeitgeist of the AFWS. It is a natural state. It is a decent, just state. It is a socially prosperous state. It is a state that defends and promotes freedom and personal growth. It is a state that gives the workers the tools they need to live an independent life, with optimism, knowledge and empowerment. In this context, facilitated by the AFWS, the workers themselves will level up their conditions to their righteous measure by means of acting and negotiating as I already expounded upon in previous pages. We are certainly blessed to own a country with such vast natural resources and markets, that the establishment of an autarky within a logical capitalist structure is not only a desirable and necessary aspiration, but rather an inevitable one.

And without more dilations, it is our will that:

Autarky: One people, sovereign, free and self-reliant.

32. Sixth founding principle: the AFWS, a logical capitalist autarky

"The economic system of the AFWS is autarkic logical capitalism. It is the most just, democratic and natural of systems, and it maximizes the prosperity of the people as it reinforces the legitimacy of the state and the solidarity within the body politic. It is both a testament to and a guarantor of the nobility and the virtuous nature of that self-loving organism, our people, the extension of the organic state."

One of the innumerable advantages of our autarkic logical capitalism is ecological. As we move from consumerism to balanced consumption, from spending on credit to spending within our means, and from borrowing from the world to lending to the world if conditions call for such an action, we are as a result moving from imports to domestic production. This in turn makes the ecological imprint of commerce to slump, since the transportation of commodities and manufactured goods is one of the most energy-intensive activities there is. Interestingly enough, the "ecologist" groups out there barely have anything to say on this subject matter; a further proof of how the partitocracy maintains a network of organizations for the sole purpose of gaslighting the people and keeping workers divided in their goals and bewildered in their thinking.

The spurious nature of a myriad of associations and organizations, underhandedly funded by billionaires and their instrument of political action, this partocracy, is irrefutable. Their only purpose is to make sure the conspiratorial state staves off the workers' criticism. To that purpose, all conceivable tangential group issues are fabricated, in an effort, quite successful I may add, to smother the overwhelmingly predatory nature of this state; predatory not on groups, but on workers. For workers are not a group or tribe within the nation, but the nation itself. Workers are the country and they should be therefore the state. It is a machination unrelentingly carried out and illegitimately funded; a conspiracy that thrives on hatred and deception, and on dirty pelf and ignorance. Rest assured that the days of that satanic enterprise are numbered, as soon as the AFWS dawns upon the land out of the righteous aspirations of hard-working people.

This thought takes me forthwith to the functional illegitimacy of the cast-driven Leviathan.

This state was created, as I already pointed out, for proprietors and by proprietors. It was the ultimate bourgeois revolution, literally sparked off by abusive taxes. From the onset, the state subscribed to a very laissez-faire view of its responsibilities, so it kept them to a minimum. And through the legal framework of the Constitution, those property rights were protected, directly and indirectly, through the various titles and amendments. But they all boil down to three fundamental tasks:

1. The defense of the country's borders.

2. The guarantee of internal peace and stability, including an independent and fair judiciary.

3. The protection of some unalienable and indefeasible

rights and freedoms among which we find freedom of speech, association, religion and the press.

⊲▸————————◂⊳

33. Immigrants as the surplus population for the expansion and concentration of capital

1. This function has not only been abjured by the state, but rather purposefully upended for the benefit of the donor caste. The violation of all immigration laws in America by the federal government is the most flagrant kickback that Wall Street receives on a regular basis to requite their contributions. I assume the reader remembers what is the sine qua non for wagslave labor and hence classical or laissez-faire, liberal capitalism: the abundance of an alternative for every worker who rejects the careening down to the bottom of the pit to meet his competitive wage. So the constitutional mandate gives way to the ruling caste's unquenchable lust for cheap labor. To procure and maintain a loose labor market, especially among "low-skilled" workers, is an ever-present priority for the illegitimate state; not because it is conducive to the weal of the people at large but because the caste for which it exists demands it as a means to lower production costs and increase profits. We have come to a point in history where the ruling caste no longer feels the need to hold back or lie about its border policies. Instead, they heavily rely on their propaganda machine and the indoctrination in schools to keep the workers diverted and divided

with tangential issues. Thus, if anyone objects to this policy, he is deemed a racist. Never mind that every wave of immigration competes with every other wave that precedes it. In other words, the immigrants of today bring the wages of yesterday's immigrants down, and the former become the latter as soon as tomorrow's immigrants arrive. It is the perfect scenario for the usufructuary caste: a never-ending influx of desperate workers, able and willing to undercut any other worker, immigrant or native. It is unquestionably established by now that most immigrants who come into the country in state of poverty, remain in state of poverty, and the cycle is reinforcing itself with every passing generation. The liberal state always has regarded workers as the fodder which the master caste feeds on through wagslave labor within the scheme of laissez-faire capitalism.

So when it comes to immigration, all the centers of power advocate for more and more, although they never argue that they do it to bring wages down, but because "somebody has to do the work that Americans no longer want". Yes! Americans and immigrants alike do not want to work many jobs at the present equilibrium wages, which are unreasonably low because of the immigrant influx in the first place. Without it, wages would be much higher across the board and yesterday's immigrants, along with their native brothers, would come out again to perform them. So the fallacy resides in a lack of predication, i.e., in stating "they do not want to work certain jobs" rather than "they do not want to work certain jobs at the current wages", which would increase to begin with once the vicious circle is interrupted. It is quite miraculous to behold the disintegration of problems once truth is allowed to shine, unhindered.

Another straw man argument is demographics. The state argues that the native population does not have enough children to keep the machine plowing on. Imprimis, workers would have more children if they could afford them, in other words, if the labor market were to stop the exploitation through competitive wages, as opposed to logical labor wages. Secondly, it is particularly alarming the voracious appetite that this state has for an ever-increasing population, in connection with economic and financial matters proper. The state's stewards claim that the only way to pay off the interest on the national debt and meet the Social Security and Medicare obligations is constant economic growth; and since productivity gains driven by technology breakthroughs have their limitations, the apologists come to the conclusion that permanent population growth is necessary to find the way out of this conundrum.

◄▬▬▬▬▬►

34. The liberal state: a mathematically unstable and hence unsustainable system

And it is here where I would like to inject a mathematical reference, although I am naturally predisposed against it. In differential analysis, a system that has to constantly grow in order to not collapse unto itself is considered unstable. By that definition, the liberal colossus is itself an unstable system. In other words, it is the mathematical definition of unsustainable. What else could we expect from a state born out of a philosophy of consumerism and predation, riddled with logical fallacies and rejection of traditional virtues!

35. Divide et impera: immigration as a reticulation scheme in the liberal state

A very important aspect of the anti-worker state's immigration policies is the reticulation factor, paramount for the state's survival. This topic will be analyzed in depth when the struggle against the state is properly defined and articulated, but for now suffice to say that the most outstanding characteristic of the laissez-faire state, in praxis, is its unquenchable drive for survival at the expense of its own people. In order to achieve that aim, and since the state itself is anathema to the people, a sort of leech or parasite growing fatter as the phalanxes of workers grow weaker, it stands to reason that the tyrant must head off any combined political action by the people which could potentially capsize the galley of the state. The usufructuary caste, and its subservient castes forming the rank and file of those manning the vessel, are existentially invested in the reticulation of the people, lest a defiant mutiny bring those marauders' scam to an abrupt end. It is thus the goal of the state to avert any possible consolidation of workers around their identity as workers. To that end, other identities must be created, promoted and reinforced. The aim is always the debilitation of the body politic along as many fault lines as possible and the thwarting of a formal, encompassing, unifying national identity around the worker qua worker.

In this regard, immigration is seen by the stewards of the

liberal Goliath as a tool for such reticulation, inasmuch as it is conducive to a multinational, multiracial, multicultural society. The fault lines thus created are too many and too deep as to allow the quiddity of workers qua workers to become the linchpin of national identity and integration. In the life of a predator, every move and action is functionally deadly; it is intended, by design, to make the victimization of its prey easier.

<hr />

36. Immigration as a thrust and an excuse for an ever-larger security apparatus in the liberal Leviathan

Another quite interesting aspect of immigration, and one that most will no doubt overlook, is its potential to prompt an expansion of the security apparatus, which is one of the main pillars upon which the illegitimate state fends off the people. In fact, no immigrant is a waste in this kakotopia; he is either a cheap and docile worker, an actuation of reticulation, or a criminal element and thus an excuse to enlarge the size and scope of the state. The functionary caste that runs countless departments, agencies and the judiciary, desperately needs objects of action so as to guarantee its survival and expansion. These are the foot soldiers or the shepherds of a state that needs to keep its ranks satisfied in order to remain as strong as necessary to retain the herd in the fold. Much more on the security state will hereinafter be discussed.

However, a large and persistent migratory influx, in the context of the liberal security apparatus, could actually become its subject rather than its object. Indeed, tyrant states, and this malformation is the paradigm thereof, are prone to use foreigners as the rank and file and even as the chiefs and managers of security and law enforcement agencies, as history has repeatedly shown. In this regard, let us read Aristotle's wise words, or shall we just say words so as to avoid redundancy in connection with this most esteemed hero of philosophy. In one of his masterpieces, *Politics*, he wrote: "Most of the cities which have admitted settlers, either at the time of their foundation or later, have been troubled by faction .... It is also a habit of tyrants to prefer the company of aliens to that of citizens at table and in society; citizens, they feel, are enemies, but aliens will offer no opposition."

My inference is straightforward from his analysis, and corroborated by historical evidence as I have already pointed out. Nevertheless, I want to make a prediction which, when it finally comes to pass, will not bewilder those keen readers and fellow compatriots who are paying heed to my words: significant sections of the multi-tribal immigrant community will become one of the spearheads of the party and the revolution. And it will not be so exclusively because of the constant exploitation that they are being subjected to through liberal competition, but also because many if not most of them come from countries where laissez-faire philosophies have not been fully absorbed by the people themselves—in some cases, owing to abject poverty and the lack of any indoctrination system in place; in other cases, because many of those nations have struggled for decades in an internecine philosophical battle between classical capitalism, socialism, communism and fascism—Those who are using workers as fodder for their predatory wagslave labor schemes will be the first ones to regret their own policies, once the sledgehammer morphs into the ax and the spade into the sword, as they march forth into the next page in that book depicted in our shield.

That being said, as a matter of practical justice for all the workers already in the land, American-born, naturalized citizens or immigrants, the state must implement a mechanism of pecuniary reparations for its deliberate dereliction of duty toward those workers, via intentional flooding of the country with an unrestricted influx of fellow foreign workers. In accordance with both this state of affairs and this principle, each and every worker needs to be properly rewarded in direct relation to the length of his ties to the land. It stands to reason that a worker who was born in the land has the uttermost natural connection with it, and as we progress in the quantitative measure and application of this principle, all workers will have to be remunerated proportionally to the time they have lived in our midst. Hence, an American-born worker will receive the maximum compensation, followed by those who became naturalized in due time. After these fellows, the rest of the immigrant population will be compensated according to the length of their stay.

The ultimate goal of this policy will be the attaining of a state of affairs in which every worker has been recompensed for the wages being artificially deflated by the state, proportionally to their vital commitment to the nation which will have to be appraised, for lack of a better metric, by the length of their stay in the land. In that way a just, straightforward and transparent retribution system is enacted based on a hierarchy which is logical and all-encompassing. In order for this scheme to fruitfully establish both an end to the injustice and the beginning of a new, fair system, it is paramount that the new AFWS implements the human parallelism to autarky. Just as the size of our economy would be the envy of all the mercantilist empires of yore, the size of our population has grown over the last decades at a warp speed, and it is now time to acknowledge our mighty and untapped potential, as well as integrate this mélange of countless tribes (adding up to a gargantuan 330 million plus) into the national organism that we call the AFWS.

To this purpose we will prohibit immigration into the country and all necessary laws and policies will be adequately implemented. It is time for this massive conglomerate of deeply divided and balkanized society, this amalgamation of tribes we call the nation, to become once and for all integrated into the organic state, on the basis of the principles and philosophies I am elaborating on in this founding manifesto. This process might take, in sooth, many decades, for the reticulation of our national life along tribal lines has reached chaotic levels. We find ourselves hard-pressed to point out what attributes and philosophies the people have in common, especially when the usage of English itself as a national language is breaking down in this Tower of Babel, and the national identity almost impossible to define, courtesy of a corrupt, incompetent and philosophically hollowed-out anti-worker state.

37. The eugenic exception to immigration policy in the AFWS

One exception will be granted so as to allow supra-men from foreign countries to immigrate into our National Liberextremist State, provided such condition can be verified without a shadow of a doubt. This policy, in addition to the eugenics tax credit (I will address this topic in the context of a sensible, organic budgetary process), are political actions toward the realization of the state's supra-race. Geniuses and other extraordinary people, whether their talents are intellectual, artistic, physical or otherwise regarded by the state as desirable according to our principles, will be allowed to immigrate and become one of us in exchange for their genetic material and the rights to use it at state-owned-and-operated fertility clinics. These nonprofit facilities will be at the disposal of all the compeers who think of themselves in need of such services, as well as those compatriots who desire to furnish our collective march toward the ideal with the most personal and powerful of impetus: the blood. In this fashion, the benefit that our people will derive from this kind of migration is twofold: first of all, as cells interconnecting with these special individuals who will be themselves henceforth members of the body politic; and secondly, as partners in the creation of that race of supra-men which is a logical aspiration of any healthy society. For who would not want to live in the midst of a people with thousands upon thousands of extraordinary men such as Carl Jung, and Gottlob Frege, and Aristotle, and Kurt Gödel, and Ludwig Wittgenstein, and Avicenna, and Mahatma Gandhi, and Baruch Spinoza, and Thomas Aquinas, and Immanuel Kant, and Gottfried

Wilhelm Leibniz, and Roger Federer, and Jesse Owens, and Charles Dickens, and Mark Twain, and Miguel de Cervantes, and Edgar Allan Poe, and William Shakespeare, and Fyodor Dostoevsky, and Arthur Conan Doyle, and Leo Tolstoy, and Leonardo da Vinci, and Salvador Dalí, and Michelangelo, and Raphael, and ... and ... and those gifted brethren with the potentiality waiting for that divine spark to turn it into actuality.

Economic autarky, human autarky. For the worker is the economy, and there is no economy or country for that matter without the worker. I hereupon deduce a simple corollary: in the hierarchy of quiddities, that of a worker is superior to that of a citizen, for a worker is immanently one unto himself but a citizen needs a state to exist. Therefore jus soli (or birthright citizenship as many call it) cannot be a natural right, since it is predicated on the existence of a state, which has been historically proven to be a contingency and not a necessity. Conversely, a worker only needs life and liberty (infused with will) to become, wherefore his nature is infused with natural rights. It is for this reason, as I have already intimated, that no man can proclaim a more exalted title than to be a worker. We are workers in the state first, and citizens of the state later. This chant is a battle cry for freedom impossible to utter within the confines of the liberal kakotopia. For how can that be done if you are just a speck of nothing in an aggregate, literally given a price tag in a market? You are a commodity for the benefit of the usufructuary caste. Sooner or later, the shattering of that delusion will resonate all over the world in ways that will defy our imagination.

A further discussion of the practical application of the

outlined reparations scheme will be carried out by the people and their representatives when the time comes. And now I declare without equivocation that it is hereafter our will that:

38. Seventh founding principle: human autarky and reparations

"The AFWS will systematically enact a reparations scheme in order to compensate all workers, US-born, naturalized and immigrants alike, for the illegitimate and constant deflation of domestic wages through immigration. This transfer of wealth from workers to the privileged financial and managerial castes needs to be offset by the state, irrespective of immigration status. Those reparations will be proportional to the length of the vital commitment of every worker to the nation as roughly represented by the length of his stay on the land. That hierarchy of payments will ensure justice through its very logical nature. The AFWS will stop indefinitely immigration into the country so all the native and immigrant tribes will finally have the resources and time to integrate into a cohesive organism as per the principles of our party. There will be a supra-man exception so as to reinforce the eugenic political action of the state in its march toward the supra-race. The AFWS is both an economic and a human autarky."

I have already stated our position and general philosophy as regards this most important subject of national defense against a foreign threat. But in connection with the analysis I am conducting in this section, I would like to underline, yet again, how unforgivably irresponsible, incompetent and corrupt this caste-driven Leviathan is in this matter. This political behemoth is the archetype of the warring dragon, the ultimate warmonger propelled in its sinning ways by its very nature. It incites a permanent state of war abroad and takes sides on every single conflict, in many cases providing free weapons and materiel. Sadly, when guns are free, wars last longer and the devastation is greater. Many of those disputes, if not all, have nothing to do with our national interest or territorial integrity. But here again, for the exclusive profit of the military-industrial complex, the aforementioned national interest is pushed to the side. The taxes raised from workers, obnoxiously crushing their living standards in many cases, are used to fulfill contracts and spending bills that are intended to fuel continuing conflicts all over the planet, as well as keeping up an oversized, domestic military establishment. Countless lives are lost abroad, whether the victims are native soldiers or civilians, or U.S. military personnel.

And yet, these foreign alignments are never properly explained or rationalized, because they cannot be. The ultimate drive of these entanglements is the generation of an excuse to set up massive payoffs and kickbacks on the people's backs, while the usufructuary caste is no longer concerned with any kind of coverup of their malfeasance. They do not believe anymore that the American people are capable of discerning between right or wrong, and between true or false. Through a multi-decade conspiratorial scheme involving mass media and the indoctrination system, it is been established that a significant majority of the people cannot effectively mount any kind of opposition to actual corruption, and the stewards of the state seem to be very well aware of it.

For what other explanation could we possibly come up with for the blatant disregard for truth, law, logic and decency, all of it perpetrated in plain sight by this rotten state? And I will not stand here, I will not! and blare that this state is altogether wrong about this. Unfortunately, it is at this juncture in our history patently obvious that huge swaths of the population are utterly incapable of any logical thinking, and their morality is likewise very questionable. Decades of propaganda and indoctrination have broken many among us; the question is, too many already to render the revolution unfeasible? Minds and souls irreparably damaged by the wayward stain of idiocy and corruption? The answer to both questions is a resounding no! Otherwise I would believe that there is no hope and I positively know, beyond an iota of doubt, that triumph will be categorically ours. My optimistic heart tells me that wickedness and dysfunction are never meant to last long in the big historical scheme of things. I only pray that the phase of pain and destruction in this upcoming internecine struggle will come to an end as soon as possible.

2. A state of internal peace, order and tranquility was deemed especially important by the Founders of this state, since it is an absolutely essential prerequisite in order to uphold property rights. And as I have profusely expounded on, this was a revolution of the propietor, by the propietor and for the propietor. So the paradox becomes even more glaring, given the utter dereliction of this duty by the laissez-faire state. But such paradox is only a mirage. Indeed, the chaos, pervasive crime and violence, and the systematic dismantling of all the institutions which so many held dear for centuries,

the tearing down of conventions and traditions and the wide range of subversive or even revolutionary activities, only affect the sections of society which are not part and parcel of the permanent usufructuary caste and its acolytes. This fact becomes particularly obvious in instances where all kinds of allegedly radical organizations hold parades and demonstrations (at times violent) in workers' neighborhoods, ripping through them and wreaking havoc in the process. However, the master caste's districts never encounter that kind of problem. Perhaps those organizations being funded by the very elites who live in the foregoing oppulent areas is the determining factor for the sparing of any unwelcome disruption?

It is certainly perplexing to observe marches of anti-capitalists and leftist groups ravaging our compeers' districts without even trying to get close to those places where the very master caste they decry abide? Not to mention the total dereliction of duty by the police forces during those riots, but God forbid anyone shows up with a harmless sign at the doors of profiteers, politicians or propagandists! The protester will be automatically repressed, harassed or even arrested and jailed. Could not I make a similar analysis when it comes to squatting situations, or DUI's, or tax crimes, or any other legal problem whether it is codified by the kakistocracy as a crime or a misdemeanor? We all know the law is a whip in the hands of the elites and a yoke around the workers' necks. The so-called "rule of law" is more than a mirage only in the dazed minds of the feeblest among us; those whose spirits and comprehension have been ravaged by the bane of propaganda and indoctrination. Generally speaking, that kind of damage could be reversible, but it will take an organic state to make it happen.

Anyway, I am optimistic that at this point most readers will have come to the unavoidable conclusion that all agencies of government in this laissez-faire mastodon exist for the sole purpose of defending the interests of the conglomerate who benefits from its very existence. These agencies engage in all kinds of schemes to ward off any and all threats to the usufructuary caste, especially those stemming from the workings of minds trained in logical and critical thinking. The state itself is illegitimate not only on philosophical grounds, but the agencies that articulate the government are illegitimate with respect to their daily activities. The bulk of their work is to protect and serve those in power and to that end they dedicate a puny amount of effort and resources to prop up the facade of public service. I could not offer any stronger example of illegitimacy than the IRS, the Fed, the FBI, the NSA, the CIA, the CDC and the FDA, to mention some of the most outstanding cases. They constitute, effectively, armies of publicly funded agencies at the service of the master caste. They are the definition of antidemocratic.

In our state, all agencies of government will be affected. Some will be dismantled and others totally downsized or overhauled in terms of internal structure, hierarchy and goals. And finally a host of other new agencies will be instituted, providing the tools that the state will need to carry out its mission according to our ideary.

And it is here where the word democracy comes to the fore. Because our state will be a state of the worker, meaning he will be the agent ultimately responsible for all the rights and protections that the state is charged with ensuring and enacting. To that end, the people themselves will be involved

*The casteless state: A rotational and perennial
regeneration enshrined in the law.*

in the managing of every affair within the public administration. In other words, all branches and agencies of the government will serve as the revolving door between the state and the people. This means bureaucratic positions will not be allowed to become careers or sinecures anymore. All jobs within all agencies of government including the judiciary will be temporary, and at the end of everyone's tenure as a public servant he will return to the private sector, to the people, as a new fellow worker takes up the vacant position for yet another limited term. The details of this process, including the duration of the public tenure itself, will be determined by the People's Council or by the people themselves directly deciding in national referendum. This constantly revolving transfer between public and private work will be conducive to two most important goals:

1. As many workers as possible will be directly involved in the administration of the state by establishing a system of term limits and rotation throughout the body politic.

2. Nobody will ever be part of a special caste of people, thereby limiting the chances and the scope of any kind of corrupt or abusive behavior.

The bureaucrat will be finally substituted by the public servant, who will always be one among other workers. Tax agents will return to their duties as accountants and tax preparers, and police officers will return to duties of private security, for example; garbage collectors and transit bus drivers will be reinstated to work again as truck and charter bus drivers, etc. We will tear down the rampart between the administration of the state and the citizenry, between the government and the governed, between the state and the worker. We will cease to be a compartmentalized organization with its concomitant hierarchy of political and financial power, and we will become an organism where the political cells are interconnected in an intricate network; always on the move, regenerating from within and living up to its founding ideals.

The people themselves or through their representatives in the National Council (more on this later) will decide upon issues of all sorts, including death penalty, war and peace and countless others big and small. And the organic state will provide the practical structure, always feeding off the people in a flexible fashion, so it can adequately and honestly carry out that popular will. The AFWS will be the first state in history where the ruled and the rulers are all part and parcel of the same people: the American worker. We will impose, with an iron fist if it comes to that, a true and democratic rule of law. The wicked and corrupt will be dealt with in a manner that the imploding anti-worker dystopia could not even dream of, because that toxic condition is precisely its nature. The word "elite" will be only appropriately used in the realm of productive achievement, and not in the murky sphere of nepotistic privilege. Ours will be a state of virtue and merit, not of corruption and upper and lower castes. The struggle will be worth it, and the conflagration ahead unavoidable. It will not be a battle for the faint of heart, because the tyrannic state will stop at nothing to get rid of all its enemies. The ruling caste will wield all levers of power with brutal force and without hesitation, for on it hinges its holding onto everything that is dear to them. It all comes down to riches and privilege acquired through the exploitation of the corrupt nature of the state itself.

And now we are ready to proclaim the following as our will:

————◆————

39. Eighth founding principle: organic administration of the AFWS; overcoming of the managerial and functionary castes

"Internal peace, order and the rule of law will be achieved in a truly revolutionary fashion, for we reject the liberal state model of castes and division between the governed and the government. Instead, the AFWS will bring to the forefront the ultimate democratic principle of the people ruling themselves. To that end, the proper mechanisms will be implemented to ensure as many workers as possible take part in the administration of the state on a limited-term basis and in an orderly and constant rotation of the people through all the ranks of government. In this fashion, we will turn the bureaucrat into a public servant, and hence transform a compartmentalized, ossified organization into the organism that is the AWFS, always regenerating from within, in lockstep with the evolving and growing of the people themselves. Private sector and public sector will be the revolving door to one another for as many workers as possible, facilitating the transition so as to identify the public servant as the worker within the administration of the state, and the worker in the private sector as the public servant working another productive job. Public and private will overlap each other because both functions will be carried out by we the people; we the workers. This mechanism will be executed by the AFWS as the heart pumps the blood full force through the entire body, its organs and tissues and cells being replenished and nourished, with the torrent of life flushing through the system like a cleansing flood. Democracy to the most radical extreme; to the last consequences."

40. The shield, the flag and the music

And is not it the time to flesh out the symbolic meaning of our party badge, our symbol and representation? As I already mentioned, symbols in general, and particularly those of an archetypical nature as observed in dreams, are the building blocks in the language of the unconscious. The collective unconscious, or the unconscious shared by the people at large, thus communicates its contents to our conscious minds through that symbolic language; and this collective unconscious is by its own very nature, the foundational drive of any movement that seeks to bring into existence an organic democratic state. Our party is the political embodiment of that movement. Therefore, it stands to reason that our party badge needs to be the most perfect reflection of our conscious goals and ethos, and also of the collective unconscious as represented by archetypal symbols. And it is for this reason that the shield combines different symbolic figures within circles and a quaternity.

The quaternity is the archetype of the Self, the God within. So it is circumscribed within a ring of meaning, highlighting the four words or motto that is both our drive and goal: iustitiam, libertatem, panem, respectum. These most decent words are highlighted in white, signifying their pure connection to the party ideary. The book within the motto circle and the quaternity and the circle of the Self symbolizes philosophy, logic and truth as a protective cocoon containing the core of the movement in its pages, namely work and revolution or struggle/action. The symbols expressing those concepts are also four, in a one-to-one relation with the words in the motto. Justice and respect are attained by their corresponding counterparts, namely the battle-ax and the sword: revolution. Liberty and prosperity are achieved through that represented by the spade and the sledgehammer: work. And work is on the right; revolution on the left. For indeed there is a natural order of things and a righteous hierarchy of values. One precedes the other, and not the other way around. The party acronym is spread around the motto circle at equal intervals, signifying a total intertwining of the party and the values that it champions and strives to materialize. The party aligns itself with the four cardinal points, or with the ever-present, all-encompassing righteous state of being. And it also represents the four projecting points of the quaternity, the symbol of the Self. It indicates that collective individuation and the party are one and the same.

All the symbolism is engulfed by a magnificent pure white, while encircled by blue, as a chromatic representation of peace and balance. There is a red outer circle surrounding all of the above and the party name is contained therein. In fact, the party and its ultimate goals and aspirations are a matter of passion, strength and sacrifice. No color better than that of blood could possible convey that meaning. Ultimately, the outermost circle is the circle of eternity, enveloped in gold. Suffice to say that the entire ethos and project represented by the logo within must be highlighted by the hue and the symbol that conveys divinity, goodness and eternity; and that is the purpose of the continuous infinity sign in gold. Indeed, our state is meant to perdure for millennia, for the weariness brought forth by the eons is never a match for the zeal brought forth by the will! On a side note, even though justice and respect are achieved through revolution, a measure of freedom is also realized in the process; hence the battle-ax is pointing at libertatem in the opposite quadrant. Correspondingly, freedom and prosperity are reified through work, but this also achieves a measure of justice in the process; therefore the sledgehammer is pointing at iustitiam in the opposite quadrant. In this way, those four symbols are not only positioned in the book of logic, but also oriented within the quaternity in the correct, significant, symbolic manner.

All this describes our shield and party badge. But the future organic state will have a flag. Since we will be in the presence of a state begotten by the people and a party, and not a people and a party born out of a state, it logically follows that the shield and the flag must be one and the same, with one caveat. The shield's background within the flag will be sable black. That color represents the boldness and power of the state and its people, and the protection thereof; for indeed the AFWS will be the safe haven where all compeers will have and feel familial bonds throughout the body politic, with relationships articulated, promoted and strengthened by the state as the intension of the people.

I do indeed place enormous importance on symbolic language. As I already established when talking about the roots of ethics, human life is essentially a narrative as we make sense of it. But it is also very complicated, at times almost impossible to understand. Thereby we are forced to use symbols in order to boil down this grand narrative to units we can comprehend on a conscious level. It is this reasoning at the core of why symbolism is so paramount, and why so much logic and feeling has been put into the design of this our most magnificent shield.

Music and lyrics must be part of the artistic expression of the state. This is a very magical albeit complicated issue, most likely due to its contradictory nature: thought out consciously but felt out unconsciously, much more so than other artistic expressions. On this subject, the party and the state must have their own music, always conducive to the homeostasis of the body politic and therefore its perfect symbiosis with its intension, the state. I am passionate about baroque music, both vocal and instrumental. Among the maestros of that era, if I had to choose one (and that is certainly a painful challenge) George Frideric Handel would be my choice. In the future, the party and the state will have to procure for themselves the composers able to raise the spirits and drive the wills of the people, especially of the youth, as high and hard as is humanly possible. Handel's heroic and religious arias come to mind. A music that can give you goosebumps as it whips up within the desire for acting out grand narratives—that is the music worth calling a party and state music. But the people themselves will have to speak, democratically, on these and countless other issues, especially important for the organic nature of the state when matters of symbolism are concerned. Whether they are shields or flags, music or uniforms, the truth is, when told out loud without artistic refrain, the most revolutionary of all devices ever imagined and implemented by man.

3. The third most crucial function of any state is the protection, preservation and promotion of fundamental rights and freedoms, among which we place speech, religion, association, demonstration, self-empowerment (the right of owning and carrying guns, along with the prudent and ethical use thereof), and press as absolute. No state is worth surviving if it is incapable of thriving in an atmosphere of true democratic liberty where these natural rights are exercised honestly and unrestrictedly. In fact, any state which is forced to curb those liberties in order to survive is by definition, illegitimate and it needs to be done away with. Its illegitimacy stems obviously from the lack of organic intertwine with its workers or citizens, since what is good for any tissue in the body politic is good for the whole body itself; and the contrary is unequivocally a sign of a dysfunctional and predatory organization, never of a wholesome, functional organism.

The laissez-faire state coopted and corrupted the nature of the rights and freedoms that I am now addressing, and they were often ambiguously enshrined in the Bill of Rights and generally to a certain extent in the Magna Carta and other "enlightened" proclamations. The Founders made them appear as if they were put forth as philosophical principles to be acted upon, as opposed to being the corollaries of a virtuous national ethic. By doing thus, they turned the quiddity of those freedoms from ethical and logical to ideological, marring this way their absolute standing among the people as it is all unraveling in the last decades. I wonder, has this wicked state ever produced or done something good and righteous, or is its nature so deviated and wayward that nothing decent could possibly come of it?

41. Of the cleansing power of the blood

A most important parenthesis must be drawn here. One of the most effective and ethical ways for the state to protect, enforce and preserve the internal peace and order, the rule of law, and all the fundamental freedoms herein broached, is the public execution of justice. For if it is not an ostensive manifestation from start to finish, from arraignment to execution, how can the people ascertain that the scales have been held and balanced according to truth; how can the body politic generally and the victims particularly be requited; and finally how the whole affair can be metamorphosed into a virtuous act of teaching and learning? In fact, I would argue that any act of justice that is not publicly executed is hardly justice at all, and the state perpetrating those acts may very well be deemed rogue and corrupt. Justice in this particular sense is the reparation to the people by the perpetrator(s) of the criminal deed or wrongdoing. By executing the acts of justice or punishments behind closed doors, in the dark of night so to speak, the state becomes one with the criminal as to the modus operandi, and also deprives the community of the satisfaction of seeing their criminal disruption properly penalized. That satisfaction is essential as a cathartic experience, as a deterrent to illegal behavior, and as a bonding event among all the cells in the body politic.

Public execution of justice is also imperative so we the workers are placed at the forefront of the reparation scheme. When the state punishes the miscreants away from the people, it effectively turns an act of justice for the people into an act of justice for the state, or even an act of revenge by the state. This concept is hardly revolutionary. Indeed, for most of human history and in most civilizations, this concept of public or just, versus concealed or corrupt, was at the core of the people's ethos on this subject matter for the reasons aforementioned. Public executions and floggings would by and large be the most ethical form of compensation to the people, reinforcement of moral behavior, punishment of unlawful and unethical behavior generally, and ultimately deterrent to crime. A public flogging rather than a cruel jail conviction serves so much better the interest of the people, serving the cause of justice without the devastating effects on peoples' lives that a jail sentence brings. Very often a painful and even brutal slapping wreaks less mental and spiritual havoc on the recipient than a protracted, low-intensity ostracizing in a dark, damp corner; while at the same time protecting and offsetting the people better, and minimizing the odds of that behavior being repeated in the future. Over the long haul, everybody in the community wins, including the culprits who no longer have their lives permanently devastated by something that in many cases could be regarded as a onetime mistake.

Regarding executions, the principle is the selfsame.

However, there is a caveat. When the crimes committed are so abhorrent that a death penalty might be warranted, these public executions will be carried out as long as the people, directly through referendum, decide the penalties and the scope and conditions under which those penalties might or not be implemented, as I already stressed in this founding work. All this notwithstanding, it is utterly unavoidable to clarify a most important point: executions must be public or not be at all and therefore be stripped off the books or never be allowed to be part of the legal code in the first place. When executions are carried out behind closed doors, they become a crime perpetrated by the state. An execution, in addition to punishment, reparation and deterrent, is fundamentally an act of cleansing through the shedding of blood. When the state excludes the people from the process, the cleansing becomes revenge, and the organic nature of the state vaporized by such a heinous act, reminding the people of their condition as mere governed subjects.

Floggings could be particularly useful on the youth, the manageable psychopaths, or when nonviolent crimes are involved (even more so given the low tolerance for public shame and physical pain that the current man has, although this will radically change over time through the development of a virtuous ethos wherewith men will grow more steely and mentally stronger and healthier overall). This kind of justice tends to propel the offender into shock and awe, facilitating the journey back onto the path of indoctrinated ethics. Effectively, they are being whipped into shape before they can go back into the realm of ethics. This, in turn, is conducive to a lessening of the prison population. For there is no doubt in my mind that many nonviolent criminals would be better off skipping the slammer and avoiding a record in exchange for one or a few public floggings. (Let us remind our people that to a large extent the prison system in its current form is a sham to generate profits for many in the bureaucratic and managerial castes, for plenty of donors and financiers, and for a slew of college graduates who end up forming the rank and file of the so-called "judicial system".) This mechanism is very much beneficial to a state of more general freedom, less waste of resources, and an immediate opening up of untapped and unlimited opportunities both for the lawbreaker individually as well as for the community collectively and organically for the state itself.

But the quest for justice cannot be circumscribed by the offering of blood, for this nourishing fluid still requires a fertile soil to soak up, and thus spark off a new cycle of life. This new life will sprout up with the impetus of redemption, forgiveness and wholeness. Indeed, the perpetrator must pay, the victim must forgive, and both must coalesce at the end of the cleansing process, within the soothing cocoon of our glorious organic state. But what is that sacrosanct soil, that perfect complement to the sacrificial blood? It is, of course, work.

Indentured labor for a codified period of time will help in the process of cleansing and reinstating wholeness and justice by repairing the relation between the two cells (or clusters of cells) involved in the criminal infection. Work (or its equivalent, money) will flow from the perpetrator to the victim until the contract has been satisfied, thereby the foregoing servitude will come to an end and the local homeostasis in the body politic will be restored.

And let us probe now into another subject germane to ethics and justice, and that is to what extent does ethical behavior pertain to actions propelled by thoughts or in addition to thoughts which never were acted upon? In other words, is a man ethical if he has unethical thoughts but he does not put them into practice? It is a very old philosophical debate and the answer to the question is, as in so many other philosophical discussions, entirely up to the philosopher who entertains it, generally dependent upon the school the thinker subscribes to. Irrespective of what the answer might be, our state will certainly ensure that not only the habits, but also the intellectual springs as well are properly modified. For, my dear compeers, make no mistake: the ethical function is comprehensively bijective, i.e., the thought impels the action as a repeated pattern of sustained action ingrains the psyche with a pattern of thought. Indeed, there are two ways of creating a habit; one is by repetition of actions which eventually will create a psychic imprint and therefore a self-sustaining behavioral pattern; and the other one is through the raw power of the will, which is a divine manifestation of the unconscious channeled through the conscious mind into the world of actuality. I want to state here unequivocally, without any wavering or pussyfooting, that the cleansing power of the shed blood is the catalyst by which the first method of habit creation can be brought about. Furthermore, thoughts induced by preceding habits become one and the same with thoughts that induce habits. And hence open-air, honest and wholesome whippings repeated over a period of time not only create a pattern of behavior, but an induced pattern of thought. In other words, there is a cleansing not only in the realm of action but in the realm within as well. The patterns of actions thus generated become the output of patterns of ethical thoughts, and not actions performed out of fear of punishment.

This is a transcendental difference from the incarceration system enacted by the liberal Leviathan on a massive scale. A very small percentage of felons change their patterns of action and thought once they are released from prison. The most hardcore among the condemned are especially immune to this kind of punishment. But the cleansing power of the blood spilled in a just manner by the people through the organic state is impossible to overestimate. It is the power exercised for millennia in countless societies for all the people to behold, as the crimson flow washes away the ignominy, one glorious stroke at the time. The blood functions as both the cleanser and the cure. The fabric of the community gets patched up and the perpetrator moves harmoniously back into that community he is organically a member of. No dwelling in a permanent circle of blame and punishment anymore; no never-ending vicious cycle of recrimination and despair; rather a tissue that has repaired itself through the regenerative powers of policy and law.

42. The synergy of virtue ethics and deontological duties

I will now briefly comment on the curious dual nature of the system of ethics that the AFWP advocates for and will institute through policy and law in the state. That duality manifests itself when the virtue ethics of the people and the deontological ethics of the state are symbiotically integrated. Firstly, right off the bat I categorically reject any notion of consequentialism. The idea that an action or behavior can be pertinently judged by the merit of its implications is grotesque to me. For how can we possibly ascertain all the consequences if we are not privy to them to begin with? As a matter of cognitive and empirical limitations, we perceive and consciously process a very tiny amount of information from the world without. The assumption that we can judge an action by its consequences implies that we are indeed capable of navigating through the world outside our consciousness with total omniscience. Obviously we are not God, so that property cannot be concomitant to our condition of human beings. Consequentialism in many different forms is at the core of many misguided political philosophies and I vehemently reject it on logical and scientific grounds.

However, having said that, it is certainly essential to distinguish between the ethics of the people as individual entities and the ethics of the AFWS as an organic political structure. The state's ethics must be compulsorily deontological, for it is moral duty and the will to carry it out within a legal framework that ultimately propels a moral state to act. Moreover, the state, when organic, in other words, when intensional, is the paradigm of a teleological entity. Indeed, since a state does not have a natural right to exist, his legitimacy must be derived inductively from a dutiful exercise of deontological duties for the benefit of the people, i.e., those duties are functional. Moreover, as I already discussed previously, the ethics of the people are based on our most sacred and proven virtues. And these virtues are, as manifested by their permanence, functional and therefore teleological. And since the state is the political organism composed of the people and their intricate multilevel relationships, it stands to reason that both sets of ethics must harmonically merge and feed on each other; and they do, because they both have a teleological characteristic. For how can a body be ruled by forces other than those that rule the individual tissues, organs and cells, and vice versa? And what is the conduit by which such a symbiotic interlacing takes place? Straightforwardly the most democratic of all powers: the referendum. The will is the mystic force sent up to the conscious straight from the deepest depths of the unconscious. When that will is the driver used by the state to carry out its moral duty, it proceeds upward into the realm of consciousness from the innermost layers of the collective unconscious. I refuse to accept the will as an entirely conscious force. It is rather the unconscious drive dwarfing our limited conscious interpretation or projection of it.

Without any more dilations, I will anon pen down our ninth founding principle. But first, please always remember that the reading and understanding of our principles must be preceded by the reading and understanding of all the reasonings leading up to these fundamental deductions. And now, it is our will that:

43. Ninth founding principle: the AFWS as an absolutist state in the defense of unalienable and indefeasible rights

"Absolute individual rights: the rights to life, speech, press, religion, association, self-empowerment and others that the people might decide upon through referendum are a function of our state indoctrination; they are part and parcel of a self-sustaining ethos. Ultimately those rights and freedoms are the covenant wherewith the state will protect the workers from within and without, carry out its doctrine, and use as a permanent lodestar of policy, enthusiastically eliminating, at any cost, any and all dangers to those absolute freedoms. To that end, the state and the people will see that justice when those rights are encroached upon is served publicly, never behind closed doors or in any kind of private or secluded setting away from the people. For otherwise the state ceases to be organic and becomes a caste-driven organization. We will be, in the defense and promotion of those absolute freedoms, as radical and extreme as a human mind can possibly imagine. Let this serve as a sacred promise to our brethren as well as an unequivocal warning to our foes."

I will now unfurl what is perchance the most fundamental of our principles, for it is the one which provides the philosophical background of our party and state with the indispensable coherence. But before I spell it out, I have to attend to the unavoidable duty to delve deep into the rotten inner workings and drives of the laissez-faire state.

44. Uncompromising rejection of the bane of political parties

Firstly, the two wings of this partitocracy are not the source of the decay, but rather the conduit wherewith the decay materializes. The state itself is unethical, and the two parties are just one among many manifestations of it. This state is inherently, philosophically as well as practically, predicated on the negation of our four cardinal virtues (prudence, temperance, fortitude and justice) and our three capital virtues (diligence, patience and kindness); and in the negation of the deontological duties of the state carried out by the power of collective will. These most grotesque and destructive negations are the direct consequence of the unscrupulous embracing of the catastrophic laissez-faire ideas espoused by the liberal revolutions, political and philosophical, that took place in the 18th century. The end result of those ideas put to work within the structure of the liberal state is a system of castes that serves only the ruling and usufructuary castes through an administrative and bureaucratic maze of agencies, departments, branches and organizations both public and private, consistently stifling any meaningful debate or opposition and keeping the population at large histrionically engaged in tangential issues. This is promoted through propaganda and indoctrination with the sole aim of keeping workers divided along inconsequential lines, always ginned up so their conscious attention is not fixed on the core, fundamental, political, economic and ethical issues that the AFWP has identified as essential for the advent of a truly democratic, organic society and state. This chronically toxic state cannot bring about the liberty, justice, respect for work and workers, and prosperity (intellectual and ethical as well as material, which I have constantly reiterated) that our ethos demands.

In other words, if these two 19th-century, wicked and barren political contrivances were not to exist, others would happily take their place within the framework of this liberal kakistocracy (I will hereinafter expound further on this topic, in the context of the struggle toward the AFWS and the four dimensions of political parties in the anti-worker state). These two parties are the symptom rather than the ultimate cause of our bane. This ideological state is fundamentally schizophrenic in nature, always in a permanent internecine strife over trivialities. It is an existence of constant wrangling over issues which are philosophical trifles at best, while all the substantive matters are back-burnered, so as to make sure that the donor caste, through its bribed lackeys in the permanent administrative structure, keeps lining the pockets through criminal misuse of state powers.

This master caste is obnoxiously present in those "political conventions" that both wings of the partitocracy hold every four years. They even book private booths and rooms up high inside the venues where those party gatherings take place, and they pay fortunes for them. As the Roman emperors, senators and patricians of yore, these modern-day overlords look down on their buffoonish minions, who down below make a fool of themselves wearing clownish customs, groveling and fawning over whoever happens to be higher

Political parties: The roadblocks to democracy through their functions as constructs, tools of political action, agents of reticulation, and as the state's escape valve.

up in the political hierarchy. They mindlessly chant trite shib-boleths, while flocks of greasy sycophants who call them-selves journalists giddily comb the arena looking for the last "rising star" or the more seasoned racket bosses, hoping to find out what they had for breakfast so such a vital informa-tion can be passed along to their brain-dead audience.

However, what appears to be a circus full of scaramouch-es and pretenders, it is in reality a chessboard where all the chessmen are playing roles at the behest of the usufructuary caste high above. In return, they enjoy a life of abundance as members of he political, managerial, propaganda, and other propping castes. All those conventions have a striking common denominator: the total absence of workers and the absolute contempt for them and their plight. No compas-sion, no empathy and no mercy; only unquenchable drive to devise and unleash criminal conspiracies on the phalanxes of the productive in order to perpetuate the ritual and ad-dictive reproduction, expansion and concentration of capital. The mechanism is always the same, namely the maximization of the ratio surplus labor/necessary labor and the concomi-tant appropriation of an ever-larger surplus value; or in other words, constant assault on worker's wages through unbridled increase of domestic labor supply and offshoring schemes.

They are not against unions per se though. In fact, this master caste is enthusiastic about their own union, which is commonly referred to as the U.S. Congress, with the presi-dent acting as the union boss. This is thus because unbe-knownst to most compeers, masses of atheists, cultists and pharisees dominate the ranks of all the illegitimate castes, including the political caste. Of course they do not noise it abroad, lest the workers draw the conclusion that a sociopolitical and economic system driven by rotten people must be rotten itself. But the degeneration of the state is becoming so extreme that the facade is crumbling down as we speak.

The conclusion is straightforward: the AFWS will be politically and philosophically articulated through the AFWP. The catastrophe of political parties or obscure, special interests will never be again suffered by the American worker.

And it follows that the AFWS is an extremist, absolutist democratic state with the AFWP as the radical glue that cements all the cells and their relations together. Therefore we will resort to any action we deem essential in order to stave off the scourge of liberalism, conservatism, fascism, national socialism, communism, socialism and all and any altered or hybrid versions thereof. We have broken free from the liberal state and all its nemeses, with that paradigm overcome for good and reduced to a baleful chapter in the book of history.

But if we are to define the core principle of the AFWS sans complicated elaborations or propositional inductions, could we somehow pull it off? It cannot be just some sort of contrary axiom to the core qualities of the political philosophies we are rising up against. (As I already discussed, a philosophy of opposite values and concepts is bound to result in disappointment and frustration, for logical and other philosophical reasons.) Happily, the answer to that challenge is a resounding yes!

I will erelong proceed on to our next principle, but first here is an apposite preface. One of the deontological duties of the state is to always lead by example, so the workers feel reaffirmed in their virtue ethics. Otherwise the organic condition of the state is not fulfilled. For otherwise, how can a father teach his son to respect women if he beats his own wife? Or how a mother can teach her daughter to be sexually prudent if she herself sleeps with a different man each night? A state that does not lead by example is illegitimate and therefore it should not exist. This dystopian state cannot help but be illegitimate on these grounds because its lack of moral compass is inherent in its philosophical genesis as well as its political structure and general modus operandi.

It is our unquenchable will that:

◂▸————◂▸

45. Tenth founding principle: the dissolution principle; a state that radically and logically lives up to the party ideary

"The AFWS will be defined by this concomitant property that results in a definition, since it is the only case in human history: total, absolute and without exception accountability measured by the standards that the workers themselves are judged by within the legal framework of the state. In other words, nothing and nobody within the apparatus of the state is above the laws which the people abide by. Worded in another way: just as the workers are subjected to the repercussions of unlawful behavior, so is the state subjected to all kinds of punishments for lawbreaking, including the dissolution of the state itself through referendum. In proportional calculus terms, this principle represents a one-element axiomatic system, ensuring that all relations and functions within the state by any worker, organization or institution, can be judged logically through its prism. This is the dissolution principle."

Forsooth, this principle alone is the hallmark of an unequal state in history, since it is the ultimate realization of the organic and unprecedented nature of this AFWS! Total, absolute, uncompromising compliance with the law by the state, which has to live up to its own standards if it is to judge its workers by them. Otherwise it would be unequivocally illegitimate. This principle is tantamount to a complete and exception-free accountability; it is the means by which the system of castes that characterizes the liberal mastodon and all its nemeses will be wiped out of existence. Or to use the old apothegm: "What is good for the goose is good for the gander". No exceptions. How gorgeously radical and righteous our state is, that it is willing to lead by example to the last logical consequences! Because of this axiom, any functions, relations and developments within the state among its people will be automatically truthful, since the environment surrounding it all is truthful. There is no environment where truth flourishes better than that of justice, equality and accountability for all.

The ultimate political goal of the revolution is to establish this all-just and accountable state. Whatever the means, the finish line will be reached when the body politic is born again so it can live in truth according to the AFWP ideary, which will become the ethos of our people as time seasons and strengthens our body of principles.

---

46. The ways of the psychopath caste

The truth: that is the core of any human endeavor worth pursuing, and certainly that of this revolution. The truth is both the means and the end of our struggle. And there is nothing more antithetic to truth, in the political realm, than this state born out of the philosophical confusion of the 18th century. All other aspects of life have been corrupted within the husk of this political malformation by this aversion to truth. Culture, ethics, art, science and dogma—all of it has been contorted into an abhorrent travesty by virtue of existing within the structure of a state which is immanently corrupt.

I must ask, what exactly are the practical means by which this innate state of deceit is present in the anti-worker kakotopia?

Depending on the sources and references, between 3% and 10% of the population at large are considered clinically psychopaths, but that percentage is naturally larger among those particular populations in fields where power of different sorts can be wielded. The psychopath has a strong propensity for positions of power over others because it is in those situations where he can inflict the maximum possible damage. I am not about to engage here in a scientific discussion about what psychopathy entails, its causes, manifestations and all the rest, for it is beside the point. However, I encourage all my readers to take a closer look at this most important and sensitive topic so he can acquaint himself with the full understanding of the context in which this subject matter will be treated.

Psychopaths are, unbeknownst to the masses of workers, and I even dare to say to the bulk of the ruling caste, the most relevant set of people involved in the most catastrophic political, military and economic events in history. In fact, at the core of many of those events there is a total and utter lack of logical reasonings and actions, which could only be explained either by the overwhelming stupidity of the actors involved or more likely a psychopathy at work, wreaking havoc on a grand scale for its own sake. But as horrifying as this statement sounds, it pales in comparison to what follows; we will always have psychopaths among our ranks, but their powers are heightened by both the nature and the structure of the schizophrenic Goliath itself.

If we go back in history to the time when this term was not even used, the psychopaths were nevertheless on the prowl as we can deduce from a close analysis of written records. As a matter of fact, what we nowadays call psychopathic used to be lumped together along with a variety of different sets of peoples and conditions under the loose terms "demonic", "possessed", "satanic", and others along those lines. I can confidently state here that those psychopaths of yore who were publicly identified as diabolical were a minority of all actual cases; just as today virtually every psychopath gets a free pass without ever being confronted publicly with his condition or the wreckage that he is undoubtedly leaving in his path.

It is also tragic that along with those sick people many other innocent men and women were punished and in many cases tortured and executed for crimes that were never such, furthering the muddying the waters and making distinctions between the wicked and the unjustly condemned almost impossible. Compounding the problem even further, the ambiguity of some records makes the problem of separating the wheat from the chaff almost unsolvable. But there cannot be any doubt about this point: scores of what we nowadays term psychopaths were put to the stake and burnt, hanged, pilloried, decapitated or shot, especially before the advent of classical liberalism in the 18th century; although many of those punishments lingered on well into the 19th and even the 20th century in a few restricted cases.

But out of the Enlightenment, the concept of public display of justice started to be frowned upon by the state, and eventually this new ethos bled off into the population at large. The laissez-faire states themselves sprang into existence, one after another, imbibing the same contemporaneous zeitgeist, one of lack of judgments on devious behaviors, for the judge was not considered the supreme ideal anymore. In a way, it was the very contradiction of the logos itself, wrapped up in a deceiving veil of modernity and compassion. It is the same compassion that the modern politician shows when instead of a whip, a hug and a plan he offers a needle to a homeless addict. It is the compassion of the psychopath, the ethos of this illogical, wicked time. Of course, if we were to approach this fundamental issue soaked up in dogma, we would call it all the wayward and twisted works of the devil, sowing discord and destruction among God's children. But we are fortunate enough to have philosophy and logic at our disposal which renders the former approach unnecessary. The conclusions, however, are eerily similar.

But the most fundamental and pertinent part of my discourse is how it came about that a state that spends trillions of dollars a year, both money that exists and that is printed ex nihilo, i.e., without any connection to actual work; a state whose scope and encroachments at home and abroad know no bounds whatsoever; a state that persecutes all those who dare to reveal its crimes against the people, alleging that "national security" has been jeopardized when the unearthing of criminality takes place (the enthymematic implications of such a fallacious argument are certainly staggering, although even more shocking is the acquiescence or even enthusiastic support of significant chunks of the masses); a state that has created the largest organization in human history, namely the US government; a state this vast, this overpowering, this massive in both scale and scope; nevertheless seems totally unwilling and unable to dedicate even the tiniest amount of attention and resources to identify the psychopaths who might be in government already and those who might be actively seeking public office or bureaucratic positions.

There is no question that whatever method is employed to analyze this issue, a simple deduction based on the axioms of propositional logic and modus ponens is straightforward and chilling. And that is that the people who already wield the levers of power for their own sake in this state are purposefully protecting the psychopathic element. Every high-level bureaucrat over at the CIA, the FBI, the NSA, and the rest of the security apparatus, is aware of this but most importantly complicit in it. The inference that many in the upper echelons of those agencies of crime and repression would not pass a clinical test on psychopathy is logically impossible to avoid.

The same argument can be used about any other bureaucrat and politician in any other department or agency of this government. However, it is particularly glaring in the case of the so-called "intelligence agencies" because they are actually the ones who are supposed to have the responsibility to protect the people from these kinds of dangers. And although it is indisputable that a few involved in this suspicious behavior are just acting out their caste powers and privileges, it is equally undeniable that their malfeasance is indistinguishable from the psychopathic majority, given the utter injustice, cruelty and ignominy these elements treat the workers with. These politicians, bureaucrats and functionaries actually wallow in their abuse overtly, poking the people with the spear of insult and disrespect. It is beyond any question that the contagion has already reached every crevice and nook in this state, and it has been happening for decades if not centuries. But this tragedy has been the result of the schizophrenic nature of the state itself, which has been, from the outset, prone to the absorption of the worst evils that society can spawn.

Ever wonder if you were a psychopath how you would proceed so you could inflict the maximum amount of damage on the body politic? If you decided to be a teacher, you would be surreptitiously driving wedges between your students and their families; you would be getting them confused as to who they fundamentally are, maybe even questioning their own sex; you would be removing any kind of religious belief from their minds because faith is the surest path to a strong virtue ethics; and ultimately you would be convincing them that their country is hopelessly wicked, because the people around them are guilty of an original sin that they cannot expiate. To sum it all up, you would be striving to make them hopeless and angry. Because a nation with its youth believing that they are powerless and wronged is a nation without any future; and with no chance to generate an organic, virtuous state. And that is the definition of a societal wreckage!

And what would you do if you were a medical doctor and a psychopath? How would you conduct your life? Would you be pumping up your patients with toxic drugs in the name of a treatment? Would you become a chopper of the unborn on an industrial scale in the name of women's rights? Or perhaps you would prescribe addictive opioids and antidepressants to children and adults alike, rather than confronting the root causes of the problems? Maybe you would take the route of cutting off children's genitals after you convince them that their apparent sex was nothing but a mistake of nature? A lot of damage can be done by doctors. Sixty million unborn babies and counting since 1973, millions addicted to noxious prescription drugs, countless irreversible life-altering surgical procedures, misdiagnoses galore, etc. The power of the medical profession is difficult to overestimate.

And what about if you were a lawyer and a psychopath? You would certainly defend somebody who is a destructive criminal and you would argue that is how the system is supposed to work; you would advance immoral causes and you would sow chaos in a myriad of ways; and if you work for the government, you would engage in all those activities above mentioned out in the open, trying to egg on the community so the people get lured into despair, rage and ultimately destructive violence.

And how about if you were a college professor or a scientist who happened to be also a psychopath? In this case, you would clearly advance corrosive, ill-conceived ideas; you would drive chasms between the students along all kinds of accidental lines; you would devise subterfuges to tear down institutions and bodies of canonical ethics and would introduce as much disarray as you can into the system without offering up anything wholesome in return. And you would also develop models and theories which are not borne out by the data or your intuition, but nevertheless passed off as valid by means of manipulating the mathematics employed. This way you would literally be heading humanity off in the wrong direction, away from truth, as you manure the fields of science and philosophy with the bitter scourge of utter confusion upon which others might unknowingly build up even more error!

So the verdict is clear. Whether professors and teachers, scientists, lawyers and doctors, or any other profession or activity we can think of, the potential for catastrophic, society-and-history-altering devices and machinations is in plain sight. It is not a theory. It is happening as we speak because this state lacks the mechanisms and the will to fend off systemic psychopathic corruption. I will venture to state that almost every time an exogenous, nonnatural event or development takes place, if it increases the amount of collective stress, anxiety, rage or fear, or sense of impotence and weakness, that event is caused by psychopathic forces. Conversely, nothing we can think of which increases the levels of peace, calmness, love or accord among the workers , as well as the will to justice and power and drive to virtuous action, ever stems from psychopathic forces. And by inductive means, this simple rule can very often help us steer clear of the wrong elements and also fall in with the right brethren.

Furthermore, people in positions of influence or power of various kinds and degrees, if they are psychopaths, will be able to cause damage proportionally to their status. If, on the other hand, because of their profession, connections or lack thereof, the scope of their influence is limited, their damage will be accordingly contained, but nonetheless real and substantial. In this fashion, a psychopath could wreak havoc in a community just by driving a car on the street and in a given moment reaching a boiling point. In fact, as I mentioned before, a substantial percentage of people at large are psychopaths of varying degrees. And it is for this reason that we constantly observe very strange incidents and interactions between drivers, many of which seem improbable to be placed, with certainty or common sense, at the feet of stress, emotional breakdowns or even alcohol and drug consumption.

I find it highly unlikely that any society, under any regime save the future AFWS (let alone this festering abomination we live in), could possibly survive, functionally speaking, the wrongdoings of a population with 3% to 10% of its members suffering from psychopathy. No wonder that even by rotten liberal standards, the current levels of dysfunction, infamy and lunacy are intolerable to those whose cognitive powers are still functioning. I am sure it is plain to all the compatriots reading this work that, for example, the Internet at large is fundamentally a psychopathic enterprise. Back in the day, the village freaks were ostracized and kept at bay, and in some cases when the degrees of psychological violence or perverse upheaval were deemed intolerable, the culprits were put away or eliminated. Nowadays, the same psychopathic freaks run channels that boast millions of visitors and subscribers, and become "trendsetters" in many different ways. This is a sick, shallow, ignorant, misdirected, desperately hollowed-out society and it has been falling prey to the psychopathic caste for a long time.

But let us focus again on the crux of the probe into this unsettling topic, which must be centered on the mechanisms of the state to guard itself against evil, psychopathic forces. As I previously stated, it is unquestionable that this liberal Leviathan, with its myriad of police and intelligence agencies, whose theoretical primary goal is to keep the people "safe" from foes at home and abroad, is not so incompetent as to ignore a subject matter which screeches of obviousness and gravity. Those agencies have plenty of departments full of analysts dedicated to studying, foreseeing, forestalling and repressing any kind of activity which is regarded as a danger for the state. But the lack of repression or basic persecution of this kind of existential toxicity in the body politic is manifest and certainly very telling of the underlying conspiracy. Enthymematically, there is no other deduction to infer that all these agencies do not repress the contagion because they are compromised themselves at the highest levels.

It is impossible to deny the conclusion that the upper echelons of the security state, along with the political caste at large, are likely part of the psychopathic intertribal caste. And if we pay close attention to their actions—the unbridled contempt or even blatant disgust they profess for the worker, and the incessant, ludicrously twisted actions and decisions, always propping up bad behaviors and putting down the virtuous ones, coming down with obliterating force on workers who might break some minor rules while protecting and promoting all kinds of criminal and pernicious behavior by the ruling elites and their managerial lackeys—there is no question that the horse has already left the barn and now we only can hope to lasso it, bump it off and burn the barn down, not hoping but rather making sure such a damning occurrence never befalls us again. There is no room for retraining. Once the animal has ventured out on its own terms and tastes the power originating from that action, nobody will be able to put the proverbial genie back in the bottle. Similarly, when a wild predator tastes human flesh, most conservation agencies are inclined to capture it and put it down because they deem the specimen likely to become a recidivist. So this course of action is natural, unavoidable and evidently effective. It will be the course of the new state so that it develops pure, strong and on the right track.

There is a fundamental connection between the catastrophic effects of the psychopathic contagion and the anti-worker state. It is precisely one of the concomitant properties of this state which suffers the psychopathic caste to maximize their destructive powers; that characteristic is the system of castes. I already expounded on the system of castes when I talked about the AFWS as an organic entity in which the people weave in and out of the administration of the state in a rotatory basis so as to involve as many workers as possible in the business of the state itself, hence invigorating and maximizing all the interconnections between the workers and their political and intensional dimension, which is an essential prerequisite for a shared quiddity. I would like to call particular attention to this most deleterious liberal caste system and its multiplier effect on the powers of the psychopathic element.

Indeed, castes exist and have been around us long before this state and its underlying philosophy were born. In antiquity and all the way through the liberal revolutions of the 18th century, the caste system was inextricably tied to the blood; in other words, to a belief system based upon tradition and land ownership with the inevitable sprinkle of dogma. Back then, that system was never considered fair per se, but natural. However, with the Enlightenment and the onset of the laissez-faire state, the ruling castes needed another justification to perpetuate their privileges, and in a gradual fashion the concept of "natural" was discarded altogether. But the problem of legitimacy was ever-present and unresolved. Eventually, as with a freak of nature which everyone gets used to by the mere passage of time, the legitimacy of privilege was canonically accepted and linked to freedom: namely the freedom of markets and classical capitalism that allowed for some to come out on top seemingly without recourse to violence, but by "voluntary" cooperation in the economy through constructs like wagslave labor.

Pray, notice here how momentous is the leap between the old legitimacy based on nature, although profoundly unfair, and the new legitimacy, which is as grotesque as the old one but misleading, for it is not even acknowledged to begin

with. Because if that privilege's source is voluntary cooperation in the markets, how can it possibly be termed "unfair"?
This state is so base as to not even have the decency to face
its own demons. It rather brushes them under the rug and
pretends they do not exist in the first place. It is a paradigm
of collective intellectual dishonesty at its worst. The castes of
today are castes of the economically privileged, the castes of
the predator within us who thrives through all the trickeries
of this creditist corporate system, and especially through
the mechanism of wagslave labor as amply discussed in the
first pages of this work. Unlike in any other epoch in history,
this privilege caste does not acknowledge its own existence,
since freedom reigns supreme in the markets and everything is done with everyone's acquiescence, is not it? They
just worked hard, and happened to be particularly talented.
Perhaps even blessed or a bit lucky, so we all understand
how humble they are. How creepy and weak that they do not
even dare to call their status for what it is, which is the byproduct of a system based on predatory laissez-faire practices
and brought about within the context of a state which exists
only to serve their interests. I respect truth and strength. If
they had the intellectual integrity and fortitude to be upfront
about the whole scheme, I would certainly feel immeasurably
less aggravated. As it stands, I feel only revulsion.

But the castes that are the most detrimental to the welfare of the people within the context of the psychopathic
contagion are the political and bureaucratic castes. The destruction, sheer horror and malaise that they have inflicted
upon the workers generation after generation is pretty much
impossible to put into words. Every major problem accost-
ing the body of the people today is a problem born in the
liberal state, caused by the liberal state, and in praxis foisted

upon the people by those two castes. It follows that at least a necessary condition to prevent the future organic state from getting infected is a total overhaul, reform and reinvention of all the departments, agencies, and the structure of the state itself, so as to not leave any psychopathic element unscathed. Here we can see how clear is the connection between an organic state and one which is not assailed with malignant actions from within. An organic state is a casteless state. In a casteless state the psychopaths can only wreak havoc within the immediate surroundings, rather than eviscerate the collective through the multiplier powers of the state's bureaucratic administration. In this sense, we can see yet another fundamental aspect of the National Liberextremist State as it relates to the workers' safety and well-being. Inherently, it is a state which by its mere existence wipes out many potential dangers to the body of the people and even better, prevents them from happening altogether. It is yet another powerful testament as to how harmonically natural this ideal state is.

As a corollary to the foregoing discourse, it is our will that:

◄▸————————◄▸

47. Eleventh founding principle: riddance of the psychopathic element in the deontological realm and beyond

"The AFWS will ensure by all necessary means that the psychopathic population is identified and adequately dealt with.

If any psychopath escapes detection, through the absence of castes and particularly the bureaucratic and political castes, the damage to the workers that their actions might cause will be minimized. We are a compassionate people and state, but compassion and kindness are virtues subjected to a hierarchy of value, and our utmost priority within that context will always be the potential victims. Consequently, justice will be systematically served as per the principles and procedures of the AFWS so as to curtail and even totally eliminate the psychopathic bane."

———————

48. The people: the state's only source of legitimacy

By now it is peradventure redundant to manifest explicitly the core moral principle which beautifully doubles as a logical conclusion of our philosophy, namely, we the people, the workers, are the alfa and omega, the sole reason for the state to exist. The procurement and protection of our moral and material welfare is the only valid drive behind the state itself. And because the AFWS is an organic political entity, each and every worker is an end in and unto himself. Just as in our physical bodies every single cell, tissue, and organ performs an irreplaceable function, so does every single worker within the body of the state itself. Therefore, every person is paramount to the people and the state, and his value impossible to ponder. As I already stated, we are not an aggregate of people, but a community and its infinite intricate interconnections. Each and every one of us performs a leading role in each other's lives, whether it is apparent or not. And it is emanating from this organic condition that in our state both the quality and the quantity of our beloved population are factors which need to be given special attention.

⬥————————⬥

49. Population size in the AFWS: an organic function

Population is to fluctuate organically so it is a reflection of the ethos of the community and not the result of a state altering the natural homeostatic equilibrium for political expediency. The increases or decreases of any population are just a symptom. The underlying causes must be addressed only if that symptom is deemed untoward by the state in the first place. The goal is to preserve the organic harmony within the corpus of the people. The workers themselves will make an organic determination as to how their own families must unfold, by exercising their freedom under virtue ethics and personal economic realities.

We have to understand that the size of a healthy nation is ultimately determined by the fruitfulness of the land, and the ingenuity and productivity of the people themselves in relation to that land. Therefore, if an ethical people is left to their own designs, the population size will always show a homeostatic trait.

Consequently, in the absence of misdirected schemes planned out and executed by the state, the population size will always be an ideal. The AFWS will never enact policy on symptoms while leaving the root causes untouched. As I already discussed, we will be the paradigm of political responsibility, and declared enemies of all kinds of expediency-driven schemes. As a logical capitalistic state on the socioeconomic front, and a National Liberextremist State on the political and philosophical front (more about this later), logic and extreme accountability by the state and the people are deemed essential for a true democracy to exist and thrive. All the devious stratagems used by the laissez-faire state to manipulate the population size for the benefit of the usufructuary caste and its spurious interests will be eradicated. This is just one reason why tax credits, immigration policy, as well as subsidies and entitlements will be entirely revolutionized, so the people in freedom and justice are moved to the forefront of the state's interests, rather than using the masses of workers as an "asset" to be disposed of at will for the illegitimate benefit of the few (more on those particular policies later).

I already touched upon the obsessive desire for constant population growth by the anti-worker dystopia, so its economic system does not collapse unto itself; as I already explained, the very definition of a mathematically unstable system. Delving even deeper into the schizophrenic nature of this state, always in constant wrangle within, I cannot help but draw attention to how the state itself is thirsting for bigger numbers but the "intellectuals" at the political and bureaucratic helms cry out for the opposite, as a sacrificial totem to be placed at the altar of climate change; hence we see the constant tug of war between those obsessed with the religion of abortion and those who attend the church of open borders. As millions are murdered in the womb, millions are rushed in from foreign lands so as to offset the number of the unborn who will never have the chance to become the pawns in the scheme of reproduction, expansion and concentration of money-capital, unlike their alien brethren. And both ends of the tragedy are called "freedom" by the ruling caste, as their message becomes sacrosanct through indoctrination and propaganda. Yes!without a question the freedom of death on one hand and the freedom of wage slavery on the other!

Rest assured that the victims who made it out alive will in due time avenge the ones who were mercilessly executed! The AFWS will be born out of many workers' sacrifices, including most of those who were lured into our ranks from without only to be exploited in a wicked scheme, just as bad or even worse than that suffered by the native population. As we can observe without a shadow of a doubt if we are curious enough, while the general policymaking of the liberal state is, on the face of it, practically psychopathic, the combination of those two particular policies acted out simultaneously is a display of unmitigated, raw schizophrenia. And thus, this compartmentalized organization resorts to the doings of psychopathic political and managerial castes so the schizophrenic nature of the state itself reigns supreme. Satan himself could not have come up with a better instrument of suffering and destruction, or perhaps this state is the proof that he has? ....

Both immigration and abortion on an industrial scale are

self-evident proofs of the unbounded will of this state to control and regulate the population, both in size and composition, so the illegitimate and criminal interests of the usufructuary caste are protected. Many other policies as I already mentioned are geared toward that final end as it pertains to population, and they will be properly addressed further on in this work.

⁕————————⁕

50. Vile ideas behind nasty words

A brief detour is here called for. Many will deem the subject matter rather trivial, but those more prone to connect the dots on the stage beyond the curtain will find it far more relevant and interesting. I am referring to the use of hackneyed words and expressions which we workers use ourselves inadvertently in doing the illegitimate elites' bidding, and which is a sign of serfdom I particularly abhor. The list is too extensive to address them all and regardless, I am not a lexicographer. Therefore, as an example, I will put forth just two modern liberal expressions and one acronym: "human resources", "human capital" and "VIP".

The first two expressions are a monstrosity of gargantuan proportions, and a grotesque affront on workers out in the open. They literally, and I stress literally, try to turn the quiddity of a worker into the quality of a thing, which is one of the vilest and most brutal actions any person can inflict upon another, from a philosophical standpoint. It is the epitome of objectification, or the reduction of the humanity within to a mere material property. The AFWP rejects the exogenous, fiat imposition of a mode of speech upon the people, so these expressions will not be prohibited in a any way, shape or form. Nevertheless they will be decried and tossed into the bin of infamy as the organic state develops new generations of free workers soaked in an ethos marked by virtue ethics and self-awareness. The people themselves will render them subwords, because they are contrary to their beliefs and principles but much more importantly, because they are objectively not true. And, as already pointed out, the sharpest and most effective weapon of our revolution is the truth.

The acronym VIP is the ignominious representation of the liberal paradigm itself. A system of castes, where the value of each and every member of the community is determined by the rung in the ladder of castes he is standing on, and this in turn is based purely and simply on material wealth. A system that is even more damaging and demeaning than the old system of castes based on blood and tradition, because it places the blame for your lack of "status" squarely on you, since the whole scheme is carried out in "freedom" and "voluntarily". A twisted and depraved instrument in which the victim is blamed for his lot. Let me state this unequivocally and categorically: there is no such a person as a very important person; or rather, we are all equally VIPs in the AFWP. Since we will be an organic state (where every member of the body politic is transcendental in its political existence and function and he's also the source of the state's legitimacy), everybody is very important, irrespective of something as blatantly accidental as his level of income, wealth, or perceived relative social status, whatever that might mean. Notice that the "leftists" or "progressives" have a lot to gripe about over all kinds of words, but when it comes to the dignity of the worker himself, irrespective of accidental features like gender, sexuality, race and the rest, they show their true colors as shills of the ruling caste and beneficiaries of the managerial and administrative state, which by and large they run. As I already intimated, those fakes will be among the first to be dealt with.

51. Population health in the AFWS: testosterone, ruralization, eugenics and more

It is on this subject matter that I wish my fellow workers to exert additional efforts of concentration so we can understand the complex radial interconnections that stems from its hub. I previously talked about the actions and destructions of the psychopathic managerial and political castes. However, there must be an explanation, no matter how simple or complex, as to how an entire population of workers can withstand this kind of overwhelming abuse with barely any kind of reaction. In other words, the success of the conspiracy is contingent upon not only the dexterity and strength of the perpetrators and the massive apparatus of the state, but also upon the weakness and passivity of the victims. And this relative debility is not metaphysical in nature, but very much the sad outcome of yet another conspiracy within this baffling realm of empirical reality. Indeed, since time immemorial, every passing civilization has been founded and upended, in an unstoppable cycle of destruction and creation, by the people who lived through it all. The civilizations created were a reflection of the people involved, and these in turn were influenced by their cultural, political and philosophical environment. So in a certain way, both the people and the civilization are feeding off of each other; hence we assume that history is a sequence of civilizations whose creators are inextricably tied down to their time. Those people created the only civilization that they could possibly create. Or we can phrase it thus: history is a sequence of deterministic epochs, where everything that happened was bound to happen as we know it. Or we can also say that everything historical that happened, creation and destruction alike, was meant to happen, because otherwise everything else that happened afterward would not have happened the way it did, including ourselves. I am not discussing the merits of this logical argument, or whether or not the latter conclusion is formally deducible from the premises. I am just laying out the argument. That being said, irrespective of whether or not historical events are contingent or necessary, or perhaps a modal predication somewhere in between, there is a common underlying circumstance to all the different civilizations throughout history all the way up to the mid-20th century, and that is the fundamentally robust hormonal health of those populations as collective entities.

Generally speaking, every known civilization has been built and developed by men with very healthy levels of testosterone. In fact, I surmise that the last three generations of men have been the first in known human history with chemically and environmentally induced, abnormally reduced testosterone levels. Through a constant bombardment of toxically grown or developed foods, massive levels of pollution and chemical contamination, saturation of plastic particles, and a sedentary urban lifestyle, all compounded by unmanageable levels of stress and anxiety (the bane of this modern civilization) ours can be termed the "era of estrogen and cortisol", as opposed to the rest of human history which could be defined as the "eons of testosterone". It is a scientific fact that the testosterone levels have fallen off dramatically over the last decades across much of the world, and to think that the tectonic shift in attitudes and fortitude that this cataclysmic decline has produced is not going to affect the relationship between the people and the psychopathic managerial and political castes is outright absurd. Yes, tragically so! Weak men are the perfect match for the schizophrenic state and its psychopathic arm, the managerial and political castes. In fact, the debility of the victims compounds the problem by reinforcing and strengthening the perpetrators; hence their assaults snowball into oppression out in the open, totally unabashed. We have apparently reached a point of no return, by peaceful means, that is.

As a logical consequence of what we have laid out regarding testosterone and hormonal health in general, the AFWS will always promote policies that enact "mens sana in corpore sano" as a matter of national survival. It will be a multifaceted approach to mental and physical health, involving regimented exercise; healthy food production and consumption and repression of the opposite; homeopathic medicine and enhanced oversight and restrictions on chemical compounds administered as prescription drugs; productive and recreational activities in nature (horticulture, forestry, trekking, bird watching, hunting, fishing, camping, etc.); and a militant attitude against tobacco and alcohol abuse.

This last point is especially important, because the ultimate goal is to wean the body of the people off those forms of poison; but it must be done organically, through the people themselves and their own moral convictions and self-awareness. After all, the will must be at the forefront of that battle and this kind of personal will is exercised by the individual himself, and it is not transferable. It is an unalienable blessing. Ultimately, indoctrination of upcoming generations will serve as the purifying flood that will wash all the rot away. Moreover, the AFWP policy on recreational (both street and pharmaceutical) drug use is one of total rejection. We will overcome, and the victory will be overwhelming and complete. As in many other situations and problems that the state on behalf of the people will confront, it will all come down to the sacrificial, cleansing power of the blood— a power and a symbolic meaning that the illegitimate state and its proponents know nothing about, as they deviously wallow in a regime of corruption and disgrace.

In connection with this crucial topic of population health is the issue of urban vs. rural and the kind of civilization we are striving for. The AFWP propounds a return to the land to the degree that it is practically and economically feasible. Cities started to develop thousands of years ago, but from the very beginning, the idea was to enhance the interactions and synergies between the people, i.e., to increase the social fortitude of the community. The first urban centers were conceived as nuclei of prosperity, strengthening tribe relationships, safety against foreign threats and an environment conducive to progress, knowledge and all sorts of human endeavors. But the incipient idea soon went astray and much of the ethos associated with the original concept became hopelessly distorted. Within the confines of this state, cities are only centers where people work because they don have any other option. As a matter of fact, those whose incomes allow them to do so, move to the outskirts and the suburbs in a desperate attempt to regain sanity for a few hours a day and two days a week. The modern American city, and I would argue most cities in the world, are nothing short of pits of filth, corruption, criminality and despair; abominations where a few get filthy rich at the expense of the many through all kinds of devious, illegitimate schemes. This moral decay comes with a corroding political and philosophical debasement. I will even take it a step further. I believe the reversal of this urban compound reality will be the greatest challenge facing the party and the new state, more daunting than anything else addressed hitherto. This urban malaise, or as I already called it, this urban neurosis, is so pervasive and reaches so deep, that it might take not only the power of the blood and of indoctrination to cure, but also great doses of time and prayer.

This urban hell was in a certain way anticipated by the ancients, as shown by written records. For example, in Genesis, we read about the Tower of Babel. Most historians and many theologians consider the story an etiology, a type of myth created to explain the origin of features in the phenomenological world—in this case, the birth of the different languages. In my opinion, however, what that tale explains is something much more sinister, namely the demonic quiddity of cities. In that narrative, the Tower of Babel is described as an affront to

God, inasmuch as it was the outcome of a people consumed by unbridled hubris. God punished the miscreants sowing confusion among them, by way of creating a multiplicity of languages wherewith communication would not be possible. In my judgment, modern American cities are not just a Tower of Babel, but indeed clusters of those towers, where throngs of people from disparate ethnic, religious, cultural and national backgrounds talk past each other—or even worse, ignore each other—because they speak, indeed, both literally and metaphorically, very different languages—rendering the logos dead in the process. Since I believe my interpretation of the story is right—and certainly the collective unconscious exists and it is not restricted by time or space—I am not particularly surprised to feel a demonic presence every time I behold one of those high-rises, a sensation that intensifies the closer I get to the tower. In any event, with or without myths and their hidden messages, ruralization will be actuated in the AFWS as a matter of national progress and in freedom, so as to reflect the ethos of the cleansed body politic according to the AFWP principles.

I will draw this commentary on ruralization to a close presently. But first, I shall approach this topic from a different angle, so our comprehension of the importance of ruralization of the body politic is beyond reproach. Everything in what we call loosely life, the empirical existence without and the psychic existence within, plus the interactions between the both in connection with what we call perception, is the field of a function with a binomial domain composed by hierarchy or order, and movement or change. (I will leave continuity aside for the sake of simplicity of argument at this juncture, but it will be wholly integrated as one of the principles of the trinity, or the three drives behind every political action by the organic state as it pertains to its people.) Everything that we know in life is a combination of hierarchy and movement or the lack thereof. All the narratives in life, both as perceived as well as invented or imaginary, are always a function of hierarchies and movement.

As I already explained earlier in this work, the ultimate narratives in human existence are what we call divine narratives, which are always intertwined with dogma. As it pertains to the AFWS, this will be a state of hierarchy and movement, since it is the intensional dimension of the body politic. The hierarchy is given life through the virtue ethics of the people and the deontological ethics of the state; and the movement is manifested through the principle of total responsibility and the permanent rotation of the people through the administration of the state. The judge or greatest ideal is the acme in the hierarchy of value, and therefore the implicit driving force behind the movement or change toward that apogee. But notice that you move toward the ideal, and not the other way around. In this sense, we are supposed to move out of the cities to the country, and not try to turn cities into the country. I do not believe that the embrace of the ideal consists in vesting the cities with country-like characteristics but rather divesting the cities entirely or as much as possible of what makes them sick, i.e., their inhuman scale, moving the source of light where it belongs.

Therefore, I logically conclude that the achieving of the ideal must be to return as many workers as possible to a peaceful, self-sustaining, virtuous and free existence in the country, which is the ultimate source of righteousness and grace. A great number of workers must be converted into small organic farm owners and dwellers. They will be the ultimate stewards of our national resources and environment (and growers of the food to sustain the AFWS supra-men; more on this later), along with a state which will consider its responsibilities of managerial duties on public lands among the most crucial within its purview. All kinds of instruments will be implemented to ensure an orderly and balanced ruralization of the country. Of course this process has a limit based on obvious economic necessities, but insofar as the people will be indoctrinated in virtue, that rural population will grow well above current levels, whereas the urban population will correspondingly diminish down to a point where cities become cities again rather than hubs of bane and destruction. I have always believed that if you cannot walk across your city in two or three hours, you probably live in a place far bigger than what is needed for total material and spiritual development. In the final analysis, people are free to live wherever they want, and that freedom will be ultimately the force behind the change. We just need to indoctrinate the people in the AFWP ideary and everything else will take care of itself.

So in this multifaceted fashion I have laid out the conditions under which we will create a healthy social body for the workers' sake, as well as for the sake of a state able thus to defend itself from the poison of psychopathic actions. Healthy workers will become the firewall beyond which the forces of evil cannot go, and therefore the state itself will be preserved this way from self-annihilation.

But we cannot close this chapter without probing further into the desirable traits of a healthy people. This is the topic of eugenics.

All throughout history, but perhaps more intensely in the 20th century, the idea of a supra-man born out of the right blood has been present both among the peoples of some nations and as a source of state policy. In places like Germany or our own country those ideas were the inspiration for policies that brought about catastrophic consequences or just unnecessary pain and suffering, including the total destruction of entire communities or the ostracization of others. As mentioned before, the liberal ideology and its 19th- and 20th-century nemeses were and still are a malaise unto themselves, and their incontrovertible rotting condition begs the question why the people continue to yoke themselves to them.

The AFWP idea of eugenics is very different. Ours is not a restrictive, annihilating, formulated-in-negative-terms idea. Rather it is an idea stated as a praising affirmation without prejudice against anybody, but just a positive judgment on some. Instead of repressing "the wrong people", we seek to multiply some workers whose organic impact on the community is markedly positive because of their cognitive, ethical, or physical capabilities. Hence ours is not eugenics based on race, but exclusively based on merit. Furthermore, it is not eugenics of contraction and destruction, but eugenics of expansion and creation. We only intend to focus on those whose merits stand out regardless of anything else.

Workers with high IQs or manifest intellectual excellence, outstanding physical or sporting achievements, or a proven record of ethical realizations or artistic accomplishments, will be targeted for all kinds of incentives (financial and otherwise) so they freely decide to increase the pool with as much new blood as they want to or can. (Consistent with this goal, an immigration exception has already been mentioned as well as the state's eugenic fertility clinics.) In any event, the choice will be theirs and it will all be carried out on a voluntary basis. Ours will be a singling out of the spearhead toward the judge or the supreme ideal, rather than a bashing of the straggler in the march forward. We have outgrown and discarded old misconceptions born out of ignorance and prejudice. We leave all those calamities for others to be judged for, and we reassert our condition of a revolution that moves forward and beyond, rather than backward and within. And as for the depth and the scope, I will leave the details of these policies to the people. Insofar as many desirable traits may or may not be susceptible of being passed down, depending on what theories or "experts" we heed, success in this endevor is not guaranteed. However, the worst-case scenario seems to be harmless and therefore this is a path worth treading in pursuit of a legitimate state goal.

Ours is the revolution forward in pursuit of the new and unmatched, and not a devolution backward into the banal and overcome, irrespective of how healthy this might be in its most unbesmirched version. Wherefore, we strive to graft the excellent onto the body politic, and not to lop the mediocre off from it. We dare to will the end of the most tyrannical of restrictions: the straitjacket of a weak blood. Consequently this is the eugenics of genesis, and not of restoration of old ideals. We rid ourselves of self-limiting beliefs and lackluster dreams, and we are at last aiming as high as our imagination and will permit.

Please notice here how a systematic and comprehensive evaluation process needs to be in place for this eugenics

Eugenics: The supra-race wherewith the people's march toward the judge strengthens.

program to be properly implemented, which is yet another unintended, but natheless positive consequence of this policy. The reason is that any time a fair judgment is passed on you, it will serve either as a thrust toward the judge or as a recognition and a respite from the hardships of daily life. As long as the judgment is righteous, there is always something to win. It is for this reason that one of my acknowledgments is to the Self within, since it is the closest source of inspiration, innnate to all of us by virtue of being humans. The Self is a constant spring of motivation and guidance—judgment—in other words, movement. It is a divine, vital source wherewith we are able to strive toward the ideal. Without it, no atainment (personal or social) could ever be consummated, since the essence of the Self is the will. Indeed, a weak man, propagandized and indoctrinated into a castrated version of himself, is the phenomenological reflection of a Self with an obliterated will, and hence an entity without a soul.

And with this, we have effectively wrapped up a section fundamental in the workings of the AFWS, and dedicated to laying out the principles and some general notions about the quantity and quality of our people as we understand those terms.

It is henceforth our will that:

◄▻————————◄▻

52. Twelfth founding principle: health policy and eugenics

"The only source of legitimacy and reason for the state to exist is to ensure the sacrosanct welfare of every single worker, whose immense value is impossible to measure. Therefore the state becomes illegitimate when as a matter of policy, corruption or incompetence it leaves anyone behind. The size of our people will be organically determined by the workers themselves as the result of the commingling of virtue ethics and economic realities. That equilibrium always will be achieved in truth, generally without pernicious manipulations by the state. However, the quality of the people will be enhanced through a myriad of health fronts: wholesome food, exercise, outdoor activities, ruralization, and many others. The goal will be the achievement of a hormonally, psychically and mentally strong population so the organic state can stave off psychopathy and function properly for the benefit of the people. Positive eugenics will be implemented on a voluntary basis so as to maximize the outcome of meritorious achievement, whether it is intellectual, artistic, ethical or physical; and all for the benefit of the whole of the people."

And the logical conclusion we are driving at is becoming more obvious with every passing page. I now unabashedly admit that we, as a party and state, are creating a now supra-man. New, because he is not the outcome of old ideas, poorly cobbled together so as to become a modern philosophy. On the contrary, we have gone to great lengths to make sure ours is truly an uncharted territory, and yet perfectly navigable with the aid of logic and our moral code, no matter the treacherousness of the undercurrents. And our supra-man is not the "superman" of old. He is not the man who chose to give up the fight because he could not win it, creating his own set of cozy rules instead in order to live in a perennial state of easiness.

We have overcome Nietzsche's defeatist concept (albeit wrapped in the cloak of debonair impudence), and decided to master God's game through the raw will of the people and the state. We have, indeed, waded through the murky waters of existential doubt and despair and reached our destination successfully; we have landed squarely at the feet of God himself. He set the rules, we abided by them and we boldly and gleefully reached the judge, the divine and supreme ideal. We are the supra-man of individuation; the man who stares at himself in the mirror and finds no shadow to be ashamed of; no unconscious content he has not acknowledged, confronted and ultimately embraced; and no dream he does not dare to dream. Ours is the paradigm of the political supra-man vs. Nietzsche's new ethics superman. He implicitly regarded the archetype of the Self as impossible to reify; thus he rejected the ideal altogether, supplanting it for his version of pre-Christian morality. We will, on the other hand, defiantly stare into the judge's eyes and march undauntedly and confidently toward that ideal, knowing that we have become its masters. For cannot we assuredly affirm that the only thought braver than the utter rejection of God (Nietzsche's approach) is the thought of becoming one with Him by his own rules and standards, and without the need for mercy but through our own achievements and merits?

I will address these ontological issues and much more in a prospective work which will serve as the compendium of our doctrine beyond the walls of political philosophy.

Ours is, beyond any doubt, a man for the ages. He is the supra-man the philosophers of old did not even try to dream of. He is the warrior, the sage and the worker; the true embodiment of the hero archetype. We have uprooted the bane of defeatism, determinism, nihilism, and atheism from our hearts and minds. And we will forge the state which will carry in its bosom, like the perfect gourd, the nectar of political and social righteousness and confidence for the world and history to behold. The power of the will and the cleansing miracle of the blood are foundations upon which this revolution will be enacted. Despair, anxiety and rot will be washed away so that our supra-man can be born into a new world of liberty, justice, true prosperity and respect for all, as we understand these ideas which are the core of our political philosophy.

PART II

THE AFWS: STRUCTURE, GOALS AND POLICIES; THE FEARLESS MARCH TOWARD THE JUDGE; REVOLUTIONARY WEAPONS IN PURSUIT OF THE IDEAL; STRUGGLE, DESTRUCTION, DEATH, REBIRTH, CONSTRUCTION, BLOOD AND TRIUMPH.

53. The National Liberextremist State

It would be certainly very easy for me to sell the advantages of a state without schizophrenic internal strife over concocted tangential issues, whipped up by the two wings of the particracy for political expediency to keep the masses of workers befuddled and reticulated; without the oppressive boot of a privileged, psychopathic and corrupt managerial and bureaucratic caste; with all the assurances of the natural freedoms, justice, respect and prosperity for all; a society that ensures no clique of conspiratorial exploiters gets control of the state apparatus to illegitimately profit from it at the expense of the phalanxes of workers; a state where work means money and vice versa; where nothing illegitimately gained is legally allowed as per a doctrinal ethical canon; nothing legitimate is made illegal in order to favor any special group; castes have been done away with; competitive wages have been organically replaced by logical wages and the state subjects itself and all its branches and agencies to the strictest of standards, so it is morally empowered to subject the people to those same standards; the workers are directly involved in the administration of the state, and the concept of a career politician or bureaucrat has been eradicated; the state lives within its means and the currency is not debased by monetary and fiscal policies not grounded on truth or the supreme maxim that money and work are one and the same; the state's legitimacy is derived directly from the ultimate purpose to be the final guarantor of justice, liberty, respect and prosperity for each and every worker in the land; the organic state's skin or its border will be protected from any infection or encroachment whether it is armed or not, by all and any means and primarily through the cathartic shedding of the blood; peace with every nation is regarded as the most natural and sought-out means of international relations and any disruption of that norm allowed only in self-defense and if the representatives of the people and the people themselves through referendum acquiesce to it; the fabric of this nation of tribes is organically made whole by an indoctrination system steeped in virtue ethics throughout the body politic, deontological ethics carried out through political actions and laws as reflections of the authority of the collective unconscious and the power of the will; militia life and training sanctioned and organized by the state so any remnants of caste structure are further demolished, and philosophy studies, ruralization and communion with nature and empowerment through gun ownership are instituted.

So on the basis of the excellency and morality of a state thus founded, structured and developed, there is no chance anybody with any ethical compass whatever could possibly object to it, right? Unfortunately this is not the case. The reason lies at the feet of a very old philosophical trope, namely, can we derive values from facts? This transcendental question has been at the core of an endless succession of metaphysical, epistemological, ethical and political debates through millennia. As is the wont in philosophy, the answer lies in the eyes of the beholder or rather the intellect of the thinker, and normally along the lines of the philosophical school he adheres to.

I will declare now that if an individual could serve as the paradigm of the broken clock, which is still right twice a day, every day, that would be the philosopher David Hume. For his insistence on the impossibility of values being derived from facts is indeed a statement I wholeheartedly agree with, and the reason why our AFWS will be born out of a flood of sacrificial blood. No doubt Hume came to his most flawless conclusion influenced by the anti-Aristotelian doctrines of his time, but nevertheless I appreciate his insight and the fact that he left his thoughts on the subject amply recorded for posterity in his published works.

The keen reader will remember that I rejected the teleological nature of human actions as the basis for a consistent and complete ethics (unless that teleological character is proven by a long history of functional success), which is the de facto reason why Aristotle embraced a set of cardinal virtues as a reasonable centerpiece of his ethics. I myself pointed to this system of virtue ethics as the soundest of all I can think of, but not as a conclusion based on teleological interpretations of actions but rather as a logical and metaphysical conclusion based on traditional and canonical convention consistent with the fundamental principles of reality within and without, namely hierarchy, continuity and movement. In other words, functional as a precursor of teleological, and not the other way around. I will expound upon all of this in a more appropriate venue, a subsequent book which will be published when the right time comes. But for now, let us focus as much as we need to on political philosophy.

Why should the impossibility of deriving values from facts have a direct connection with the way our state will come to be? The answer is quite straightforward: because one can only link up our organic state to a most desired ethical state if he can also line up his ethics to the ethics fostered within that state. In other words, for a worker steeped in the moral philosophy of virtue ethics, this state we propound is the most excellent we could contemplate; but if his ethics derives its canons from other sources, the dichotomy with our AFWS manifests itself. If, for example, your ethics, no matter how inconsistent or incomplete or just about the opposite might be, render a state righteous if and only if it hinges on a multiplicity of political parties operating within, then our AFWS is not righteous or ethically desirable. And because our initial premise is that we cannot derive values from facts, the aforementioned conclusion is not formally invalid but nevertheless we qualify it as false because the premise it is based upon (there are other ethical systems better that the canonical virtue system) is false. But this is a matter of dogma or modal logic at best. Regardless, it will take a nation steeped to the hilt in blood to link up actuality with potentiality, or a state with its most virtuous and phenomenal version. For nothing that is worth something was ever born dry.

And thus we have already anticipated the stubborn resistance to the virtuous state, on the basis that the prima facie facts alone cannot procure a meeting of the minds because the brutes will not accept self-explanatory evidence as the basis for righteous actions, and the wise will not accept them either on the philosophical theory that values cannot be derived from facts. So in consequence, we are doomed to fight to the last breath if necessary. However, I must draw the attention to the faulty reasoning of the wise. For indeed, if we accept the precept that values are not derived from facts, I cannot understand how anybody would possibly object to violence to reach a virtuous end (and the wise and "sophisticated" certainly do), not on the conjecture that virtue ethics are teleologically explained in an Aristotelian way, but on the realization that we cannot deductively judge violence as spurious per se if we are to be consistent with the initial premise.

Yes! Indeed a state born out of blood is far superior to one born out of political intrigues or academia, even without considering the merits of one or the other, since force is a syllogistic consequence of the necessity to overcome the conundrum just laid out: a virtuous state on its merits being rejected by some because they possess another set of canons, and by others because they do not accept facts as a causal source of values. So force is a logical conclusion in the march forward in pursuit of the ideal (or the supreme judge, whose quiddity is transcendentally shared by the people, at least partially, through the collective unconscious), represented in the individual psyche by the archetype of the Self, borrowing the terminology of my most esteemed Swiss shaman, Carl Jung. I find it quite amusing that one of the founders of this babelic state, and with whom I share nothing philosophically speaking, put it well when he wrote: "The tree of liberty must be refreshed from time to time with the blood of patriots and tyrants." It is an undeniable statement of fact.

All of the above notwithstanding, I will explain later on why life manifests itself very often in various stubborn and uncompromising ways, to the degree that philosophy and aye! even logic itself must give way. Because of it, practicalities trump theoretical reasonings, and thus the sequence of events leading up to the dawn of the organic state will have to mirror the struggle between David and Goliath and not the slaying of the dragon by Saint George, which is what my narratives always tend to imply, perhaps carried away by the heart of a rebel and not of a sage.

I already established the economic system the AFWS will adhere to; I have minutely described it and baptized it autarkic logical capitalism, primarily because it is a descriptive title. I also termed the AFWP platform and hence the AFWS itself as a program that renders the National Liberextremist State. And here I will expound on this concept.

It is a national state because the nation is recognized as the natural social basis for the articulation of a body politic. Our nation is a cultural and historical reality and she will be properly actualized as an organic state under the AFWP.

Consequently, any kind of membership in supranational political, financial, military and commercial structures will be terminated, since those institutions are by their very definition antidemocratic and spurious, and therefore illegitimate, expensive, corrupt, dysfunctional and prone to generate unnecessary confrontations with analogous, parallel organizations and their members.

The state will negotiate appropriate and mutually beneficial trade agreements when there is no other choice to procure essential raw materials, and cooperative treaties conducive to an expansion of scientific research. Worthy cultural and academic arrangements will be signed and enacted. That will be the extent of our entanglement with foreign nations aside from regular international travel of people for personal reasons. Immigration will be brought to a halt as we already discussed, so the organic nature of the state can be realized within a stable framework. If we are asked to mediate between nations so peace agreements can be brokered, we will engage in that kind of diplomatic enterprise as well, provided the ensuing status is not deemed a threat or an actual injury to the national interest. We will strive to be in peaceful and even friendly terms with all, but we will nevertheless always reserve the right to engage only with the nations of our choosing based on national interest and political ideary.

We will not, however, partake in any kind of alliance which by its very nature poses an antagonistic or yet worse, bellicose threat to anybody else. We reserve the right to steer clear of states we do not approve of without aligning ourselves with those who wish to confront them. Our active friendship will have to be earned, and never taken for granted based on alleged cultural, religious or historical grounds which we do not recognize as bonding. By the same token, our enmity should not be assumed based on the same irrelevant grounds. Our peaceful and distant neutrality will be, however, the general rule of our foreign policy. The best contribution to the world we can possibly offer is an unrelenting and strict observance of our founding principles, thus providing a paradigm of justice, liberty, prosperity and respect for the whole of the people which has never been and will never be equalled in the history of the world. Our impact abroad will be measured by the sheer power of righteous example for everybody to behold, and the inspiration without precedent that will undoubtedly bleed into the collective unconscious in this plane of existence, one shocking and marvelous milestone at the time.

The world, indeed, will come to know we are genuinely a new state, and no tainted baggage will be dragged along by the newborn, this Ground Zero of the paradigm lost.

It is paramount to address the issue of reciprocity and proportionality. The AFWS will never uphold any kind of proportional reciprocity whatsoever within the context of international relations, especially in crisis situations or the preludes to them. We will make crystal clear, for the whole of the world to pay heed to and understand, that we will never bind our state to the illogical constraints of proportionality. This most damning principle of foreign policy subscribed to by so many states in the course of history, and especially framed by the babelic behemoth as a virtuous and rational, canonical modus operandi, is indeed a catastrophic source of wars and strife. So much so that putting up a comprehensive list of the conflicts sparked off by this policy would prove a mission impossible.

If the actors involved in these schemes of foreign policy had a basic understanding of propositional, predicate, or modal logic, undoubtedly none of this nonsense would ever become a tragedy to contend with; unless, of course, we understand the fundamental, underpinning drive of all things within this ill-begotten state: an insatiable thirst for unearned profits to benefit that elite of plutocrats for which the state itself exists and operates.

For war must be regarded as one of the most lucrative businesses for a few and yet one of the most destructive occurrences for the many and therefore for the organic state. And the proven guarantee of the outbreak of war has always been, still is and will always be the principle of proportionality. In other words, the solemn a priori declaration by a state that it will de facto make its response to any foreign attack commensurate to the magnitude thereof. There is no possible argument that makes that principle logical or functional on any level if the ultimate goal is to avoid conflict.

If, however, the aim is a quasi-sempiternal state of war, that doctrine is difficult to improve upon. Conversely, if the ultimate goal of a virtuous state is the avoidance of war, the wonted policy should ineluctably be unpredictability of actions, of intensity and of qualification for causation (i.e., a plan of attack on us is an attack in and of itself and it will be treated accordingly). The precept which should be conveyed as the solemn epigram of foreign policy in the context of hostile environments should be "do not conspire against us and make sure we never believe otherwise". That is the logical proposition upon which meaningful conclusions can be inferred in an effort to not become embroiled in conflicts with others. This is the ultimate logical maxim of an ethical and strong state, rationally steered, and willing to execute whatever action is necessary to survive and thrive.

This course of action, both in theory and in praxis, confronts a direct question: do we regard our people as more valuable than others? Immanent to our foreign policy framework within unfriendly environments, the answer is unapologetically yes. I already discussed the nature of the organic state, and the fact that its foundation and reason for existence is the people themselves, our workers. So we are indeed establishing a hierarchy of value between peoples and therefore all the inferences deduced afterward need to be consistent with this doctrine: we do not regard the people of other states as our equals, because otherwise the existence of this state is a fallacy unto itself. Our workers are obviously not better or worse than others; that is not the interpretation of our hierarchy. Our workers are just different and unique, insofar as their weal is the first and only purpose of the organic state. We are a deontological state; we are not an Asiatic religion, even though the ethics into which our people are indoctrinated have partly Asiatic roots. We do not exist as an archetype of self-immolation, but as an actual state whose only purpose on this Earth is the actualization of each potentiality within our body politic. That is our creed, our foremost principle, and we realize to the utmost logical conclusion. For this reason, ruthless means consistent and complete; it means propositionally logical. It means rational, virtuous, honest.

And as without, so within. We will obliterate any bane to our people, foreign or domestic; and we will finally be a state with the people, and a people with the state, living in truth, proudly professed out loud for everybody to heed. The hemlock will be austerely, uncompromisingly uprooted and trampled, and the sap will flood the land so the laurel and the olive can feed on the sacrificial ambrosia and grow strong and proud.

I want now to take a detour to emphasize the importance of the national character of our revolution. National Socialism was a racial ideology. Fascism was based on pride of history and national identity. Communism is a class ideology. Liberalism is a caste ideology revolving around the expansion and concentration of capital. The AFWP ideary and philosophy are based on an ethos of logic and virtue ethics and the will to politically instantiate every conclusion regardless of any further predication. But such an instantiation requires an object, precisely the nation in which the foregoing ethos is generated. When the liberal hegemon embraces globalism, or the obliteration of national identity, nothing is left to glue the body politic together, since it has already been reticulated to the maximum by design through all the devices already discussed (modern-day religions built upon government, science, sex, sexual orientation, race, national origin, political parties, etc.). The usufructuary, administrative and generally privileged castes still have at their disposal elements of internal cohesion, like attendance at the same Ivy League institutions, membership in elite sects, clubs and associations, and the like. But the only source of oneness for the productive caste is national identity. Once this identity is watered down to its minimum expression, the feebleness of the body politic at large ensues. Hence our revolution and party, and the future National Liberextremist State, are national as a matter of logical consistency and survival.

Our state is defined as liberextremist. I have already used this term before, but what does that mean? Liberextremist is a neologism I have gingerly chosen so as to be immediately descriptive and as encompassing as possible. The etymology of the prefix liber is very symbolic on different fronts. It links up graphically with our party badge as it means "book" in Latin; and it goes to show how magical the Latin language is, not just for being the father of so many wonderful Romanic languages and a rich linguistic source for countless others, but also on account of homonyms such as this one, which I regard as almost a semantical example of synchronicity. For is there anything more beautiful than the sharing of the same word (albeit different declensions and vowel pronunciations) to label such a priori disparate concepts as "book", "free", "unrestrained", "child" and the god of viticulture, male fertility and free speech, worshipped particularly by Roman plebeians? For what are we, if not the plebeians of the liberal state? And I cannot help but wonder, are those seemingly unrelated words truly independent from each other, or we can perchance perceive a common trope, a spiritual source from which all of them imbibe in a sense, making this homonym a supra-word? We would be painfully mistaken if we fall prey to the belief that words are just the building blocks of languages rather than the repositories of unlimited powers passed down through countless generations through the subtle and mysterious influence of the collective unconscious. Much more on this topic will be addressed in another work, but for now let us go back to politics.

Liber is indeed, a powerful word and symbol. It needed to be part of our definition and conceptualization of the AFWS and therefore it is. The suffix "extremist" is of course a word on its own and very much straightforward. We are a state which abides by its ideary and principles without equivocation or hesitation, and logically follows through to the last actions and consequences. We are extremist in the sense of maximalist and radical: a state free from political compromise to appease agents at home, let alone abroad. A state born out of a revolution; a state rooted on a soil nourished with the blood and the logos; a state for the sake of free people who meant all of it. Ours will be the revolution of the hero, he who faced down the worst of dragons and prevailed. What our foes will call cruelty and barbarism, we will call the triumph represented by a snake well slain. And once the state is established, there will not be a change of course and we will not forslow fundamental duties. The state will not be a culmination of a revolution, but the start of a glorious journey toward the judge, for we will never relent until we place ourselves, self-assured and defiant, at the feet of the ideal. Others will live in doubt and fear; as for our people, they are decked in virtuous armor which has passed the test of time, consistent with our principles and goals.

And now it is time to lay out the structure and policies of this ideal state.

A National Liberextremist State, such as I have defined it, is a radically democratic state. It is a casteless state, as I already discussed—a state which has rid itself of professional bureaucratic and political castes and any trace of psychopathic abuse across the ranks. It is an organic state, where the people themselves run the agencies of government on a temporary basis and the rotation of public duties through the body politic is enshrined in the law. It is a state that has utterly rejected, in theory and praxis, all the residues of the liberal fraud, including its constitution, laws and canons. The workers themselves will have to build a new structure, from the bottom up, through their democratic representatives and the most democratic of tools: the referendum. We envision a state without the absurd baggage of the superannuated federal structure, where the people articulate politically through the county and the electoral district and where the betterment of the nuclear family is the ultimate aim of any political action; a state where the workers actualize their political inclinations not only through the polls but also through their participation within the union. Each individual company or in some cases entire productive sectors will be integrated in an all-inclusive union, as we talked about when addressing the wage labor vs. logical labor dichotomy. This union will serve not only the purpose of connecting marginal utilities of labor taken with marginal values of labor given, but also as the locus and the conduit for political feedback which will be adequately gathered and acted upon by the representatives of the people. So party, union, county and electoral district. This is the quaternity upon which the political action of our people will be built and transmitted upward and outward throughout the structure of the state.

At the bottom of this hierarchical structure are the county and the electoral district, and above the union, articulating economic relations across the forenamed political and administrative units. These linchpins of the National Liberextremist State are where much of the people's civil life unfolds, and therefore they must be legally empowered so as to procure the maximum symbiosis between the body politic and its intensional dimension (for otherwise the AFWS would not be organic), as well as to guarantee the most efficient allocation of public resources. And at the acme of the hierarchy, the party, which orients the state as this is the most ideal reification of the party ideary.

Our National Council will be formed by 500 outstanding workers, and it will be an assembly whose members will come from every district in the nation, proportionally to its population and size. To start with, both factors will be weighted at the same rate, so as to recognize not only our people but the land itself upon which this unprecedented effort in liberty and dignity will be enacted. A posteriori, this design could be changed according to the people's will. The workers themselves will redraw the electoral districts through local referendums at the county level. The newly formed districts will consequently be assigned a number of representatives (as we already hinted at, that number is dependent upon population and acreage) and the people will choose democratically those representatives from open lists. The money allocated by the state will be evenly doled out to all candidates. Needless to say, no private pelf of any kind will be allowed and it will be a punishable offense to engage in illegitimate money-raising schemes. The lists themselves, however, although open to all, will only be slated by persons of extraordinary qualities previously assessed through standardized and public procedures. These extraordinary workers will be the best the body politic will have to offer on the basis of combined and outstanding intellectual, physical and moral prowess. Yes! effectively the people will be represented by our archetypal supra-man. This national liberextremist democracy is a radical meritocracy, and we will enforce this principle without exceptions as a matter of collective survival. The criteria to fill the ranks of public servants weaving in and out of the different departments and agencies of government will not be as stringent, though, since that rotatory nature is paramount for the state to be organic.

It is already stipulated that the National Council will be a representation of the people and it will take into account the sizes of the districts as well. Hence there is no need for ludicrous bicameral structures and cumbrous legislative modus operandi which nowadays are the remainders of an absurd, archaic founding document. The federal character of this weird liberal creature stems from the national and independent nature of those thirteen colonies of yore, and the ensuing expansion westward, which was designed upon the extant political and institutional framework. Indisputably, that is not a reasonable way of enlarging a nation or constructing a new state. Today, we are used to maps all across the Central Great Plains and the American West full of squares, rectangles and a myriad of other quasi-perfect geometrical figures. The lunacy of such a contradiction should be apparent to any discerning observer, but sadly the power of paradigms ingrained into laws and canons, as well as the overwhelming weight of tradition and history, is the reason why the peek does not turn into a horrified goggle. Nations and states are supposed to be cultural and historical entities, normally born from the bottom up. In the case of this liberal swindle, the expansion took the form of a colonial enterprise, establishing arbitrary borders from the top down, and endowing those territories eventually with statehood status, in an attempt to artificially recreate the genesis of the original states. This development is such a de facto snafu that I wonder how miserably deluded anybody who sets out to defend it has to be.

Term limits will be the law of the land, for otherwise the complete intertwining of the people with the state would not be possible. We will hold elections to the National Council once every four years, and each representative will serve a maximum of two terms, if reelected to office. All workers age 21 and older will be eligible to run themselves and to vote for any compeer slated based upon merits. The age limit is essential so we can indoctrinate the youth into a life of philosophy, work ethic and virtue, as well as practical camaraderie through the National Liberextremist Youth (as it could be named), before they are deemed ready to exercise their right and duty to run and to choose. Indeed, a duty it is, since how can a drop of blood refuse to run through the vascular system propelled full force by the heart into the furthest confines of the body? It certainly cannot. Likewise, a worker is admittedly responsible for the democratic sustenance of the organic state through a range of actions, in accordance with the AFWP program, the laws and canons, and their own conscience and inclinations; but surely compulsory suffrage is essential for this state to be all-inclusive and functional. All workers will have a designated day to vote in person, and their identities properly verified at the polls. Allowance will be given for those who can adequately prove they cannot nourish our organism in person due to medical reasons or other well documented and justified circumstances. In such cases, a well organized and supervised mail-in system will be implemented. And finally, anyone who does not meet his obligations will be punished according to the spirit and the letter of the pertaining laws.

The term limits for any other office or bureaucratic position will be strictly enforced too. Eight years of service to the state and the people, as well as to the ultimate purpose of becoming one with the state, is considered generally sufficient and adequate. The details of this revolving system will be ironed out by the people themselves through their representatives, and enshrined into the laws and regulations of the state. The democratic procedures of municipalities and counties will mirror the state's and vice versa. As compounds of cells form tissues and these in turn entire organs and the physical body itself, so the organic state is an organized and infinitely interconnected web of singular cells whose quiddity is one and the same throughout the entire system.

We are laying out the only possible state for our supraman, since this entire enterprise is logical, not ideological! How sickening the babelic state, as a wicked, illogical, stale and empty organization appears to us now, in the wake of an organism which is the vivid political reflection of the workers themselves, as virtuous and logical singularities!

But what about the biggest obsession in the shallow freak show of American politics? What about the presidency? This institution is antidemocratic both in its genesis and in its membership. When the liberal states came to the forefront of international politics as the laissez-faire ideology actualized at different stages during the 18th century, the intellectual temptation to anchor them in the ethos of the monarchic states that they were supplanting became irresistible. A president in an alleged "constitutional republic" such as ours is the liberal interpretation of an absolutist king. In fact, the original idea of many among the so-called "revolutionaries" was to endow the first president with royal powers and institute an actual dynasty.

I will take it a step further and I will say that most of this state's founders were monarchists in principle; they just rejected the abuses and encroachments of a particular king, but not the legitimacy of the institution politically, legally or historically. They just happened to care about their property more than about the British royal family's interests, which I do not find reprovable. Much has been embellished and tergiversated about the lives and drives of those who invented this state, for obvious political reasons. But the facts remain stubborn: they founded neither a democracy nor a republic since, based upon their actions during the revolutionary epoch and later writings, they never believed in the merits or legitimacy of either one. Instead, they invented what I would call a rotatory monarchic republic, that is to say, a monarchy without a dynasty and therefore without blood heirs, and with a restricted suffrage system in lieu. Anybody who has seriously studied the classics, those who gave intellectual form and philosophical explanation to the actual democracies, dictatorships, autocracies, plutocracies, republics and monarchies that sprang up all across southeast Europe and Asia Minor 2,100 to 2,600 years ago, knows the absurdity of the nomenclature used by this state's founders.

Our country used to be, indeed, a constitutional rotatory monarchic republic, although nowadays the first word in that predication has been obviously obliterated. The modern liberal sham is a bureaucratic administrative state; a political structure operating for the profit of a plutocratic oligarchy through what most would term a partitocracy. It is quite something, actually. It has morphed from a traditional proprietor-driven presidential system to a state which has no precedent in human history. It is theoretically a constitutional state, but where those in power never abide by that document. It is a state with an alleged separation of powers, but where all the branches of government are controlled by the same two wings of the partocracy; a state where the president is kept at bay from the public or any real conversation or debate, aloof in a house where criminal deals are struck behind closed doors for the benefit of the donor caste; a state with a massive corpus of laws which the executive branch only enforces at its discretion based upon the interests of the few, always at the expense of the many; a state where judges are appointed by politicians, and the highest court in the land is formed by political activists from both wings; a state where a caste of professional politicians becomes ever richer while in office and afterward, through a medley of criminal subterfuges, more and more out in the open: assets revaluations induced by convenient budget allocations for public works, inside trading, government contracts for kith and kin, bribery and influence-peddling, massive book deals and lucrative sinecures—and the list goes on.

These same politicians remain in office in many cases throughout their entire lives, literally for decades, while receiving absurd amounts of campaign contributions directly or through criminal enterprises called political action committees. The state media will ignore the decay of all institutions which they are part of, while the national security assets working within their ranks spew out lies on behalf of the gatekeepers and engage in massive coverups, lies, hate-promoting campaigns and all sorts of propaganda operations, all of which are immoral, criminal and illegal. They count on a gullible and ever-less-discerning population at large rendered uncritical thinkers by an "education" system engineered for that purpose; that and to make workers slave away without questions, of course.

The laissez-faire state is a state hellbent on a cruel and obliterating scheme of reticulation and division of workers based on hate and resentment, along lines that can be controlled centrally by government agencies and corporate / state media. It is a state that articulates itself so only rich people can run for office (due to the absurdly high cost of running a successful campaign), and those stooges lackeying for a chance to make pelf without working. It is a state that steals from some workers to arbitrarily give to others, so the people keep on being at each other's throats, consumed in rage and envy, while the puppeteers keep winning on this demonic battlefield. And then, in the ultimate display of hubris, the logos itself is accosted and repressed; the people themselves gagged, and their sacrosanct right to speak the truth suppressed by technology companies inextricably intertwined with the state in the pursuit of dirty, illegitimate money and power. Believe me when I say the cleansing flood will have the power to redden the land from Babylon to Santiago or it will not be cleansing at all ... and it will certainly be.

From a strictly historical point of view, before the total bastardization and disintegration of morals, institutions and policies, as I already mentioned in this work, this state is a spinoff of the Lockean social contract. This was the most timorous articulation of a body politic imaginable, ideated around the interconnected obligations derived from property rights. Alas!

as if the quiddity of a man can be defined in term of his possessions! I argue that such an accident is not even the concomitant property of any Self, at most contingent and not in any serious way essential to any particular man. The revolution of 1776 drew heavily from Locke to conclude that a rebellion is justified if a ruler does not uphold the aforementioned contract by means, for example, of capricious or abusive taxation. Undoubtedly, the revolution itself was much more impetuous and bold than the political philosophy from which it drew its justification. Nowadays we perplexedly contemplate a state that has grown its political structure to unprecedented dimensions in human history, and all on the basis of a ridiculously constrained social contract to protect property rights. In other words, we are beholding the archetype of the schizophrenic state, one which is in contradiction with its own alleged nature.

We can further define this parasitic outgrowth within an Aristotelian framework of causation as:

- Finally plutocratic;

- Efficiently kakistocratic;

- Formally partitocratic;

- Materially immoral, submissive and obtuse.

The people will have to be reeducated, indeed, if we are to create a moral, just, prosperous and respectful society in which workers can actualize all their potentialities in organic cooperation with one another as a body politic sustaining the AFWS. To this end, no doubt the youth will have the stellar role and all our hopes will be placed in them.

But back to that Frankenstein of an institution, the American presidency. It is not the legitimate daughter of republic or democracy, if the conceptualizations of Plato and Aristotle were to be taken seriously. But it is certainly the bastardized consequence of the liberal revolutions of the 18th century. I must admit, among all the institutions and mores we have been yoked to for hundreds of years now, the presidency is the one which I find the most repulsive. Perhaps its sophistical character—passing itself off as a republican concept, and concomitantly counting on the ignorance and feeble acquiescence of the people—is what disgusts me the most. Or perchance its utmost character as the byproduct of an immanently caste society, because the presidency is indeed the ultimate caste. It is actually a caste unto itself. On philosophical grounds it is hopelessly contaminated. But in praxis, I can assuredly proclaim that the presidency, as is defined and legally delineated in America, has caused incommensurate damage to the body politic over the centuries. De facto, that institution has contributed more than any other to the development of a serfdom mentality throughout the phalanxes of workers.

Because of this, the new state will have to dedicate a great deal of resources to stomp out the idea of that institution. The inappropriate and untoward deference that the people, propter honoris respectum, show to the president, elevating his figure grotesquely to that of a modern-day emperor, is truly pathological. We can mention his wasteful journeying around in expensive aircraft, limousines and else; his constant vacations in publicly funded mansions (very often bringing along extended family and friends), etc. All of it is funded by overtaxed wagslave sweat. But even worse is his never engaging in meaningful and serious public policy debates; his lack of philosophical acumen and ethical standards; his meritless existence in the spotlight of the American political empty circus, devoid of content but with plenty of glitter; his illegal and criminal decisions through the security state involving Americans at home and abroad; his enforcing some laws while flouting others for political expediency and the profit of his donors; and the emetic display of sycophants galore in corporate media when engaging with the holder of that office—the list of grievances is too long to detail, and it is so because of the putrid nature of the institution itself.

It is immanently inconsistent with the political system that claims to be part of and consequently it is an illogical institution in the deepest sense. It is very prone to corruption, and to excesses of all kinds. It is the direct product of an illegitimate caste system. And it has been the cause or the medium of unjust wars, repression, wickedness, manipulation and dishonesty, waste and even economic distress and abuse. Particularly insane is the tradition of building multibillion-dollar "libraries" to honor former presidents, in displays that remind us of almost pharaonic settings. Those cringing monuments are funded by the special interests protected ex officio by the president, serving as a surreally overt and obscene demonstration of bribery. This custom began in 1941, and continued on by a series of presidents with wits and decency severely dwarfed by their narcissistic personalities. Prior to that, presidential documents and records were securely kept in different locations, one of them Congress itself. But the degeneration and decay of this state through the centuries, which seems to me its only organic aspect, knows no limits.

And the pernicious character of this institution is so un-mitigated, that with every passing generation the holders of that office have become more ostensibly outré and detached from the phalanxes of American workers. Nowadays, most compeers would consider the behavior, mannerisms, speech and even looks of many of those presidents or would-be presidents quite unnatural, awkward or downright bizarre. Although pathetic, that is not necessarily harmful to the body politic, unlike their ego-driven scorn for the people's natural rights. And this is the most destructive implication of such putrefactive institution: the uncontrollable presidential hu-bris, which in synch with the rest of the partocracy, can ren-der fundamental freedoms a target for obliteration. Indeed, those disturbing liberal concepts (misinformation, disinfor-mation, and malinformation) are nothing but the symptoms of an ideological beast willing to resort to anything to survive its own people, no matter the cost. (I'll hereinafter elaborate on the mark of the liberal Leviathan in the context of the deontological reasons and justifications of the state's exis-tence.) More specifically, those three terms are the instan-tiation of a lese-majesty imposition on our mores—by fiat and law—whereby the ruling caste implicitly identifies itself with the state, substantially predicating free speech beyond the limits of one of the state's founding document—thereby further demonstrating the schizophrenic nature of this liberal kakotopia.

Thus the presidency will be no more in the AFWS.

We also have rendered the federal structure of the state and the Senate unnecessary as the rollover of a colonial era. The idiosyncrasies of our people and their electoral districts are already factored in by considering not only population but land size in the process of allocation of representatives.

The executive branch stands no more as a separate entity and opposed in many regards to the people via their representatives, but rather is a projection upon the structure of the state itself of the most excellent among the forenamed body of representatives. The executive will be designated by the Council out of its own ranks, in a public and deliberative process. The executive will be in essence the ideal collection of supra-men, or the real-life archetype of the ideal body politic, since the chosen will be the cream of the crop within the legislative body. The same rules of term limits and else will be imposed upon the executive, which will lack a "president" or "prime minister" but it will nonetheless furnish the rest of ministerial posts according always to the state's needs. Decisions within that cabinet will be made by majority rule and will never be in contravention of the party principles. In order to ensure this is the case, the Council will debate and vote on the measures passed by the executive according to the aforementioned principles and program. Thus any executive decision will be subjected to the will of the people through their representatives, thereby reinforcing the organic nature of the state, the strict adherence to the party principles, and ultimately a perfect integration and compatibility of executive decisions with the ethos of our people.

As we have pointed out several times in this founding document, the ultimate weapon of this organic state is the referendum. Accordingly, when the Council cannot reach a certain threshold of approval or disapproval on any particular legislative action or executive policy, if it is manifestly important to do so, the people themselves will be asked to cut the Gordian Knot. For in the AFWS it is the people who rule, and not any king or president or would-be Council leader. And the details of the internal rules and procedures will be left for the supra-men themselves to figure out, since that is not an ethical or philosophical enterprise but rather administrative minutiae, and therefore I do not need to entangle myself in it.

Let us now flesh out our thirteenth founding principle, for it is our will that the structure, goals and policies of the state itself must be axiomatically put forth.

<hr />

54. Thirteenth founding principle: the structure, institutions, functions, and policies of the AFWS

"Our state is an autarkic, logical capitalistic state, and we call it the National Liberextremist State. It is politically articulated through the party, the union, the county and the electoral district. This radical meritocracy is an organic democracy where the worker is always the master of his reality and his destiny. The National Council is the legislative body of the state, slated with 500 supra-men so established on the merits of their combined intellectual, ethical and physical prowess. To this end, ours is a state of judgment, where the appropriate mechanisms are established so the best represent the people. The executive is a democratic offspring of the legislative and the obnoxious figurehead of the president/king replaced by the whole of the collective executive, one of the most meritocratic subsets of supra-men within the Council, and subjected to the same strict rotatory rules as everybody else so as to actualize the ideal organic nature of the state. The local councils are a mirror of the National Council and vice versa, and the lists are open and publicly funded by the phalanxes of workers. The money is evenly apportioned and the referendum is the ultimate tool of the people to resolve important issues of the state when the representatives cannot reach a sufficient majority."

It is worth mentioning that all laws and dicta of the Council and the executive branch within it will be subjected to the same standards the people themselves are subjected to, and therefore breaches of substance or inadequate execution will be punishable offenses as per our tenth founding principle. Ultimately, the party and its tenets will be the ultimate judge of any activity within the bounds of the Council itself, and the people themselves will be the executioners of that bonding judgment through the multitude of party cells and offices throughout the country, and the self-realizing powers of the people already discussed. Ours is indeed the ideal of radical democracy taken to its logical conclusion, and particularly vigilant regarding any deviations within the ranks of the administration of the state itself; anguished as we are about the possibility of corruption of principles and canons, abuses galore and mischief, but relieved with the acknowledgment that the cleansing power of the blood knows no bulwark that could not be torn down, so as to restore dignity where she can forevermore pair up with law. Ours is a state where every worker can happily look up to everyone else, and where those with rotatory political and administerial powers watch out with healthy fear lest the people judge that the party ideary is not being fulfilled. From the standpoint of a worker serving his tenure as a public servant, the only cure for fear is a clean conscience.

It is mandatory that we turn now to the most important subject of the judiciary. In this Leviathan it is called a branch of government, but I would call it instead a political extension of the partitocracy and a tool to repress people without caste status. Indeed, the politicization of this judicial system has reached such obscene levels that it is truly shocking and frightening to observe so many people who still believe in its legitimacy or independence. Most judges, at least those in higher courts, federal or state, are directly appointed by the government, whereas the people generally elect some judges in the lower courts. This fact alone is indicative as to how much politicians disdain and mistrust the people. Without equivocation, judges in the higher courts are in essence political activists. Otherwise they would not have a career. Those individuals are partisan hacks whose judicial decrees follow party lines so the corresponding donor subcaste is rewarded accordingly. When no apparent donor conglomerate is involved, the rulings are made based upon the canonical set of policies toward different groups fleshed out in different ways by both wings of the partitocracy.

The state is, de facto, a political entity so vitiated and warped that has become a construct relative to its purported deontological duties. The institutions and agencies upon which the state itself rests are spurious and corrupt. They are illegitimate, and they do not represent the interests of the whole of the people; neither do they abide by their own laws and rules. This has been thus since the state's founding, because it was predicated on an intellectual rot. You cannot repair what is wrong, only potentially what goes wrong or that which breaks down. But you cannot fix what is essentially, in the literal sense, a wicked creation, because you cannot transform quod semper manet, i.e., its quiddity.

55. The supra-man of the judiciary: the logician

In the AFWS, judges will never be elected by rotatory public servants, whether representatives or administrative workers. Neither will they be elected by a body of workers who do not know them well enough to render a just verdict. In our state, judges will be replaced, as always on a temporary basis, by the most extraordinary of man, by the quintessence of thinkers: by logicians, the most excellent breed of philosopher, who will be assisted and informed about the laws by interim lawyers or paralegals. We will replace a legal system based on internal strife with one which is invested only in the pursuit of truth. We will get rid of the old formula of plaintiff vs. defendant, since neither one will have a lawyer. On the contrary, the logician will evaluate the merits of a dialectic disputation of both parties, in which he himself in a scholarly fashion will participate, on the basis of the law and the general principles of the party and the state. No lawyer will be allowed to muddy the waters with sophistry or conniving deceit, but they will be there only to assist the logician in the interpretation of the law.

Lawyers will dramatically diminish in numbers in the AFWS since frivolous lawsuits will be eradicated. And because the state is organic, and it is ultimately the political actualization of the people, the lawsuits involving the state itself will be treated under the same set of rules and canons, that is, with a logician at the helm, someone to inform him about the particulars of the law and the relevant implications of the principles and ideary of the state, and a scholastic type of academic disputation involving the private party and the logician. This philosopher will be in charge of handing down the verdict and the sentence as well, once a logical conclusion is achieved based upon law, principles and canons in the AFWS.

Of course, appeals will be available and the same procedure will be carried out but with a different set of public servants. The logician is indeed a paramount element in our judicial system, and even though he will serve on a non-permanent basis, it is essential to the state that a supreme philosophical curriculum is administered to those students who choose that professional route. This will be, as is patently obvious by now, a state of the philosopher—not because they will be especially rewarded in any way or allowed to form any kind of caste, but on the contrary, because through their work and selfless sacrifice the state itself will be able to endure in order and justice for all.

It is also a direct consequence of how we are laying out the structure of this organic state that prosperity will be a welcomed byproduct. Without a doubt, countless persons nowadays involved in unproductive, or even destructive activities, will be given the opportunity to work for a living, hence increasing the output of the state and decreasing wasteful spending. One radiant example of this will be the class of lawyers, which will be dramatically reduced in size as a direct consequence of the radical restructuring of our legal and judicial system. First off, frivolous lawsuits will be tossed out by the court and fines imposed upon those who brought them, since it is imperative that the organic ethos of the party and the state prevails over internecine and petty disputations. It is without question a matter of national survival to indoctrinate our people into a truly communal and solidaric society, and recidivist gnawers will not be tolerated. Secondly, since only one lawyer or paralegal will be assisting the logician in the procedures, right there we can cut the number of lawyers in half. His fees will be paid by the losing party, and this will occur independently of the matter, civil or criminal. Both policies combined could reduce the number of lawyers by three quarters at least, which would be a revolutionary boon for the economy.

Let us remember now the connection between money and illegitimacy in our economic model. An activity which is regarded as illegitimate should be also illegal, and everything that is not in accordance with our ethical canon is not legitimate. But let us also remember that money is fundamentally work, and so an economic activity that does not increase the output but only distributes it, is an unproductive activity and hence illegitimate and illegal. This enthymematic inference was the basis for the outlawing of lending at interest, which was called usury throughout medieval Europe, and regarded as sinful and teleologically unproductive. The practice of law in our state will not be considered illegal because logicians need to be advised on the contents of the law in their deliberations and dialectic disputations. However, the curtailing as much as possible of this activity is axiomatically conducive to economic activity and prosperity, since we free up a lot of potentiality from those involved in unproductive activity. In other words, people who were engaging in the production of nothing valuable will now have the opportunity to work for a living and truly contribute to the body politic with real output or money. It is painfully clear how parasitic is the action of a lawyer within the present legal system. On the one hand, he is producing nothing but receiving money nevertheless. On the other hand, people are benefiting or losing out from his actions. If they are unjustly losing out, the damage is double. If they are justly benefiting, it could be achieved through our much cheaper and more efficient legal system. In any event, it is a logical inference, after the propositions established within our economic theory, that the falling off in the number of lawyers will be a blessing to both justice and prosperity, at least from the standpoint of the body politic rather than individual interests.

56. Intolerable crimes; punishment and cleansing

And now we focus our attention on the especially egregious cases against the people and the state. The adjudication of these extreme cases that involve issues of a fundamental nature cannot follow the regular channels, because it is imperative to maximize deterrence, requital, and concomitantly the ostensive power of the judgments. Unfortunately, extreme violations of fundamental law are intrinsically incompatible with organic reintegration, which is also a goal of the state when minor crimes are involved. We consider this particular class of crimes to be the following unholy quaternity:

1. Child abuse, especially of a sexual nature.

2. Activities contributing to moral decay and the disintegration of ethical standards and the principles of the AFWP, especially those perpetrated by public servants while holding office, whether the crime itself is contingent or not upon the power derived from the office.

3. Predatory offenses of any kind by psychopathic persons or by profit-driven criminals. In this category, particular attention will be given to murder, rape, animal cruelty and ecological crimes (wildlife crimes, pollution crimes and wildfires caused by pyromaniacs and other miscreants).

4. Crimes against the public health, physical and mental, and the destruction of any constructive potentiality of our people. For example, drug trafficking, production or trade of substandard or toxic consumer goods, especially foodstuffs and prescription drugs (when done knowingly and hiding relevant facts from the people), and others that on their demerits the people consider appropriate to include in this list.

Unless otherwise determined by the workers, marijuana and psychedelics are not classified as destructive of potentiality, due to relatively mild effects in the former case and a non-addictive nature in the latter. Regardless, all drugs, tolerated or not, legal or illegal in whatever degree, will be deemed pernicious to the people and therefore their consumption will be discouraged through education and propaganda, with the workers the ultimate deciders regarding legal status. But I firmly believe that the organic state will eventually succeed in spreading throughout the body politic the most exhilarating and addictive of all drugs, and the only one whose consumption will be protected and promoted starting with the youth: the drug of idealism, wherewith our supra-man will forevermore fuel his enthusiasm in the indomitable march toward the judge!

And these four categories we regard as transcendental, meaning we cannot go on as an organic state and live by the AFWP principles if they are not to be brutally eradicated, and properly punished and cleansed. These classes will be logically codified, to the minutest of detail, as it is indeed a matter of literal survival for the state. It is our will that the wolves among us, and those who are looking in, are made aware of the fortitude, radicalism and logical intolerance of this state toward those crimes. The brutality wherewith such scourge will be requited is worthy of a thousand gilded pages in the annals of history, for everybody within and without to behold, to remember, and to heed. The logicians in charge of these proceedings will be selected from a special pool of professionals; namely those with the grit and the severity to match their logical prowess and take each proceeding to its most logical conclusion.

It is in this context that I would like to broach the theme of "torture". This concept has been perversely and intentionally muddled by the liberal philosophers, perhaps to such an extent that only true indoctrination can restore it to its proper meaning. There have been many different types of torture through the ages, but its nature is to be judged teleologically if it is to be judged rationally at all.

Torture served many purposes throughout history, and many of them were certainly spurious. The purpose which I am interested in, though, is what I call differentiated instantiation of maximums. For a legal system to be philosophically logical, it ought to be consistent and complete. And both properties must be predicated on the principle of induction. To make it all clear and as simple as possible, every crime must have a punishment attached, and every distinctive punishment necessarily attached to a particular crime. In other words, crime and punishment should be the domain and the field of a bijection. A legal system actualized otherwise is thus illogical and unethical. So I will unabashedly state that the legal system in America is illogical and unethical, as is the case, as far as I know, in virtually any other liberal state.

Nowadays, in this dystopian state, we dumbfoundingly observe how the punishment for the murder of two people is, in praxis, the same as for the murder of ten people. Or the rape of ten women or children would equate in actuality to the rape of fifty, and so on. These examples of what I call undifferentiated instantiation of maximums are not curious oddities in our legal system, but daily doled out and shown shamelessly to the people as something perfectly normal, and not to be considered a subversion or a miscarriage of justice. It is tantamount to an annulment of the value of the victims number n plus one, n plus two, n plus three, etc. beyond the last victim or victim n, for whom a punishment has been formally issued, adding to the punishments issued for all the preceding victims in the series. That is a catastrophic obliteration of the principle of induction, and without it, no system can be deemed logical.

Indeed, that is not an inductively generated series and therefore it cannot be the basis for a logical or ethical legal system. As I have said multiple times, the quiddity of this state itself is illogical and unethical. And it shows every step of the way, in every realm we delve into with the sufficient degree of critical thinking and insight. And as I also have repeatedly indicated, because of the force of convention within paradigms of this nature, they become canonical in the ethos of any society, and therefore very difficult to combat by means other than those of a cleansing revolution. Case in point: plenty of people these days do not even object to this kind of nullification, and even worse, they do not perceive it to begin with. Surely the intellectual lobotomization of the masses through indoctrination and propaganda are the underlying causes of this moral decay. I am not by any means suggesting the people are wicked; what I am saying is that most wicked paradigms are meant to burn down through the just and brute force of a violent revolution. It is hardly ever happened in any other way, although I hope the upcoming, ineluctable schism will prove to be an exception. (The final pages of this work will be dedicated to predicate the latter statement.)

It is precisely in this context where we have to debate the means of instantiating differentiated maximums. The people themselves will make the corresponding decisions through their representatives and through referendum. But there is no question that the AFWS will be a logical and ethical state where every victim needs to be counted and cleansed, or otherwise that state will not be at all. It will necessarily be a state where deductive inferences will be acted upon congruently with our laws and founding principles and as brutally as possible. We will never be a mawkish and unethical state where so-called civility will be dumped on the shoulders of victims so that elitist sophists get to carry on without enduring any of the pain. Yes, in sooth we are enduring the common suffering too, so we can proudly and morally proclaim we are all imbibing from the same chalice. A caste of sufferers and another of high-ground hypocrites will be no more.

In order to carry out justice in these particularly baleful cases a special court will be instituted. Unlike the secret, illegal and criminal court of the liberal state, the Foreign Intelligence Surveillance Act (FISA) Court, where the government breaks the laws of the state to accost political dissidents, our special court will proceed out in the open, for every worker to observe and ponder. And adherence to the laws of the land will be scrupulously maintained. Let us remember that justice in the organic state, from arraignment to execution of a sentence if declared guilty, needs to be acted out publicly, always according to the law without exceptions. Of the worker, by the worker, for the worker. Who would have thought that this most banal liberal slogan would be realized to the last consequences by the AFWS?

But in praxis, what does it mean to differentiate instantiations of maximums? It means not all death penalties are created equal, for example. Just because a criminal has been sentence to death by the people, the way to carry out the sentence should not be the selfsame, but actually cannot be the selfsame. Pain and suffering preceding execution are the ultimate means of differentiating instantiation of maximums. He who has murdered two will have it easier than he who has murdered four and so forth. The mechanisms by which that extra measure of pain will be actualized will be up to the people themselves, and its materialization will occur as an ostensive expression of ethics, for everybody to learn from and pay heed to.

The whip is the perfect instrument of both justice and deterrence in some cases. Certain crimes carry enormous ethical implications and a dour cleansing action in the light of day is the only solution. No need for absurd prison sentences, which only compound the problem by destroying lives in perpetuity and causing unnecessary expense to the people; that is the dark, nonsensical solution or rather colossal failure of the behemoth state. A failure which as in so many other instances, is actualized in the form of a corrupt industry for the profit of well-connected scoundrels and the administrative state itself.

An important question concerns the hierarchy of tribunals within the judicial system. In our state, the hierarchy is horizontal and contingent upon the nature of the crime, and that includes the appeal courts. There is no vertical hierarchy regarding the authority of the judge in his interpretation of the law. The reason for this is twofold:

1. The laws themselves are unequivocally written up; that is to say, there is no possible semantical equivocation. Our laws are indited and passed by the Council of the state's supra-men, assisted by a body of temporary lawyers and logicians so as to fine-tune the redaction of every dictum.

2. The application of the laws themselves is carried out by logicians who are, as I already said, the most sterling and sage subset of philosophers. Upon considering this second filter of objectivity, the few cases which still cannot be adjudicated will move on to another court of appeal where a third whittling of equivocations, fallacies and invalid conclusions and inferences will render the process consistent and complete.

Jurisprudence and a vertical hierarchy of binding judicial dicta are only necessary when the laws are poorly drafted or judges and not logicians muddy the waters with faultily deduced rulings; events that in the liberal hoax are as rife as corruption or incompetence. Moreover, jurisprudence and the Supreme Court are the nefarious consequence of a state ruled by spurious interests that weave their way into the drawing up of laws and the sinful obsession of this state with castes, with hierarchies not predicated on merit but on politics and decisions driven by illegitimate and unethical reasons. Therefore, in praxis jurisprudence will disappear through the operation of supra-men and logicians, and concomitantly the Supreme Court will be henceforth rendered an obscene concept and eliminated. Every case will be considered on its merits through disputation by the logician according to the law; every case is a singularity in and of itself, and through logic a just verdict will be rendered without resorting to the history of judicial decisions. Otherwise we should indirectly infer that the law is inadequately drawn up and/or the logician is incompetent at carrying out his duty. In either case the solution is not jurisprudence or a higher court, but rather to solve the root causes of that deficiency.

I now set out to formulate our fourteenth founding principle. It is thus our will that:

57. Fourteenth founding principle: the judiciary and scholastic logical disputations; the principle of instantiation of differentiated maximums

"All the offices within the justice system will be filled on a temporary basis by workers. Judges will be replaced by trained logicians assisted by one lawyer or paralegal in the task of informing themselves about the details of the law. The classical plaintiff-defendant binary setup with two legal teams representing each respective side will be supplanted by a scholastic type of academic disputation in which the logician himself will partake. A system of cunning and deceit will be replaced by a collective effort in seeking truth. All the process, from indictment and arraignment to final and conclusive sentence and execution thereof will be carried out by the people, and the organic quiddity of the process reinforced by totally transparent proceedings, always publicly conducted. Moreover, special tribunals to try a particularly baleful class of crimes will be enacted, but the nature and the workings of the aforementioned tribunals will follow the general rules. In order to enforce an instantiation of differentiated maximums, an additional set of punishments will be established so every victim is individually recognized in the sentencing process. The particulars of this set of supra-punishments will be contingent upon the people's will and carried out, yet again, in the open so they become the ultimate ostensive manifestation of ethics and justice, for everybody to behold and to heed. If the dragons and monsters among us do not fear God, we will make them fear the organic state through a flood which will fill with awe and terror every crevice and nook deep in their Jungian shadows. Victims no more!"

I am delving deeper into the structure of the state. This structure must be not only compatible with, but conducive to the organic nature of the AFWS. Consequently, we have determined that the people themselves will carry out the business of managing the state through a system of mandatory and rotatory service, so as to make sure as many workers as possible weave in and out of that administration, whether the vacancies filled are political positions and therefore elected by suffrage or bureaucratic positions. But since public service is axiomatically work, how about the working conditions and clauses that pertain to that service?

The ethics involved in the administration of the state must be all-encompassing because they need to configure a set which is both consistent and complete, i.e., every potential conflict should be evaluated and judged univocally through that set of ethical rules. Therefore, they have to be laid out painstakingly so as to assure the people that no remnants of liberal-caste corruption bleeds off into the actualization of our political collective self, this utmost effulgent citadel that will by and by replace the depraved colossus born out of abuse, trickery and mischief, or that trite intellectual revolution that was wrong at every turn.

58. A fair state

As a general principle never to be broken for the sake of consistency and orderly development of rules and laws, the public servant, who is the actual repository of the social will and trust of the people, will always earn either his salary prior to taking office or the median income within his electoral district, whichever is the smallest. This simple set of rules aims to achieve two goals: firstly, nobody in the administration of the state will earn more money than they did previously; in other words, no public post will be personally lucrative for anybody while holding that job; and secondly, the organic nature of the state and intertwining of the people will be at all times reinforced by ensuring political representatives and administrative personnel are not better paid than the median of their compatriots and compeers within their given district.

Indeed, this scheme will result in some fellow workers serving at a personal financial loss, namely those whose income is above the median. For first time in history, in some cases the expression "public servant" will become more than a trite misnomer; it will represent instead an instantiation of true camaraderie within the ranks of workers and a selfless contribution to the political organism. Of course, all kinds of pelf-making schemes that try to leverage any political or administrative position will be codified as illegal and severely punished. In fact, even crimes and misdemeanors committed by fellow workers while in office but without any abuse of power or misuse of the office will be, regardless, brutally castigated so the appearance of impropriety is nipped at the bud, as I had already indicated.

The state cannot afford the spread of disillusionment or ennui over suspicions or misunderstandings. The collective spirit of enthusiasm and purposeful struggle must be protected at all costs. The aging of the state will be much slower than any other case in history, and to that end any vestiges of sloppiness by people holding public offices will be unceremoniously wiped out. The increase in personal wealth while working for the state is a detestable footprint of corruption and it will not be tolerated under any circumstances. Wherefore, corrupt machinations so widespread in the tyrannic Leviathan will be codified as criminal, and the brutality of the corresponding punishment will be something glorious to behold. Examples of the aforementioned unethical practices are, as I already pointed out previously in this work, absurdly lucrative book deals while in office or soon thereafter, massive public speaking fees, revaluation of assets as a result of legislation passed by the Council, insider trading (or any kind of short-term trading which is not directly linked to an index fund), inappropriate government contracts indicative of influence peddling, employment as board members with high remunerations (or rather payoffs) … and since the proclivity of broken souls for devilry and malfeasance knows no limit, the list indeed goes perennially on.

One of the quintessential issues for the maintenance of a state and the execution of its functions and goals is taxes. This is not only a matter of economic policy, but also of raw deontology. More broadly, the budgetary process is one of the paramount mechanisms of the state, politically, economically and ethically. You can tell more about a state by how it deals with taxes and spending than by any other accidental or fundamental policy. The budgetary process and its execution, taxes and spending, will make or break a state, i.e., it will determine whether a body politic flourishes or dwindles. By analyzing some fundamental features of this process you can unequivocally judge the merits of the state as to its ethical standards, competence in carrying out its duties, legitimacy of its ultimate motives or lack thereof, and finally its worthiness as a political entity. In the course of this dissertation about the budgetary process, many of the premises and their logical conclusions will come as a shocker for those who never dreamt of breaking free of the liberal paradigm. Much of what will be related will be regarded as trivially obvious, and yet it is not much thought about by most readers hitherto. I want to reiterate what I have continuously intimated, and it is the fact that this will be a logical state or will not be at all. And only sophists and other intellectually dishonest people fear the last logical consequences of any valid and proven theory practically articulated.

Let us start this critique by stating what should be obvious to any moral person: taxes are not a punishment for any wrongdoing. I am considering each and every word very precisely, because all what follows are enthymematic, if not syllogistic conclusions. A punishment implies, among other logical consequences, a deterrence. Much has been written in the corpus of moral philosophy about punishment. This is not a treatise on the subject matter and therefore I will cut straight to the chase. A pecuniary punishment is a fine; it is never a tax. Thereby, as a matter of principle, a tax cannot deter or modify behavior. The only purpose of a tax should be to procure the resources to fund the administration of the state and all its programs and goals as established by law and executive fiat.

It follows that if a tax alters behavior by way of punishment, either it is not really a tax but only a misnomer, or it is an ill-conceived tax. The way the liberal tyrant has laid out and developed taxes is a mafia-type operation: it punishes its enemies and rewards its friends through the parameters that define the tax system (how much to collect and from whom), and through the priorities put forth by how the revenue is spent, i.e., how much is spent and who receives the bulk of the money raised. The budgetary process represents at once a repression of unwelcome behavior, an incentive for desired behavior, and finally a reticulation among the people based upon who become the recipients of the government's projects and policies.

It is quite clear that the objectives of this process as it stands are twofold: firstly, to punish foes and dissidents, and secondly, to reward those who cooperate whether with pelf or votes and submission. It is also a very straightforward mechanism to keep everybody at each other's throats on both sides of the process (taxes and spending), so this competition for the state's favors keeps the state itself above the fray and out of danger.

Nowadays, we can observe the devastation this kind of sophistical and cynical process is causing throughout the land. People resent each other based on the perceived (and very often actual) advantages of some groups or tribes over others, on the basis of specious reasons which are neither logical nor ethical, but purely ideological and tactical. This way, the destructive energies of rivaling identity groups are focused on one another, canceling each other out as the kakistocracy and the infamous state itself soars in power and control over the people.

Divide et impera has a lengthy history as a successful political strategy going all the way back to Philip II of Macedon and in praxis it is much older than that. It is the default strategy of this kakistocracy, and in all fairness it is not only in America where this devious design is ruthlessly enacted but all across the Western world and beyond. Without this subterfuge, it would be impossible for the masses of workers to support and even endorse a political system that primarily protects the interests of the plutocratic usufructuary caste. Very clearly, beyond any confusion or equivocation, as univocally as possible, the laissez-faire state determines the groups it is going to buy up and those who are going to be punished, and it expects total obeisance in return from those who are illegitimately propped up. The cruel reticulation of the body politic maximizes at every turn the division and the hatred of the people for one another.

Based on this alone, the upper echelons of this administrative state ought to be considered hostis humani generis, since they prey on defenseless people as did the pirates of yore, and they actualize the slavery of workers through the wagslave labor institution, as slave traders were instrumental to the actualization of slave labor. As a matter of fact, without the systematic division, envy and vitriol among the phalanxes of workers caused by a rotten budgetary process, the institution of wage labor itself would be in the crosshairs of the people, and so the budgetary diversion becomes existential for this criminal state.

The state's deviously designed taxation and the national debt are the fountainhead of the bankocracy caste, and ultimately the precursors of the most infamous layers of unproductive scum (financiers and banksters, stockjobbers, pettifoggers, bureaucrats, criminals working for the national security state, etc.) and of unsound money. Together, those two juggernauts have propped up and corrupted the institution of wagslave labor to such an intolerable degree that only the advent of the organic state out of the crimson corpse of the liberal kakotopia can bring this hellish nightmare to an end, and the means to achieve this goal of decency and reason will be sorted out later on in this founding work. This bankocracy is in charge of issuing interest-bearing banknotes or what the laymen mistakingly call "money" or "fiat money". The Federal Reserve and central banking in general will be hereinafter treated at length on the topic of logical capital.

It is true that some specific taxes are overtly in the business of behavior bending, as well as a money-raising scheme for an ever-hungry state, like some kinds of excise taxes which are levied on certain goods as if they were proportional mulcts. But the right word is the latter, the former just a misnomer to keep people befuddled and confused.

A tax, whether it is on flow, source or nature, i.e., on income, wealth or property, or activity, is the means wherewith the state funds its existence. Period. Everything else is either fallacious or inadequately defined and codified. But the different administrations within the state weaponize the tax code and the spending bills against anybody not willing to partake in the orgy of hatred and permanent confrontation that keeps the gatekeepers in charge of a state marred by inherent corruption since its inception. It is quite shocking to think about how America has been bogged down in a mire of debt practically since her founding, even though the constitutional duties of the government were always supposed to be very limited. The reason for this strange phenomenon is quite obvious: the budgetary process is neither formally logical nor congruent with the true meaning of money that we have been elaborating upon throughout this work.

And this is precisely the crux of the issue: the mismatch between what money is, or its economic quiddity, and the processes by which the money is taken from the people and later on distributed among the people. Since money is work, only the sustenance of the organic state can be adduced to take that money from the people without calling that robbery. Any money taken from the people and spent on issues not existential for the state, or fundamental for its legitimate goals, is an act of violence against the people. The liberal state's apologists claim that one of its most essential roles is that of an agent of wealth distribution. They fail to mention that the disproportionate concentration of wealth and the endemic income inequality is one of the hallmarks of the predatory capitalistic system, or the ever-present economic system in this illegitimate state. This situation is an instantiation of the infamous paradigm of the scoundrel who is both the arsonist and the firefighter.

On the other hand, in our AFWS, logical capitalism reigns supreme, and within this system employers and employees meet in a conjoining of marginal utilities and marginal values, as we exposed in the first pages of this founding work. Wagslave labor being substituted for logical labor, a dynamic sequence of macroeconomic equilibriums ensues, and each one of them is characterized by higher wages compared with the predatory model, and more organic integration of all the people within the all-encompassing state, including a radical narrowing of the income and wealth gap. And this most harmonic state occurs peacefully as a result of direct and enclosed negotiations between all the compatriots involved. Under our model, the people are not beholden to the state, but rather to one another. There is no caste component whatever, no figurehead on whom our hopes and well-being are dependent. In our system, the organism has supplanted the putrified organization only to bask in the glory of a nation of workers carving out their own free and prosperous destiny.

Back now to the central issue: taxes and spending bills and the process whereby they are coherently intertwined. We are shedding light on the motives that compel the monstrous Leviathan to turn a logical and deontological exercise into a cruel game of winners and losers. The central motive, as I already said, is purely existential. It is derived from the eternal need of this state to keep the people fractured along lines that can be controlled and exploited for political purposes by the permanent ruling caste, the administrative caste, and the myriad of satellite agencies and organizations which work on behalf of the state; namely, corporate media, academia, the security state apparatus and the multifarious grievance industries. All these toadies are ultimately at the service of corporate America for which the state itself exists. With the exception of some gaslighting operations here and there, the scheme is so obnoxiously obvious that it becomes outright disturbing to recognize how so many compatriots seem to be incapable of connecting the glaring dots. Certainly, one more reason, this time around of a practical nature, to enforce to the last possible extremes the meritocratic nature of the organic state, if we are to fend off the catastrophe of a state steered by people not up to the task, their good intentions notwithstanding.

I will not dwell for long on the description of the ins and outs of the budgetary process in this state. However, it is unavoidable to delineate the fundamental features so we can denounce them and put forth our organic alternative.

To start off, let me make as clear as possible this fundamental point: the process in place nowadays is not logical, responsible, legitimate or sustainable. It is the projection, in the realm of fiscal policy rather than political philosophy, of a state that is not on the level with its people; a state that should not exist; a state which will be overcome. This state cobbles together twelve independent appropriation bills, negotiated among the two wings of the partitocracy, so both get plenty of money allocated for different causes, industries and all kinds of instantiation of special interests; the very same special interests that in turn fund the politicians' campaigns, not to mention all the kickback schemes after these venal characters leave office. Up to this point, no serious conversations about revenue are included in the process, just piles after piles of money taken from the people so the donor caste, a particularly indecent subset of corporate America, get ever richer as the nation goes bankrupt.

A second tranche of money is that reserved to pay off the foot soldiers of both wings or the different groups or tribes that are politically aligned with either party and the multitude of satellite organizations which, directly and indirectly, sometimes covertly and sometimes overtly, do the politicians' dirty job of spreading hatred and resentment so the workers remain divided, unfocused and enfeebled. So if the spending side of the budgetary process is a manifestation of punishment and rewards along political lines, as well as a fundamental way of breaking up the power of the people to rebel, the revenue side is even darker. On this side, work itself is stolen, its quiddity rejected and sullen, and the ominous power of the state to choose winners and losers and to reinforce an atmosphere of dependency and submission brutally exercised. The tax codes are craftily written out by the lobbyists so the workers believe they have a "progressive" tax law to abide by, but the loopholes are so massive and apt to be taken advantage of by cunning elites and corporate lawyers that it all amounts to an ugly ruse. Masses of workers are ripped off and others prima facie propped up with the work extracted from the former, always making sure the people understand who is being abused and who is being guerdoned so the hatred and envy is planted on fertile soil.

In addition to all of the above, we still have to reckon with the sheer waste and fraud at every step in the process, coupled with the purposeful neglect of fundamental duties by the standards of the state itself, and the incompetence in the execution of other duties. And all of it is topped off with an overt, obscene and defiant lack of accountability or responsibility of any kind up and down the political and administrative echelons of the state. It is incontestable for being the only explanation based on both anecdotal evidence and more importantly ineluctable deductive inference, that this aggressive display of indecency and refusal to accept accountability is the inevitable conclusion of a deep-seated feeling and belief. The ruling caste firmly believes the whole of the people is as immoral as they are; and consequently they feel disgust for the people, because that lack of moral compass in themselves is seen as the prerogative of the strong, whereas the same lack of moral compass in the people is regarded as sheer contemptible weakness.

Why is this? Let us recall now the caste of psychopaths within the political establishment and the administrative body of the state. The AFWS will aim to ensure no caste is allowed to exist and thrive within its apparatus, especially the caste of psychopaths which is securely lodged deep inside the fabric of this administrative state; but this brutal behemoth goes to great lengths to never design and enact any kind of protection of the people from those predators, since the corruption is so extended and systemic that no possible reaction from the state could realistically be conceived. It is therefore incontrovertible that the castes within this administrative state feel nothing but disgust and contempt for the people. These feelings are so ingrained in their psyches, and they are so empowered by a history of docile submission throughout the phalanxes of workers, that the expressions of calumny and obloquy against the masses are evermore expressed out loud, without any fear whatsoever of any consequence. These devious and psychopathic individuals, wielding enormous power within the state, cannot see the incongruence of their feelings toward the people versus their feelings toward themselves for the same lack of moral compass, because that narcissistic lack of fair analysis is actually one of the concomitant features of that mental malady. As the abuse becomes ever greater and more vile, the reaction of the people as time goes on will be very telling. The wolves will roar ever louder while the sheep will continue to bleat, and we will pay close attention to tell them apart, so when the time comes we will be sure that we will not mistake one for another.

The final chapter in this grotesque game of punishment, reward and domestication that the liberal state is dependent upon for its very survival, is the schizophrenic mismatch of revenues and expenditures, and the insane machinations this state stoops to in order to fictitiously close the gap. Indeed, spending always dwarfs the revenues, even though the latter never stop their upward trajectory. To pay for the structural deficits, the state engages in political chicanery and all sorts of financial skulduggery, including enlarging ad infinitum our national debt, quantitative easing (the expansion of the monetary supply in exchange for government bonds bought by the central bank), or in other words printing money ex nihilo, and purposely giving inaccurately low readings of the impact of inflation on prices, so the monetary policy favors a never-ending expansion of the monetary base. This expansion is carried out at an interest, of course, since that is the mark of the central banking beast. Much more about this later.

The result of all these policies is more debt, more inflation, ever bigger cycles of pumping and bursting financial bubbles with an increase in job destruction over the long haul, a massive upward transfer of wealth through personal debt and inflation of consumer goods and assets, and ultimately a total debasement of the currency and the erosion if not total obliteration of workers' savings or their accumulated work over the years. And all of it while at the same time the essential functions of the state are utterly neglected and actions that are inimical to the safety and the common weal of our people are unrelentingly actualized: unprotected borders for the sake of special interests and to the detriment of workers, massive homeless encampments and a total lack of interest in proactive, comprehensible and compassionate solutions, violence and crime everywhere only to be addressed when the donor caste is affected, promotion of proxy wars galore, a befuddling education system where castes are perpetuated and sophistically justified, and fundamental rights attacked (freedom of speech, empowerment rights, right to life, etc.).

It is an unmitigated catastrophe. The longer we take in our march toward the definitive action the more destructive and violent that action will have to be. For in political philosophy as well as in praxis, for every action there is a reaction of equal force in the opposite direction; and this is a law of politics as much as it is a law of natural philosophy. As the state unravels and its depravity reaches new highs, as the elite castes ramp up their onslaught against the people and their disdain and scorn grows unbridled, the watershed comes ever closer, but tragically its violence a fortiori will wax with any unnecessary delay. Let us hope that reason triumphs and we forslow the genesis no more.

And this is what greener pastures look like: pastures flourishing on truth, collective sacrifice, responsible policies and an organic effort, by the people and the state, toward the forthright ideal.

The first step in the budgetary process must be the assessment of forthcoming revenues. And based on that, a prioritized, publicly discussed and debated list of bills conjoined into a budget simultaneously. The reason for a contemporaneous debate of all the spending bills is to guarantee a comprehensive mechanism of hierarchical priorities, according to the needs of the people and the state, and consistent with the party ideary. The end result must be a match of revenues and expenditures, in order to ensure a balanced budget and consequently no accruement of debt. In other words, ours is a process which starts on the revenues and moves on to the spending part, which is the total opposite of the way the sham state proceeds.

As I previously said, in the AFWS taxes are the means by which the state funds itself and its policies. They are not meant to change behavior or punish anybody, and they are supposed to not disrupt the macroeconomic and microeconomic equilibriums. Or we can say taxes are supposed to be designed in such a way that they organically blend into the economy so if they were removed from it, the relation between all the economic variables in the descriptive and projective models stays the same. Of course, in order to achieve that holistic goal we need to understand two fundamental factors that always affect the workings of taxation:

1. Taxes tend to be passed along to others if not properly configured, often resulting in unwanted altered macroeconomic equilibriums of wages and prices of goods and services.

2. Taxation needs to be easy to enforce, simple and straightforward, and to guarantee an atmosphere of justice and universality to minimize the risks of lawbreaking behavior and resentment within the body politic, which leads to reticulation of the people, confrontation, envy, and ultimately an impossibility to maintain and develop the organic state.

Now our state is organic. That means the state itself is made and run by the people, and it is the people themselves who contribute to the synergistic workings of the state with either one, sometimes both, of the assets that they possess. In a general sense, those two assets are always money and time. Money is actualized work, and time is its potentiality. This means that both assets would have, in their relation to the state, the same quiddity and thereby one can perfectly substitute for the other and vice versa. It is upon this principle that the state must create a fair tax code, able to fund its structure and functions, without unduly deleterious effects on the economy of the people, and reinforcing the organic bond of the workers with the state and with each other. I will forthwith enumerate the five rules that logically supervene upon the foregoing two factors:

1. This code must be simple, to make it accessible to everyone without unnecessary additional costs to understand and comply with. And it also needs to be so in order to ensure an equal treatment of money or work across the board, irrespective of familial or personal circumstances. The place to address those issues is the body politic itself, the civil society and their institutions properly managed according to the party principles and program. Complex situations will be addressed using multifaceted approaches, not by codifying privilege and difference in the tax code, which is anathema to the organic nature of our state. We abhor any policy that promotes caste formation within the state on basis other than sheer merit. Income within a bracket should be treated equally regardless of exogenous considerations. Those peculiarities, if they are legitimate issues to be solved, will be addressed accordingly by the people through the political powers of the state, without resorting to a massive unethical distortion of the tax code.

2. This code must be univocal, or in other words so properly indited that no clause could possibly be misconstrued by a logician in a court of law.

3. This code must be a tabula rasa so as to not have any kind of preconceived notions or influence from the codes in the laissez-faire state. It must be a clean slate, a start from scratch in the deepest sense. This code must be a revolutionary code.

4. This code must be organic in the sense that it must treat the people as compatriots and compeers, as workers already synergistically integrated in the state, and it must account for all of the contributions that the people already make on a daily basis, as per the actualized institutions and programs that are part of the AFWP ideary. The concept of a taxpayer will be eradicated, because it is an idea only sensible within the context of an organization internally compart-mentalized and in strife along the lines of personal interests. It is a concept which reeks of a caste based on money and not raw merit or variegated contribu-tions, and therefore illegitimate. That is because it is a concept with a misleading hue around it, namely one hinting at the existence of a superior caste based upon money contributed to the state and therefore acknowledging only the actuality and not the potenti-ality. Consequently this liberal concept, which cannot encompass the true quiddity of time, which is poten-tial work and therefore money, is to be utterly rejected on both logical and ethical grounds.

5. This code must not be a tool to extract from some and give it to others. In the National Liberextremist State, under an autarkic, logical capitalistic economy, people are already freely matching utilities of work

absorbed with values of work created. The income gaps have organically collapsed and have been reduced to a fraction of what they used to be under the liberal regime. In the AFWS the people themselves are the masters of their lives and futures, and the exploitation of competitive wages washed away and substituted by logical wages. The people thus owe nothing to the government of the state, and they are effectually their own providers and liberators. No more will the workers be forced by the state to partake in the massive financial rape of others, whether more prosperous or not, through a tax code which condones that kind of violence for political expediency. The illegitimate state needs to ethically blacken as many workers as possible, to drag them down into an abyss of corruption and theft, so the ruling caste can claim everybody is equally immoral. That ruling caste needs total obeisance from the bulk of the workers, and they achieve that goal by, among many other devious schemes, making the people dependent on the government and thus forestalling any kind of virtuous collective behavior. It is a monstrosity that knows no precedents in the history of the world (at least not with this intensity), and this depravity and those who have articulated it, will be addressed as they deserve.

The above five rules, as they have been laid out, constitute a formal logical system of generation, consistent and complete, of the kind of tax code we wish to actualize.

A code thus created is a code with very few brackets, with

no deductions or credits (two exceptions will be established later, nevertheless consistent with the system of generation), where all the income no matter the source is treated equally, with non-pecuniary contributions to the state factored in, so as to make the taxation fair. It is a code not conducive to a transfer of taxation through wages or prices and therefore as output-neutral as possible, with limitations.

A code so ideated would be similar to this hypothetical example:

NATIONAL INCOME TAX

Married filing jointly or single

- $0 to $50,000 taxed at 0% or exempt

- $50,001 to $150,000 taxed at 10%

- $150,001 to $500,000 taxed at 30%

- $500,001 and above taxed at 50%

A structure of income tax like this is, with no deductions, credits, loopholes or subjective differentiations based upon sources or nature of income, a revolutionary code. It is the simplest and fairest of codes, one that cannot be exploited by people with sufficient resources (although that would not be an issue within the organic judicial system previously expatiated upon). A code that taxes only income, and not contingent situations. A code that implicitly recognizes non-pecuniary contributions of workers to the sustenance of the state through the organic mechanism of temporary work in its administration. It is a spartan code, wherewith most workers would pay much less in taxes than under the liberal regime. And it is neither predatory nor caste-generating, but equal across the board within the same bracket; therefore it is a code that does not raise suspicions among the people. It is a straightforward code that does not incentivize cunning schemes in a gluttonous search for deductions or credits. It is plain, honest, modest and hardly disruptive of equilibriums in the economy compared with the current code, which is an incongruent maze.

It is also a code that does away with the rest of payroll taxes. Those taxes are based upon laissez-faire concepts of contributions that make no sense within the AFWS. Some of those taxes are de facto very poorly designed. For example, the Medicare program is structurally underfunded and thus the corresponding tax a facade. And the Social Security tax is another massive liberal-state misappropriation since the fund allegedly created by that tax has been chronically pillaged and used for all kinds of nefarious ends by the political caste.

The AFWS code blots out some other taxes in addition to the payroll taxes already mentioned. The corporate tax will have to be eliminated altogether. The reason is purely economic, as it is a massive disruptor of efficient macroeconomic equilibriums, or in other words, they are always passed along to the workers themselves either through lower wages or higher prices of consumer goods. It is, indeed, the archetype of the liberal-state scam. This is a tax sold by politicians as an act of solidarity, economic justice and ultimately compassion for the people, when it is in sooth yet another scheme to transfer resources (money=work) upward through altered prices and wages. It is a regressive tax, not progressive. It is a destructive tax. And it is, simply put, an act of robbery on workers disguised as the opposite by the state academics and the state media.

Every time you tax a flow midstream, the final output of prices and wages will be correspondingly manipulated so as to compensate for it, resulting in workers paying for the transferred tax. That is why the plutocrats enthusiastically keep on funding those politicians that advocate for higher corporate taxes. It is all a trick, intended to obfuscate the comprehension of the entire subject matter. The only tax that will not be passed on to workers is a tax on all personal income or in other words, the flow as it is once it has run its productive course through the supply side of the economy. Then it cannot be retroactively passed back and upstream to others. It is not feasible. That is why phony "leftist" paid actors and shills focus so much on the corporate tax and so little on a truly revolutionary tax on personal income. The same reason why they claim to be pro-worker, but they never prop up local unions independent of the politically controlled, establishment unions; and the reason why during decades of "progressive" political action, they never dared to bring up the concept of a countrywide general strike, which is something unheard of by most Americans, although a rather common occurrence across Europe. A wicked syndicate if I ever saw one, they are the overseers and the drivers of this plantation state, and they will be dealt with appropriately.

The estate tax, also called death tax, will be stripped from the tax code. It is the very definition of predatory. To be wealthy relative to others within reason, as long as it is achieved legitimately, is not a crime and should not be subjected to an untoward punishment in the form of an obnoxious double-taxation scheme. Furthermore, nobody will ever be able to become wealthy in the AFWS without being ethically and organically intertwined with the rest of the body politic, doing legitimate work. Therefore confiscation in the form of a tax will not be necessary. Moreover, our state will not get itself sullied by the collecting and spending of money deviously taxed. Our state is the most ideal, organic state; therefore all people within the state are an integral part of it, and they are not supposed to be ripped off through unethical laws. That is the bare minimum a deontological state should guarantee. However, it is undeniable that the accumulation of capital and wealth in our AFWS will be radically more difficult than it is now, as radical as the difference between liberal capitalism and autarkic logical capitalism. So we are solving a problem organically, rather than managerially. We are nipping at the bud before its solution becomes a logical and ethical conundrum. Ours is here, as is everywhere else, the ultimate, most complete and consistent answer.

An especially grotesque tax, from a logician and moral philosopher's standpoint, is the abomination called the excise tax. This tax (specific or ad valorem) is a Quasimodo-like hybrid between a sales tax and a fee. It is a tax levied on the consumption of specific goods and services, most of which this state has deemed deleterious to the people in differing degrees. After collecting, the state theoretically uses the revenues to somehow counteract the aforesaid negative impact, although in praxis much of that revenue is used elsewhere. The state also claims that this extra taxation is an essential part of a scheme to eradicate the pernicious behavior in the first place, but this eventuality has never materialized and the taxation remains ad infinitum.

I will be as succinct as possible on this matter: an ethical state cannot profit from taxing activities that harm the people, regardless of how it uses the money after collection. In fact, anything that harms the people should not be tolerated because it is not legitimate and therefore should be illegal. If the state taxes something harmful to the people, it effectively becomes accessory to the crime. And if on the other hand the consumption of those goods and services is legitimate and not particularly inimical to the people's health, then it follows than it should not be additionally taxed on baseless grounds. It is one or the other, so we can logically infer that the tax is illogical or immoral. Consequently, any product or service allowed to be consumed by the people in the AFWS will not be additionally taxed beyond the regular sales tax. Some goods, like tobacco or alcohol or even many prescription drugs and many processed foods, have negative health consequences; but the AFWS might choose to remove them from the market gradually, through virtuous indoctrination in an intergenerational struggle, so as to not cause massive social pain and chaos. What the state should not do in any way, shape or form, is to become complicit in the damage by profiting from it through taxes. The state must at all costs remain pure, logically consistent. It cannot, under any circumstances, become entangled in any activity that it wishes to obliterate in the short or long term. This should come hardly as a surprise to any philosopher or historian of philosophy, for since the times of St. Thomas Aquinas and many other scholastics, the aforementioned conclusion is pretty straightforwardly derived, in my opinion, from their moral philosophy.

The counties will be funded through sales and property taxes, favoring as much as possible the latter, as the former is a much more regressive tax and also in and of itself in a certain sense inflationary (for actual price hikes are really a function of a compound rate: the tax rate applied concomitantly with the inflation rate). Since we have dispensed with that colonial type of political construct (the federal structure of the state), many of the duties will be centralized, reinforcing thus the administration of the new AFWS, and some will be decentralized, invigorating the political realm of the county. Two levels of administration have been thus strengthened, and one totally eliminated, making the resultant state much more efficient and cheaper to run and maintain, and minimizing the chances for possible overlapping of functions and expenditures.

The spartan nature of the AFWS will rub off on the administration of the counties themselves, by virtue of the fact that both the state and the counties are organic with the people, as the policies and procedures of both are congruent with the party principles.

Before we continue on, I must now shift my attention to two particularly revealing cases where the wickedly illogical nature of the dystopian state manifests itself so clearly that I wonder what kind of moral and intellectual stupor is seizing the philosophical community (if that even exists), given the fact that it seems utterly uninterested in exposing the folly.

The first case is what are commonly known as traffic and parking tickets. Those penalties are mulcts (fines), and they are not prima facie intended to fund the administration of the county or state, but rather to punish certain untoward behavior and thus curtail its occurrence as much as possible. As a matter of principle, that is a legitimate goal and a mulct is a legitimate instrument to achieve it. However, we have to start off accepting the premise that that particular behavior is equally noxious to the state and the body politic regardless of who is doing it. This is a democratic principle, where privileged castes are not allowed. In other words, the state is interested in minimizing the occurrence of that behavior, which is contingent on the actions of an active agent. Thus the state has to punish the agent or cause of the unwanted effect, rather than the effect itself. And it has to instantiate that punishment in a manner consistent with the initial premise, namely that the effect is equally deleterious irrespective of the causal agent.

Therefore it stands to philosophical logic that the lawbreakers cannot be punished equally across the board, in nominal terms, but rather contingently upon their circumstances so as to produce a similar deterrent effect irrespective of the causing agent. In other words, the miscreant must pay according to his means so the real pain is the same in all cases and thus the potential causing agent is equally deterred regardless of personal financial circumstances. That translates into a progressive ticketing system linked up to the financial status of the causing agent. This conclusion seems to me inescapably obvious. Indeed, a speeding ticket could represent a catastrophic financial event for a worker and something trivial and barely noticed for a rich man. And yet, the liberal mastodon gets away with a ticketing system that is designed contrary to its purported goal. Of course, the conclusion that we infer from all of this is that either the major premise is untrue; the minor premise is untrue; or both are untrue. In other words, the state does not fine lawbreakers as deterrence; or the state does not subscribe to the belief that real deterrence across the board after factoring in financial circumstances should be equal; or both. Syllogistically speaking, the deduction is etched in stone. Therefore, nominal traffic and parking tickets are a swindle on the American worker. In the AFWS, those fines will be articulated in a way congruent with the major and the minor premises. That is the logical way; and of course it is also the moral way, since the state must always be honest with the people as to its actual aims in all cases. The state must be truthful, always, if it is to be legitimate and organic.

The second case of study would be government-sponsored lotteries. Hardly revolutionary on any grounds, whether logical or deontological, is the critique that I am inclined to make here. Up until not that long ago, any respectable moral philosopher or logician would have forcefully decried this kind of scheme. Now they are too busy endorsing genital mutilation of children for the sake of the post-modernist academic pride, and industrial-scale abortion lest prospective mothers become too anxious or inconvenienced by their own flesh and blood. As I result, practical proclamations of moral philosophy and logic are entirely blown off by those geniuses.

Government-sponsored lottery is the quintessential example, without being drenched in innocent blood like the two others above mentioned, of this state's deviousness. Predictably enough, that blood, pure and innocent, is the only kind the liberal dragon is hellbent on shedding. But returning to this little dirty device that the ruling caste so cleverly has designed for the debasement of all involved in it, the lottery has devastating consequences in the body politic.

To begin with, it makes a very few rich while impoverishing the masses even further. It torpedoes the organic nature of the community by reinforcing two castes, that of the rich who are so with no connection to work, and the governmental caste in charge of the administration of the lottery itself. Secondly, it generates envy among the people, furthering the destruction of the organic fabric of the state. Even worse, it creates addiction in some cases, which is literally the negation of prudence and temperance, two of the cardinal virtues at the heart of the people's ethics in our AFWS. With addiction comes pain and suffering for the victim and the people around him, with the concomitant destruction of work as he spirals down into an abyss of unproductive life. Finally, the state itself profits from the trap it set up, cannibalizing in the process its own people by degrading their life standards, their moral standings or both. The state argues that most of the proceeds go to fund public education, for example. This way, the state as a profiteer further smears the body politic by piling the mountain of guilt and wretchedness on top of children and their families. To top it all off, the process becomes canonically accepted, so those who are allegedly benefiting from it do not flinch or even think about the scheme. That is the ultimate goal; to create a society where something potentially good is manured with sin and those who imbibe from the chalice do not even have any qualms about it. In other words, the utter obliteration of conscious guilt. The philosophers of old, the giants of thought and wisdom through the ages, would call this crafty ploy satanic. I call it psychopathic, and that is close enough.

Many critics accustomed to the babelic-state paradigm would adduce, in rejection of our philosophy of taxation, that a code thus structured cannot meet the fiscal obligations of the state, and that it is also massively progressive. Others would call it simplistic and dangerous since it does not provide allowance for different circumstances like family size, mortgages, medical expenses, etc. To all of which I say guilty as charged, because this tax code is meant to operate within the confines of the AFWS, and not in the schizophrenic state. Their philosophies are completely antithetical to one another and the tax code is a reflection of this.

In our organic state, accidental circumstances within the nuclear family are not treated as a class-generating factors in the tax code, but as situations to be addressed on the body politic front, through the AFWS institutions and agencies according to our principles. In other words, they are not treated on the revenue side of the budgetary process but rather on the spending and political side of it. The reason is both ethical and economic. Ethically speaking, people should not be treated differently, sometimes better or sometimes worse within the same income bracket, because they have chosen one path or another in their lives. If we are to be an organic state, everybody's path is intertwined with one another in a synergistic fashion, and so the creation of different classes by the state through the tax code is in contradiction with its deontological duties. The economic reason is more technical, and it is this: in the ideological state, with the creation of classes along accidental circumstances within a given bracket, the collective economic decisions within the class change in order to take advantage of the tax reward, so essentially many people change their behavior to put themselves in that privileged class. The result of this collective behavioral shift can be defined as a set of unintended consequences that disrupt the efficiency of the macroeconomic equilibriums, making the body politic worse off mainly through waste and misallocation of assets. It is a destructive policy.

To reiterate the driving point of this section, the AFWS is interested, on economic, logical and deontological bases, in taxation of the receiving end of the flow, and not in taxation based upon sources, activities or circumstances. We do so because in that manner we do not need to qualify the object of taxation, and in this way we are able to levy fairly and efficiently across the board and percolate through the body politic a conviction of justice and appropriateness; a conviction that is paramount in sustaining the organic nature of the state. Our tax code is nominally very progressive, but really neutral after the potentiality of workers' time has been actualized into work through the organic administration of the state.

And to wrap up this topic of taxes, we need now to bring up and elaborate on the only two credits that should be present in our income tax. These two exceptions are still, as I observed before, consistent with our axiom schemata at the core of our tax code. Those two credits are:

1. Inflation credit;

2. Supra-man or eugenics credit.

These two financial boons, to all of the people in the first case and to some meritorious compeers in the second, need to be expounded upon so we ensure the people that they are consistent with the generating set of axioms and rules of inference.

1. As I already explained, inflation is either a purely monetary phenomenon, or a monetary phenomenon originated by an expansive fiscal policy actuated through debt and not taxes. True inflation manifests itself eventually through an increase of prices beyond the normal sectorial fluctuations due to competitive market forces. Thus, inflation is a destructive monetary event whose formal cause is the state. Of course, inflation cannot occur in the AFWS since our fiscal and monetary policies will be rooted in permanently balanced budgets, expenditures to always match tax revenues without resorting to government bonds, with a monetary supply that closely reflects the real output of work in the economy, and with fiat money rather than bank notes issued through interest-bearing debt for the benefit of banksters and other racketeers (more on central banking later). Simply put, it is an economic policy based on truth and virtue rather than falsehood and vice. Under those conditions, inflation cannot occur. However, if due to short-term misalignment of monetary base and output some inflation befalls the people, the state has the deontological obligation of making it right, since it is the culprit in the first place. The people should never pay for mistakes in the administration of the state; that would be a gross misplacement of responsibilities and pain. Thereby, the AFWS will enshrine the proper compensation in the tax code. If we use the example above (and we consider the American

dollar the currency of the new state for the sake of simplicity), and the debasement of the currency is measured at let us say, 3%, the credit would be up to $1,500 for the lowest income bracket, and up to another $1,500 for the next bracket, totaling $3,000 for those making $150,000 and up. Notice we have applied a credit of 100% of the inflation to those incomes up to $50,000 and 50% of the inflation to those incomes in the second bracket. And we apply 0% of the inflation to those in the third and fourth brackets. The reason is simple: increased prices impact principally money spent in basic necessities and therefore the first segments of income are affected. Beyond those thresholds, inflation can be combated by reducing discretionary spending, something that is not possible with items like housing and foodstuffs because we cannot do without them.

In this fashion we have made the people whole for any errors committed in monetary policy, and the existence of that credit will serve as an invaluable incentive for the state to get its policies right.

And because the AFWS is an organism synergistically composed of all its people—rather than a compartmentalized organization at the service of a caste— the measure of the final cost of inflation, or CPI, will be honestly computed rather than artificially concocted in a corrupt attempt to make it appear smaller—as is the illegitimate state's wont— in order to protect itself from the ire of the people and to continue on the path of monetary and fiscal mischief.

2. As regards the supra-man credit, this is truly an organic credit insofar as it is the ultimate blood credit; a practical policy whose positive reverberations throughout the body politic are second to none. This is a credit designed to reward and more importantly incentivize the reproduction of as many biological supra-men as possible. It is the instantiation of our founding principle of positive eugenics. It has to be a credit relatively proportional to income rather than a flat amount so everybody feels rightly compelled to take advantage of it, but concomitantly the proportionality must taper off in order to not introduce unduly privileges which could be misconstrued as caste-generating policies. This is not a credit to be cancelled beyond a certain income threshold, and such contingency should be avoided at all costs. There is nothing better than a state can do for all its people than to maximize the number of supra-men across the body politic, because everybody, without exception, will benefit immensely from the most exquisite of all synergies; namely the derivative of excellence radiating outward in countless ways from those who can create exceptionally well in the different fields of human endeavor. This state implacably pursues its holy grail, that never-ending race for the most powerful computers, robots and AI technologies; we, on the other hand, relentlessly will pursue the actualization of that man who will, undeterred, make it all the way to the pedestal whereon the judge stands. Instead of dead circuitry, our creation will have a soul and an iron will, and that most human spark of divinity within. To this end, we will credit those who are assessed to be exceptional in some relevant way:

intellectually, artistically, ethically, physically or a combination thereof. And in order to ascertain that, much effort, investigation and imagination will be poured into the creation of comprehensive standardized tests and evaluations, so the process is straightforward and beyond reproach. The AFWS will overcome the insatiable appetite of the old satanic state for weaklings raised, indoctrinated and used as wagslave labor; and so will we dwarf the pathetic pursuit of master races in some of the liberal state's past nemeses, only to create an ideal actualization of the hero archetype as a symbiotic miracle made out of the best in each and every race that we can put our hands on. We will usher in a new era of excellence, freedom and achievement … the era of the AFWP supra-man!

On a side note: how much easier to comprehend and endorse all these tax concepts it would be if we were steeped as deeply as possible in philosophy, which here as in many other crossroads, provides us with the answers that many geniuses thought out for us, and whose writings through Providence have been preserved for posterity! Indeed, I would like to simply state that in an Aristotelian way, the AFWS will be the formal cause of every compatriot's self-realization or the actualization of all his potentiality; whereas his personal will and the synergies within our body politic, will be the efficient cause. It follows from this that every compeer and the organic state are mutually vital to one another; the former by materially sustaining the latter in a literal sense, for without the people there is no state; and the latter by being the formal cause of the former self-realization. Both contributions cancel each other out so nobody ends up a debtor. Conversely, each compeer plus his relations with everybody else within the organic state, is partly the efficient cause of every self-realization, so by the same reasoning every compatriot within the organic state owes to everybody else as much as he is owed, and therefore balance is achieved on this front as well.

And by looking into taxes from this prism, the logic and legitimacy of it all becomes impossible to deny. I have to confess that among all the peoples in the world and through human history, the classic Hellenic Greeks are probably my very favorite, and not because they had all the answers but because they came up with most of the transcendental questions. A good question requires active imagination, the most magnificent of the intellectual faculties; whereas a good answer requires only raw intelligence. And through a life of observation and reflection, I have come to the conclusion that people with imagination are more exciting and rare than people with intelligence, although it is always a pleasure and an honor to surround myself with either one and perhaps a life blessed with the presence of both would be superior to any other.

Moreover, our state is like no other, because we have broken free of the paradigms of the past. The AFWS is indeed immensely bigger than the Leviathan in scope but much smaller in size. In other words, it is a state with many more and deeper onuses, but carried out through work by the people themselves and not by a professional caste of bureaucratic types. The state is commingling with the people by providing order, discipline, orientation and thrust. But it is not encroaching in people's lives through the mere spending of public money. This is a spartan state, imbued with a spartan ethos, and determined to protect and lead a spartan body politic. Over the next pages we will flesh out the various ways this idea is actualized in praxis: how much more can be achieved with much less; how people can be radically more helpful to themselves and others, led by the organic state, without the obnoxious waste of what we call money, which is work; how the state will be the port where ships of dreams and ideals will moor for protection from the tempests of life, or the road on which brave trailblazers will traverse in fearless search for the judge. Finally it will be the safe haven in which intelligent and virtuous ideas will have a chance to be acted out and prosper, knowing they are protected and impelled by a force like no other: the national family articulated through the AFWS.

Once we have successfully established for what purpose, how, and relatively how much we will be collecting from the people, we move on to the spending side of the process so as to reach a harmonic equilibrium, or a balanced budget—year upon year, repeating without deviations, a state living in truth, without deficits or debt, emerges victorious.

But before we delve deeper into this most important topic, two fundamental points need to be sorted out. These two issues are interconnected and foundational to this new state: the present currency and the present national debt.

A currency is the monetary expression of a state's output and the means whereby all actualizations of economic and financial activities take place. The currency is inextricably linked to the ways the state orients itself in the international exchange of goods and capital, as well as the relations established within the body politic and with foreign peoples, institutions and governments as it pertains to procuring funding through debt and the corresponding paying out of interests on that debt. I am convinced many incisive readers have already anticipated a conclusion which is logically un-avoidable, given the tenets of our revolution and the found-ing principles of the party and the autarkic logical capitalist state: the U.S. dollar, as a national currency, will be termi-nated. And it will not be substituted by the gold standard, but of course, by the work standard. A work standard will be therefore the monetary standard of the AFWS. This stan-dard means in actuality that this state's bank (the bank of the people, not the bank to serve the interests of private bankers as is the case in the laissez-faire fraud) is in charge of match-ing the monetary base with productive output on a regular basis so as to ensure null inflation over the long haul and a totally predictable and stable financial environment in which a misallocation of assets becomes a rare occurrence.

This bank of the people will not be responsible for pump-ing up financial bubbles to benefit the plutocratic caste. Neither will it be the last-ditch guarantee of a safeguard against irresponsible banking and investing activities per-formed mainly for the benefit of the few. Our new currency will be in fact a fiat currency, but strictly based on work and not political expediency or the protection of special inter-ests. It will be a radically sound and predictable currency, thereby becoming a nonfactor in any kind of economic deci-sion within the body politic. Our currency will certainly not be tied to gold in any way, shape or form, since we are an autar-kic state. We will not be affected by the stockpiling of gold by foreign entities, public or private. And any country that wants to purchase goods from us will have to pay for those exports either in our own currency or through a standardized bartering mechanism when they can supply raw materials that we need to acquire. We will not be part of the World Bank or the International Monetary Fund. We will cease to be, in fact, a participant, an accessory, or an accomplice in the raping of "underdeveloped countries" for the tainted benefit of a plutocratic internationalist caste. And by the same token, we adamantly refuse to partake in an international financial farce whose main objective is the impoverishment of workers all over the "industrialized world" in a grotesque orgy of unbridled avarice by a relatively small satanic clique. We will appropriately deal with them at home and shun those who live and operate abroad. The name and design of the new currency will be decided by the people through their representatives in the Council. I will further expound upon this crucial topic of the central banking racket and the nature of a currency when I treat the subject of logical capital.

Concomitantly with the creation of a new national currency in the context of an autarkic economy is the liquidation of all state's holdings and reserves denominated in any foreign currency or gold, for their value is subjected to international speculative forces and hence untethered to the actual productive output of the nation. Our state bank (whose name will be chosen by the people through the democratic institutions and instruments of the state) should hold only reserves of our own currency, for otherwise their exchange value is not predicated upon the exchange value of our national output, but rather dependent upon short selling and stockpiling schemes carried out by international shylocks, banksters and speculators in general.

The national debt is a matter of paramount importance for the actualization of our state. This will be a state born out of a cleansing revolution, a true tabula rasa with no connections to its metastatic predecessor. We will not recognize or accept any level of responsibility for the debt created and obscenely accrued by the laissez-faire state. Those dozens of trillions of dollars are the debt of the United States of America, not the AFWS. Many compatriots and foreign nationals, and a number of foreign governments, will lose their stake. The possibility of losing your investment is always real and must be internalized and factored in, especially when investing in a state that is fundamentally bankrupt. Are not asset assessment, risk-taking and the potential consequences thereof what they normally call part and parcel of capitalism? Just about two thirds of that debt is held by institutions and private investors at home, and the other third by foreign governments and nationals. All of them will be participants, although perchance unwillingly so, in the most exhilarating political liberation that man ever dreamt of. They will not be given the chance, ever again, to fund vice and lunacy domestically, because there will never exist again such a dystopian instrument as an "interest-bearing government bond".

So our revolution's first fillip to the people, even before any instantiation of our ideary through the powers of the state, will be the riddance of the yoke of national debt. The workers will be effectively dozens of trillions of dollars richer and freer than before, although the amount will not be computed in dollars anymore. Of course this will be the case because most of the bonds held domestically are the investments of institutions and the financial elites, although a small tranche of that debt is undoubtedly also owned by fellow compeers. This relinquishing will be their first sacrifice toward the ideal, and so it needs to be honored by a fanatical pursuit of success in our revolutionary endeavor by the whole of the people.

Once we have addressed currency and debt, we can now proceed on to the debit part of the budgetary process. We have to conceptualize this process as a formally causal sequence, for otherwise we will fall prey to the vices and failures of the illegitimate state, which articulated the entire budgetary process as a distinctly compartmentalized mechanism, where both sides once ideated are integrated without input from one another. The result is a monstrosity glued together through deficits, debt, inflation and the destruction of the currency.

The schizophrenic process of that state will be replaced by a harmonic process in which revenues are calculated and spending bills engage in a competition for funds within the boundaries established by the totality of resources raised through taxes. The spending bills will be debated conjointly and not separately, so the enmeshing of one into another in an open debate yields the most efficient and just results. The debates will be televised live in their entirety for all the people to witness, and they will take up most of the representatives's time and effort for several months a year. Every compatriot will be able to find out in real time who is voting for what, and who is voting against what, and in any case what are the reasonings for it. The entire debate between the councilmen will be closely assisted and framed in a comprehensive way by a rotatory group, acknowledged already as the epitome of our supra-men: the logicians.

It is undeniable that spreading the information about the process all throughout the body politic is absolutely essential on two fronts:

1. It guarantees the organic nature of the state by including the whole of the people in the analysis, debate and deliberations on a local level.

2. It keeps our representatives on the straight and narrow, because they know the people are watching so they need to do their utmost to uphold the ideary and to procure the most perfect of possible budgets for the people. In other words, here, as was the case with public courtroom proceedings and ostensive executions of justice, accountability is an unavoidable byproduct which will have eventual political repercussions.

It follows from all of the above that the budget needs to be negotiated in a fashion where all the bills are debated contingently upon one another within the framework defined by the revenues as we already mentioned, and not like a piling of independent bills summing up to a certain amount to be funded through deficits and debt. Our organic process thus structured equates to a causal sequence predicated on the concept of "priority". This is one of the most important concepts involved in the action of the state. A priority is a mark, a stepping stone, a reference along a hierarchical sequence and it predicates and is predicated upon any other priority in a logical fashion, attending to the maximization of the well-being of the body politic, as defined axiomatically by the party platform concomitantly with the ethos of the people.

A set of any decisions, let us say budgetary decisions, made according to this definition will entail a set of logically consistent and complete decisions not possible to improve upon. It is the ultimate budget. It is a budget of truth and reason. It is a budget free of mischief and corruption. It is a budget that represents the national reflection of the budgets every family has to put together every time there is a significant money restriction, and therefore this budget is the quintessence of an organic budget; one that is of the workers, by the workers and for the workers. Of course, a sacrifice could be defined in propositional logic as a "no priority", and if we use this terminology in our discussions, all conclusions will be syllogistically deduced in a way consistent with our underlying goal as we expressed it earlier. All this will sound no doubt like twaddle to many, but it is actually the implicit way working families go about the not-always-pleasant duty of laying out a budget. It is the most natural and wholesome way of approaching this issue, although most compeers do not flesh out the process this formally. But the state must, in principle, be aware of the logic behind the entire process and act it out appropriately.

When we talk of a spartan state articulating and integrating a spartan people, we certainly mean it. An austere life as a cardinally virtuous life, rooted in truth, and in conviction or faith in that kind of ethics, is the best life because it is the freest. And this background Zeitqeist is what makes the AFWS budgetary process not only ideal, but fundamentally possible. A life in truth is a life lived within your own means, whether it be the family or the state. Moreover, it is a life enjoyed in freedom rather than suffered in privation, and the difference between those two propositions is to be found more within than without. We are striving for the ideal man, capable to produce an ideal society or a community structured and aided by an ideal state. In consequence, we are designing an individuated man with a radically different set of principles and norms he abides by, and whose feelings and attitudes toward the world without are holier than any religion ever was able to contemplate. We do not want a man who stoically endures a spartan life; we want a man who loves it on philosophical and spiritual bases. We want to create a man who sees a divine reflection in the mirror, and not a "consumer", or "citizen", or "white man", or "black man", or "straight man", or "gay man", or "rich man", or "poor man", or "successful man", or "unsuccessful man", or any predicated man whatsoever with the possible exception of "good man". Finally, we want him to see in that mirror our holy "supra-man". Ours will be a revolution within, preceded by a revolution without. And I judge the former even more transcendental than the latter in the march toward the ideal, although nevertheless caused and not the cause: first things first.

Indeed, if I cite my personal example, through the study of moral philosophy, natural theology, logic and epistemology, the desire for anything material has receded into oblivion. It all happened organically and without any planning and hence, any struggle. I was blessed enough to fall in the footsteps of those mystics who found themselves wanting less and less, the less they had. It all happened inevitably, as I became addicted to the truth, which became my only pious master. Without the want of riches, power, fame or beauty I found myself empowered to extremes difficult to put into words. With close to nothing in my name or any source of egotistical pride, maybe we can say I was propelled to the realm of the logos, paradoxically making it really difficult to explain. I guess I became the perfect tabula rasa for the Jungian individuation and that is exactly what followed. Unfortunately all the people whom I admire the most are dead, so my only possible interaction with them is through reading their corpus, but that interaction is less passive than you might expect. In fact, I have been involved in my own mind in dissertations and certain types of personalized academic disputations with a number of the greatest giants of thought that ever lived. These were learning experiences, and learning is the only passion that I never could refrain from. And speaking of passions, I do not have many anymore. Perhaps an uncontrollable love of animals and other sentient beings, physical exercise, banter with good friends, shotgunning, and traipsing through rough and lonely parts pretending that I am hunting. The philosophers of old were right when they deemed the lust for truth and knowledge incompatible with other drives and ultimately ever-consuming. I have the greatest respect for all those juggernauts of wisdom to whom my debt of gratitude will never be fully repaid no matter my efforts.

After this brief detour, we move back to the austere nature of the AFWS as an organic reflection of the same nature present in the people. The state is spartan out of necessity, because of the budgetary process earlier laid out, and out of philosophical conviction, because the AFWS is the political actualization of the AFWP ideary. Conversely, the people are spartan out of necessity, because they are living virtuously within their means, and out of philosophical conviction, because they are the actualization of the ideal body politic according to the AFWP principles. And thus, yet again, the organic quiddity of the state as a reflection of the people, and an organism whereby the people can traverse from potentiality to actuality, is patently manifested.

The final budgetary equilibrium is undoubtedly one of massively reduced spending. Cuts include: the elimination of debt and interest payments, the suppression of all kinds of foreign aid and interventions, the massive reduction of the military budget through the effects of the policy of no proportionality and the national militia as a precursor to the draft in the unlikely contingency of war (the publicized promise of a quick resolution to war by any means is an essential prerequisite for the avoidance of war bonds), the elimination of all military bases abroad or the participation in supranational military alliances, the falling off in spending on bureaucratic salaries and pensions as a direct result of the organic administration of the state, diminishing incarcerated populations, a cheaper and faster judiciary as previously expounded, etc.

The AFWS treats every monetary unit as what it is, i.e., the work of each and every contributing compatriot. Or posited in another way, the AFWS is the most frugal of states because it is one with the people and no differentiated caste is in charge of its administration. It stands to reason that administrative abuse, waste and fraud can only be actualized by a caste that does not feel part of those who will be at the receiving end of the abuse—a caste subservient to the special interests for which the state itself exists. The organic nature and administration of our state makes systemic incompetence and waste virtually impossible. Conversely, the schizophrenic state is a system of legally empowered bureaucratic or political castes that make the instantiation of corruption and waste of resources ineluctably prevalent.

It is an organization bound to evince dysfunctional behavior within, stemming from the natural competition between departments and the schizophrenic nature of that wrangle, accentuated by the presence or even the preponderance of psychopathic elements; whereas an organic state is bound to function harmoniously, for each and one of its parts is consequential to the realization or even the survival of everyone else.

If we take a quick look at the United States federal budget, it becomes glaringly obvious how unnecessary or even deleterious to the people many if not most of the allocations of that budget are. If we strip from the budget the cancerous influence of castes and special interests, protected industries, donors and the rest, the budget could be slashed massively and the people would be better off, not to mention the state itself.

However, I must make a special mention about the so-called "non-discretionary budget", principally the programs of Social Security and Medicare, Medicaid and Unemployment and Disability Insurance. Since they were instituted on fiat powers and the people were forced to contribute their entire lives through payroll taxes and otherwise, it is without a question that these payouts have to be preserved for those who need them as we phase them out; not to do so would automatically turn the state into a highwayman-type archetype. The alternative though, will be a radically new, organic solution to those needs which I will explain in detail later in this work. These new policies plus those involving discretionary spending will suffice for a massive cut in the national budget while we observe a gargantuan expansion of the organic state into the body politic, not to spend people's money, but only to facilitate the actualization of their potentiality and their individuation.

Each and every possible surplus will be stashed away in a fund to be used only in cases of national emergency thus declared by the Council and the executive, or by the people themselves through referendum. This fund will play the part that nowadays is reserved for tax increases, debasement of the monetary base through quantitative easing and the wholesaling of government bonds, all of which result in an upward and indecent transfer of wealth to those who are already rich enough.

We can now proceed to the announcement of our subsequent founding principle. It is our will that:

59. Fifteenth founding principle: organic budgetary process; deontological duties involving taxes and spending; goals, principles, and mechanisms

"The budgetary process will start out from the evaluation of revenues and all the spending bills will be publicly debated and money will be allocated in a comprehensive and logical manner through the establishment of priorities, in such a way that no deficit spending will arise and hence no debt will accrue. Taxes will be enacted only as a means to fund the state and all problematic situations within the body politic addressed on the spending and political side, never on the revenue side, so as to not alter or disrupt the efficient equilibriums beyond what is inevitable. People will never be punished or differentiated through taxes on the basis of their free choices, but rather they will be taxed within the same bracket equally on the money at its last stage through the productive cycle, i.e., as personal income. The deontological legitimacy of every tax will be determined, and only those that are logically and morally sound will be accepted as part of the tax code, as per the analysis made in this work. And logicians and even moral philosophers will have a central role in the transformation of these principles into an actual code, according to the AFWP principles herein put forth."

Notice yet again the important role that logicians play, not only in the structure but also in the instantiation of policies in the AFWS, according to the philosophy of the AFWP. To the best of our abilities, we will keep pettifoggers and shysters away from the business of the state, and they will be prompted to embark on a process of skill recycling so they can make finally an honest living, especially considering our revolutionary reform of the judiciary, for which these characters will not be required anymore.

60. Economic intertwining of interests: the organic approach to capital

We have said that our national liberextremist democracy and state is economically an autarkic logical capitalistic state. We have analyzed in depth the concept of logical labor as opposed to wagslave labor or wage labor as it is normally called. But to make the idea complete and functional it is paramount to switch now to the capital side of the employer-employee relationship within the AFWS.

In wagslave labor, the equilibrium happens on a macro-economic scale when every worker accepts the minimum wage he is willing to work for, created as a result of competition in a workforce that is always guaranteed by the caste-driven state to exceed the demand for workers (a significant unemployment rate is required and created if necessary for this artifice to work). In logical labor, the functions of supply and demand of labor are substituted by closed negotiations between workers and employers where the former obtain the maximum wage beyond which the utility for the latter ceases to be enough to continue operations. In this fashion, the worker as an individuated man with an innate and distinctive quiddity, is recognized and realized, overcoming the old rot of laissez-faire wages.

Now in order to instantiate a totally organic and inextricably commingled interest between employer and employee, it stands to reason that when the former needs capital to operate or expand his business, the latter must cooperate with a percentage of his logical wage (the minimum will be sensibly established by law). That contribution will be in the form of a stake in the company, never in the form of debt. To the myriad of reasons already mentioned to reject debt in principle and on its demerits, we must add here another one: since the workers now have money to turn into capital as a result of the dynamic wage increases above and beyond the wagslave equilibriums, as we already extensively discussed, it would be utterly obscene to turn that excess of income (which proceeds from a reduction in profits and margins for the employer) into debt. Otherwise we would be witnessing a parasitic situation. Therefore, the contribution must be in the form of an investment, or a share in the company, making the worker a minority partner. If an employee, however, refuses to accept that partnership, the employer automatically has the right to fire him, for it is evident that belief in a cooperative enterprise is nowhere to be found and thereby no organic interdependence is being actualized. The worker will be better off going somewhere else, where perhaps he can find a valid reason for a stronger commitment and in this manner better himself as well as the community and the state.

In the AFWS, real interest rates are zero and nominally nigh on zero because monetary supply always matches output and it is never used to cover for fiscal shenanigans. This implies inflation over the long haul will be virtually eliminated. Besides, as we adumbrated earlier, the Bank of the People as wo could baptize it, through a network of brick-and-mortar offices will exercise a monopoly on credit. Only worthy and legitimate businesses with a history of success or with a certifiable chance of success will be entitled to apply for financing up to a limit and only in the excess above and beyond the capital already raised internally through the instrument of logical capital. The credit limit will be logically and financially calculated attending to factors like the amount of funds at our bank's disposal, the number, size and merits of the potential applicants within the body politic and others that might be judged relevant to this calculus, and consistent with our principles and the size of the monetary base.

We can conclude this commentary on logical capital, an instrument indisputably essential to squarely and logically consolidate the access to capital of those who legitimately need it for business, given the constrictions that we deliberately place on money supply, in this way: the monetary system in the AFWS posits an integrative and syncretic system that embraces the best of fiat money and the gold standard without the restrictions of either one. Indeed, the AFWS would have the power to control the monetary supply without creating inflation. Here we are again going beyond the constraints of the liberal paradigm for the empowerment of the people, through an exercise of logic and raw will encapsulated in our virtuous doctrines.

And regarding an issue I am sure most readers are wondering about, I certainly have something definite to declare. That question is credit for personal consumption. Our bank will not feed the compulsion of spending above and beyond one's means, gambling on future earnings, for all the economic and ethical reasons already sufficiently discussed. However, we will encourage the formation of local and sectorial credit unions or associations which will be funded on a voluntary basis by the workers in a specific county or economic sector on a local level. Those workers in turn, as paying members of that association, will be entitled to apply for personal credit at no real interest to be repaid as per the contractual clauses agreed upon by the parties, as long as his application is accepted. The rules and norms regulating those credits are to be internally approved by its members and no discrimination of any kind whatsoever will be legally tolerated. In any event, these financial associations will operate as private, not-for-profit membership clubs. In this fashion we are reinforcing even further the interdependence of the people within the structure of the organic state, encouraging solidarity and co-operation rather than exploitation and predatory behaviors, and all of it actuated congruently with the austere nature of the people and the state itself pertaining matters of money or work, as it will be customary to be called.

———

61. The paralogisms of Immanuel Kant

Logical capitalism is thus the logical and ethical rejection of the corpus written by casuists in the 16th and 17th centuries, which is an affront to our conceptualization of credit and debt. Those sophists rejected the scholastic view of credit and interest using two paralogisms (as Kant would say):

1. Damnum emergens, or unforeseen damage;

2. Lucrum interceptum, or cessation of gain (called opportunity cost in modern economic theory).

I believe that at the core of those fallacies lies dormant

the subtle phantasm of a confusion (probably deliberately generated): that of mistaking contingency for necessity, hence warping the meaning of the modal formula, especially in the second case.

Here we shall overcome as well, delighting Aristotle, St. Augustine and St. Thomas Aquinas, if they only deigned attention to our endeavors.

62. Central banking: the transformation of money into a criminal enterprise in the liberal state

This is a topic of the most consequential nature for the AFWP, and in connection with the institution of logical capital and all what it entails. For indeed, no nation in the history of mankind has heretofore been free or will henceforth be free unless the state itself issues the currency at no interest, debt-free. In other words, money created at an interest through debt will always be the conduit for massive transfers of wealth upward, the debasement of the currency through inflation, misallocation of assets and malinvestment, deindustrialization, deleterious concentration of capital, unemployment, poverty and financial enslavement.

This liberal state and many others use banknotes as money and as such they are used in all economic transactions. However, that is not fiat money or real money, but rather a

Logical capital: Property and communion rather than debt and disunion.

debt for the people and the state since the central bank (the Fed in this case) issues it at an interest, creating bonds that must be repaid at some future time. In other words, the monetary base is expanded through interest-bearing debt. They use the assuaging words "quantitative easing" to describe the scam. On the other hand, real or fiat money, also called Treasury notes, must be controlled by the state; its central bank must be a mere agency under the management of the Treasury Department, or the Finance or Exchequer Ministry, or any other name we desire to give it. Through this agency, department or ministry, which is in charge of the allocation of the state's expenditures and the collection of taxes, the organic state supervises the creation of fiat money by the Bank of the People, in such a fashion as to render such monetary supply the mere reflection of production within the body politic and the borders of the state. Under this regime, money is work or output. Therefore it is issued interest-free, without saddling the people with a debt whose origin is unproductive and hence criminal.

Consequently, America today is a nation with work but without money. This means that the equation, or rather, truism, money=work is not being instantiated. It is an unbearable situation, and the source of collective puzzlement, dissatisfaction and even rage, at least among those who are able to espy the beast, knavishly hiding in plain sight.

But to be fair, there was a time in America and in many other countries today enslaved, when money was not a subterfuge for a clique of banksters to extort inordinate amounts of wealth from the people creating nothing in the process. Tragically, through assassinations, bribery and blackmail of

Congressmen and Presidents the Fed was finally instituted in 1913. During the next six years, the dollar lost 60% of its value. A few years after that, that same central bank created an unprecedented bubble which ended up in a burst and a depression where millions lost everything, including their lives, while unemployment and hunger spread all throughout the land. However, the money lenders or credit mobsters and speculators for whose benefit the Fed exists profited immeasurably from the widespread deflation and the defaults that plagued the country for many years after 1929. Today those facts are so indisputable that even Ben Bernanke (chairman of the Federal Reserve from 2006 to 2014), in response to a question posed in 2002 by the famed economist Milton Friedman when Bernanke was serving on the Academic Advisory Panel of the US Federal Reserve Bank of New York, said "Regarding the Great Depression. You are right we did it. We are very sorry."

On June 10, 1932 the former chairman of the House Banking and Currency Committee (1920-1931), Louis T. McFadden, gave a very lengthy speech on the Floor of the House of Representatives. I will quote a few excerpts which convey the gist of the entire diatribe:

"The Federal Reserve Board ... one of the most corrupt institutions the world has ever known ... has cheated the Government of the United States and the people of the United States out of enough money to pay the national debt .... This evil institution has impoverished and ruined the people of the United States .... Some people think the Federal Reserve Banks are United States Government institutions. They are not Government institutions. They are private credit monopolies which prey upon the people of the United States for the benefit of themselves and their foreign customers; foreign and domestic speculators and swindlers; and rich and predatory money lenders. In that dark crew of financial pirates there are those who would cut a man's throat to get a dollar out of his pocket; there are those who send money into the States to buy votes to control our legislation; and there are those who maintain international propaganda for the purpose of deceiving us and of wheedling us into the granting of new concessions which will permit them to cover up their past misdeeds and set again in motion their gigantic train of crime ...."

A few years later Congressman McFadden died in mysterious circumstances, after he had previously been the target of two reported assassination attempts.

In every "crisis" breaking out "unsuspectedly" in the liberal hegemon, this curious occurrence is ever-present in the aftermath of the disaster: massive amounts of wealth are siphoned upward into the pockets of financiers and other miscreants always using the same tools, viz., runaway inflation (and sometimes deflation), debt and default. We can think of the Crash of 1929, the Crash of 2008, COVID-19, etc. The list is actually as long as our memory allows and it has been amply documented throughout history.

To sum it all up, the National Liberextremist State will have, as per the party principles, fiat money issued interest-free by a central bank owned and managed by the state and unshackled from the price of any commodity artificially set in international markets by speculators and profiteers, and a monetary base established always as a reflection of actual production in the real economy; or in other words, our people will enjoy the blessings of real and sound money.

We are now primed to enunciate our sixteenth founding principle, relating to logical capital.

It is our will that:

◆————◆

63. Sixteenth founding principle: logical capital and its conceptualization, workings, and goals

"Logical capital is the counterpart of logical labor in our system of logical capitalism. Capital necessary for business will be firstly procured within the bounds of the company, sector or county by the workers themselves through their logical wages, and the minimum percentage to be allocated for investment will be determined by law. That capital will make them effectively minority partners in the business. Hence capital will never be raised through debt, but through investment. If a worker refuses to supply at least the minimum legally established, and if asked to do so by the employer, the latter has the right to terminate the former, in view of his refusal to organically intertwine his interests with that of his employer. This way, the worker will be freed up to pursue other venues and opportunities that will better suit him so he can fully invest himself in the work, and the employer will have the option to hire another worker perhaps more inclined to eventually become a partner in the enterprise. Through this mechanism, the organic nature of the productive part of the economy is thus reinforced to extremes where all the relations among the people are suitable for all the organic institutions and duties of the state to be possible. If more credit in excess of what can be raised internally is needed, the state-owned and operated central bank will provide those funds based upon credit worthiness, availability of funds (money-capital in the organic state is a genuine monetary expression of actual national output and hence strictly limited and bounded by that metric), nature and size of the enterprise and other factors, all of which will be scrupulously and publicly assessed according to criteria univocally codified into law, so as to guarantee the impartiality and transparency of the process. Use of credit for personal consumption will be limited to not-for-profit private credit unions and clubs funded by voluntary contributions of their members, who will have the option to apply for credit if they are deemed worthy of it. Those members will receive loans in an amount consistent with the financial health of the club and the members' own contributions, never to be discriminated against for exogenous reasons, and always at no interest."

We will treat now the subjects of retirement, unemployment and health insurance covered in this state under the titles Social Security, Unemployment Insurance, Medicare, Medicaid and more broadly commercial insurance.

These are some of the most relevant topics that any functional state must address, because in a general sense they could be a matter of life and death for the people, or at least a question of financial survival. In the current state, there are public and private instruments which purportedly address the issues but in praxis nobody believes that nonsensical propaganda. Most workers retire after a life of service virtually destitute or at a minimum in dire straits. In fact, dozens of millions barely can come up with a few hundred dollars in cash if their lives depended on it, and their Social Security payments hardly cover the essential necessities. Millions slave away to barely keep up with their health insurance premiums and when a crisis strikes, they still struggle to pay up the co-insurance and copayments. Unemployment insurance, due to how scanty the payments are and how stringent the rules to be considered unemployed have been laid out by design, barely could keep anybody alive, especially considering how insanely expensive the cost of living in America has become. And what is termed "commercial insurance" is actually an illegitimate industry based on sophistry and deceit.

Our solutions to these problems created by liberal capitalism and a state that exists for the profit of the caste that controls it will be expounded upon over the next pages. They are, indeed, revolutionary policies, based on logic and the morality of work as formulated in this work. They are policies consistent and comprehensive within the context of the AFWS as the actualization of the AFWP program, and only within that political context and its concomitant ethos would those policies make any sense or be possible to be instantiated. For this reason I urge all my readers to break free of paradigmatic presuppositions and approach these solutions on their merits and the solidity of their design in accordance with the principles of the AFWP herein brought to the fore.

Our logical capitalistic alternatives within the backdrop of the National Liberextremist State will be:

1. Contingent post-factum inversion;

2. Necessary ante-factum conversion.

These two terms have been chosen because of their descriptive nature, and once we define them properly this circumstance will be made perfectly clear.

1. Contingent post-factum inversion will replace the failed and insufficiently funded programs of unemployment insurance and public health insurance, as well as the casino-like scheme of commercial insurance.

2. Necessary ante-factum conversion will replace Social Security.

Let us start with commercial health insurance. Under this device, workers incessantly drudge so they can pay exorbitant premiums to these companies. Sometimes the workers split that bill with the employers and sometimes they do not, depending on whether the employees have or do not have a "benefits package". In any event, the middleman is the health insurance organization which effectively produces no work, no service or good, but rather turns itself into a gambling operation altering the relationship between medical providers and patients. A commercial health insurance company is an organization whose business model is based on fear; namely that of people thinking they will not be able to afford care on their own if they eventually need it. As happens in a casino, the house always wins, most clients lose, many lose a lot and only a few reap some benefits. Unlike a casino, the clients here partake in this scheme out of sheer fear of what the future might hold; whereas the gamblers operate out of a search for unearned riches or just for some misguided excitement or entertainment.

Comparatively speaking, a health insurance company is more predatory than a casino by an order of magnitude because indisputably fear is more self-sustainable than greed. Indeed, well-nigh everybody is hooked on insurance or the illusion of safety, but only a fraction are addicted to gambling. A health insurance company charges everybody a regular fee or premium, and when this is exorbitantly high, the copayments and coinsurances are contractually waived. Only sick people or those who visit doctors often and undergo extensive or permanent treatment, and those who have to face some kind of medical emergency, profit, to a debatable degree, from this setup. But the premiums, copayments and coinsurance are so designed that most people put in much more than what they take out, so the company turns this revenue into profit after covering the operational costs including the expenses of the minority who put in less than what they take out.

As I said, the analogy between casinos and these companies is direct and irrefutable, except for the even-more-egregious drive of fear versus avarice. But as we have discussed in the context of our concept of money and work, these companies are the epitome of illegitimate activity. They do not create new goods, services or, therefore, money. They just extract it from people by exploiting an instinctual fear of impoverishment. To give money to some at the expense of the many is an act which does not require active creation of any kind; it does not imply the instantiation of any potentiality; it is mere air disguised as a legitimate service. In fact, even by the liberal state standards, health insurance companies are quite a stretch and rather a new phenomenon in historic terms. For centuries, people used to pay for their care directly to their providers, sometimes with money, and sometimes by bartering commodities of different kinds when patients did not have money to spare. It stands to reason, or rather to business theory and even basic propositional logic, that when we add a layer of administration to any economic exchange, the final cost of the goods and services exchanged will increase proportionally to the size and cost of that middle structure.

Indeed, very often that increase in cost is more than proportional due to the compound addition of margins and profits. Health insurance is the archenemy of healthcare, because it increases costs for the whole of the population seized by fear of the unknown, and therefore in the equilibrium quantity and quality fall off and price increases compared with a system that lacks a middleman. It is an illegitimate, destructive industry and it will be eliminated. The people involved in the health insurance industry possess all the skills necessary to make an honest living elsewhere, and the freeing-up of these workers can offer a tremendous impetus to the whole of the economy once they orient themselves productively in old as well as new enterprises and entire industries (which perhaps we cannot even dream of at the moment), and all of us will benefit from this newfound potentiality.

Public healthcare is instantiated in this state through different programs, of which the most universal and best known are Medicare and Medicaid. The former is chronically underfunded, partly covered by a special payroll tax and partly by debt. The latter is also manifestly insufficient and paid for by what the government scrapes together after it fills the pockets of the donor caste with absurd spending programs that benefit particular industries and companies, including allocations of war materiel deployed in wars of attrition overseas, where countless lives are tragically lost or irreparably altered by crippling physical and psychological injuries. So much for healthcare! Medicare is roughly intended for seniors and Medicaid for those without the means to fend for themselves, without going into further details. More importantly, Medicare and Medicaid are corporate welfare disguised as personal welfare, for the phalanxes of workers are inured to subterfuges whereby they become the excuse for massive transfers of revenue (raised through taxes and debt concomitantly with inflation) from the citizenry to conglomerates owned by the usufructuary caste. As we well know and has been amply discussed, it is the wont of this state to turn itself into the customer that the master caste needs in order to effectuate and accelerate, beyond what free-market forces would render, the concentration and expansion of capital on a grand scale.

Unemployment insurance is self-explanatory, and again it is grotesquely insufficient even to cover basic necessities of life, and therefore in and of itself a pathetic act of wishing rather than an act of will. In addition, the corruption and gaming within that program, involving recipients and administrators alike, is painful to behold; indeed to the point of being downright comical.

The artifice generally called "food stamps" defies explanation and it is an obnoxiously evident manifestation of the emptiness of the liberal kakotopia and its disturbing and shameless refusal to accept any kind of responsibility for its colossal failures. For how can it be that in a country with so many resources of all sorts, where over a trillion dollars in yearly net domestic consumption is produced abroad by foreign workers in exchange for paper money issued through debt; and yet there are millions of compatriots out of work living in abject poverty, and many more working full time without making enough to survive? What is relevant about this program is not its alleged purpose, but rather the startling reality that it purportedly tries to address; a reality which is one of the damnedest condemnations and the smoking gun showcasing that this state exists in permanent dereliction of duty, under the most brutal and immoral indifference of the caste in power. This program is the realization that cheap labor in our land through open borders and slave labor abroad through open trade have had the intended consequences, as we had already pointed out.

The victims of this scheme, obviously, are workers, both immigrants and natives. Food stamps are a type of welfare, a subsidy, which would completely disappear organically in the AFWS. That would take place in the context of an autarky and logical labor, with the state controlling the educational system and in charge of implementing and developing the best orientation courses imaginable, so the prospective workers are propelled right off the bat into the most adequate field, where they can maximize their personal satisfaction and hence productivity. In those cases where serious mental issues are involved, the state will always proceed to address the underlying issues, and not engage in makeshift contrivances that solve nothing except the compunction of some in the upper castes; but this aspect has already been previously addressed.

Notice now the words unemployment insurance and health insurance (private and public) are exactly what the titles clearly reveal. They are instruments to turn resources in the present into solutions to future health or unemployment situations. Therefore the state or private companies are the active agent that converts the nature of the funds from a deposit to an allocated withdrawal. The practical and deontological issue here arises when we question whether the quiddity of the deposits matches that of the expenses; because money is work, and consequently that nature should be present in both ends of that equation. But if we take from some workers and we dole it out to others, potentially taking work from those who have less and transferring it to those who have more, contingent upon the instantiation of the conditions contemplated by those programs, we are ultimately plundering the weaker in order to cover for ill-devised state instruments.

Based upon all that has been posited, contingent post-factum inversion is the only possible solution to the problems expounded upon if we are to have an organic state based on work. This instrument is called thus because the situations confronted are unpredictable and the solutions to them must be enacted after the situations arise, with the ultimate goal of reversing the final outcome to the terms prior to the occurrence of the event. In order to achieve this goal, the state must become the insurer of the people, but without the spurious motives and means by which the insurance companies operate. The organic state must be the catalyst to a transformation of work into the funds wherewith the people affected can get back to the antecedent situation, without any predation on fellow workers. This mechanism thus predicated logically implies the state will articulate a policy whereby the worker can work within the organism, to the extent that the money generated can cover for his contingency as he gets back to the initial state. The organic state, in this manner, does not charge anything to anybody, nor distributes the funds to others, but rather it becomes the medium through which the people who need it can work their way out of their situation and pay for their own medical care. The state therefore will allocate not the money, but rather the opportunity to work within its organic structure so every man becomes his own master even in the face of unexpected and expensive occurrences.

We talked about the state and all its agencies and operations being carried out by the people themselves in a permanent and well regulated succession. In that rota, those who have medical bills who cannot afford to pay by their own means, will be given the opportunity to serve beyond their established stint, as long as that emergency and insufficiency of means is properly validated by the state. The people will also be given the opportunity to defer their assigned work to others within their kith and kin, so as to increase to the largest degree the flexibility and the interweaving of this organism that we call the AFWS. And in order to ensure that the medical costs do not become an instrument of untoward and dangerous caste generation, the state through its monopoly on education and indoctrination will stir into the medical field a sufficient number of youth so as to guarantee a healthy level of competition in that market, which is evidently insufficient today. Nobody should expect to become rich doing his job, and everybody should expect to be free and comfortable in self-actualization. Of course different income levels will continue to exist and that should continue to be the case given the fact that not everybody is equally productive, and money is work.

By linking up the ultimate cost of medical care to the work of the patient and of his friends and relatives in the political articulation of the state, we are ensuring the most efficient decision process in the choice of the medical provider by the patient, relative to his means. If once the provider, the treatment and the means to pay for it (including if necessary a measure of organic work within the administration of the state) are established, and if there remains a balance to be offset, the worker will also consider his membership in the local credit union as we defined these institutions in the framework of logical capital. Notwithstanding this membership or the lack thereof, if there is a final balance after all the mechanisms have been used, the organic state itself will be the guarantor of last resort of that outstanding balance once all the aforementioned institutions have been instantiated in the process of providing care and rightfully paying for it within a competitive and free market.

Some considerations must be brought forth in this analysis, which will shed necessary light on the whole of the issue as it pertains to our system's superiority with regard to its financial viability, efficiency and fairness:

- This policy must be understood in the context of our National Liberextremist State, which is an autarkic logical capitalistic state, and all the institutions and legal framework that will make the articulation of such policy possible.

- The people will only pay for care after the event takes place, thus "contingent post-factum". Our workers will benefit not only from logical wages (substantially higher than those present in the liberal Leviathan's wagslave-labor scheme) and from radically reduced taxes, but for the absence of monthly premiums paid in many cases only as a means to subdue the fear of the contingent. In some other cases people are forced to pay for costly health insurance so the donor caste rips off the workers through the plundering of tax money in the form of subsidies for those who cannot afford the market price of those insurance policies. Here once again we observe that this laissez-faire kakistocracy is turning people into pawns for the benefit of the plutocracy whose interests are the ultimate reason of this state's existence.

- Our mechanism is a ploy to pay work with work, predicated on the individualities of both provider and patient, without intermediaries or undue and potentially regressive transfer of work from those with less to those with more, as is the case of commercial insurance in the liberal state.

- The instantiation of this institution on a case-by-case basis is an act of inversion to that state of affairs prior to the contingency, and all carried out through work and not debt, nor predation in the form of untoward transfer of work.

- The organic state is reinforced thus in four different ways. Firstly, the people meet their financial obligations through the organic nature of the state's administration. Secondly, the people strengthen their interconnections with the cells all around through the transferral of duties to others who are willing and able to pick up the slack. Thirdly, the workers deepen the organic interconnections with one another through logical capital and the local and sectorial credit institutions when available. And finally, the state itself and the whole of the workers who constitute its tissue, are the guarantor of last resort to cover outstanding balances left unpaid by the previous instruments. Because in the final analysis, the whole of the body politic and its integrity is predicated upon the integrity of each and every of its cells, and therefore our organic state employs all the resources necessary to quell an infection, no matter how minute and localized it is, lest it spreads like wildfire throughout the entire system.

I regard the existence and proliferation of credit card companies as well as health insurance companies the canary in the mine that foreshadows a regime approaching a systemic failure, doomed to collapse unto itself; a regime in the cusp of disintegration. However that foreseeable future is only thus in historic terms, so its demise could potentially take several generations during which the level of abuse and violence against the people could increase dramatically, as its last gasps for political and economic air become ever-more desperate. In the end, this forthcoming epic confrontation will be unavoidable and potentially bloody; and it will be up to the workers themselves to make it worthy and final.

It is quite obvious that the issue of unemployment insurance is analogous to that of health insurance in any of its forms. It is in fact a clear case of contingent post-factum inversion and hence the policies and mechanisms set out to address and solve these situations virtually identical. However, it is indisputable that in the AFWS the concept of "long-term unemployed" is void of true meaning, for the ethos of our body politic and the institutions that articulate the state would make the instantiation of such a concept an impossibility, except in cases where massively debilitating mental or physical issues manifest themselves. In such cases the organic state will proceed on with the resoluteness and compassion which are the hallmark of its deontological identity. This state will never leave anybody behind, for an organism is not an addition of components but rather their individualities traceried in a political act of defiance and love as we brazenly advance toward the judge.

When workers reach a certain age, they have to retire. That age varies depending on the industry, type of work and even personal preferences. In our state, where wagslave labor and abusive taxes have been eradicated, the disposable income of workers across the board has increased dramatically, as has their capacity for saving and investing through the mechanism of logical capital and any other traditional form of investment either in equities and commodities, real estate or others which are compatible with the philosophy and the laws of the AFWS.

The organic state places the uttermost importance on the freedom and personal responsibility of each worker to conduct his own financial matters, because he is not only responsible to himself and his immediate social circle, but also responsible to the whole of the body politic—responsibility that entails decency, according to the ethics of the people and the deontological duties of the state articulated through its corpus of laws and regulations, consistent with the ethos of the AFWP.

If somebody is obscenely irresponsible with his work, or money, he will be held accountable by the people not by punishing him, but by avoiding the punishment of others through immoral transfers of work to cover for his egotistical ways. A necessary ante-factum conversion is, unlike the contingent post-factum inversion, an action to be executed by the workers themselves as an act of ethical behavior, so as to not foist themselves in the most selfish fashion imaginable upon the whole of the body politic, ultimately cannibalizing the tissue of the state at the altar of their hedonic and self-serving actions and habits. With a conversion, understood as a forward transformation of present work into future money, the workers have the moral obligation to be thrifty and dutiful in their finances throughout their lives. Acts of egoism and gross negligence will not be requited with the sacrifice of dutiful and responsible workers. Predatory or parasitic behavior will not be guerdoned with the sweat of virtuous workers. Unethical people or cancerous cells cannot be sustained at the expense of those who kept the organism healthy and strong; and the state cannot be organic if it descends into the depravity of polluting its deontological duties with actions against the virtue ethics of the people. That is a state disintegrating at its very core.

This general principle notwithstanding, it is within the realm of the possible that a virtuous worker cannot take care of himself by the time of his retirement, as a consequence of events or circumstances whose causality is not directly or indirectly to be ascribed to his actions. He might also lack the immediate support of the surrounding tissue for many different theoretical reasons. In such situations, the necessary ante-factum conversion that is supposed to be done by the worker will be turned into a simul et factum conversion by the state through organic work in its administration. If that does not suffice or it is not plausible to instantiate, a budgetary solution will be implemented to cover for the most basic needs of the affected so as to ensure a life of dignity and peace; and to this end an appropriate agency within the apparatus of the state will be adequately funded and regulated, and the conditions and circumstances covered by its functions minutely detailed and codified.

It is now that we are prepared to inscribe our seventeenth founding principle as a matter of historical record, and not just as a formal political declaration of intentions, for our founding document will be thoroughly studied through the ages. Not in vain are we creating a new state steeped in the ethos of a revolution like no other in history. We are in fact inventing the state of the moral philosopher and the logician, superannuating the state of the politician, the shyster and the capitalist. Let the logos spring forth as we write our manifesto, hopefully one day etched on a shrine proverbially soaked in the blood of the righteous for the people to behold, to revere and to live by.

64. Seventeenth founding principle: contingent post-factum inversion and necessary ante-factum conversion; work as the solution to health and retirement needs

"It is our will that the state will actuate a contingent post-factum inversion and a necessary ante-factum conversion as a replacement for all the different programs and insurances run in the liberal state on the workers' sweat, whether through taxes or payments in the private market, pertaining to healthcare, unemployment compensation and generally social welfare. Our structure will be predicated upon an instantiation of potential work into actual money by the people themselves through the organic administration of the state, avoiding predation on other less-fortunate workers or exploitation of the workers themselves in gambling schemes. Our policy will be a reflection of the organic nature of the state and a reinforcement of such a nature, and prosperity and justice for all its concomitant properties. Our invention is predicated upon the existence of the proper institutions and legal framework within the AFWS and an ethical and adequately indoctrinated body politic, where each cell-man is aware of his obligations toward himself and all of his brethren."

65. Absolute ante-inference self-defense: the most radical and purest of natural rights

The theory of just war, which constitutes the philosophical underpinning of our causally very restrictive but operationally unbounded theory of war, is very much interconnected with the theory of self-defense. Lex naturalis, ius naturale (natural law or natural right), is the foundation of just war and personal self-defense. Hence, the consideration of the people and the state as organic reflections of each other is made glaringly evident by the laws and mechanisms which ensure the survival of both. A just war is an unavoidable war, a war of self-defense. As we stated before, it has to be a war over our physical borders or over the necessary conditions for the AFWS to remain functional and intact. Wars are waged against foreign governments and any hostile organization and are only intended to reinstitute the original conditions before the aggression was actualized. Just wars thus are never wars of occupation, exploitation or nation-building, practices categorically prohibited as an axiom of foreign policy in the AFWS. Throughout history this state and most others have witnessed countless sophists and psychopaths cloaked in the mantle of statesmen making decisions for their own sake and that of the plutocracy they serve, and the upshot is a constant occurrence: vast fields of ignominy manured with the blood of legions of workers.

As I previously expounded upon, formally, honestly, and publicly stated intention of non-proportionality is a sine qua non to minimize the probability of occurrence of a war and to maximize the probability of it coming to a quick and satisfactory conclusion in the unlikely event of its outbreak. Similarly, as the organic state is a cognate entity with the body politic which is its material cause, the theory of just war is analogous with our theory of what I term "absolute ante-inference self-defense". Self-defense, as an absolute natural right preceding any historical political structure whatever, must be at the foundation of any moral state. This right, thus stated, must be non-proportional, which is essential to serve as a mechanism to discourage aggression. And it must be prior to any inferential calculation as to the actions and counteractions potentially caused by the meddling of the state through the law. But that contingency is impossible to actualize unless we dispense with the state meddling altogether, because once the law is factored in, the inferential assessment of the sequence of potential actions will inevitably produce an immoral outcome. For in that scenario the cunning will always prevail over the just.

In other words, we seek for the state to get out of the way in the exercise of this most fundamental right in order to avoid the restriction of legal interpretations by the parties while in the heat of the confrontation; otherwise moral hazards and unintended consequences will be the result of such encroachment, leading to a situation akin to an organism consciously doubting its own cells in their fight for survival; a fight which is supposed to be unconsciously carried out. So we cannot elude the logical conclusion that any trespass on this personal, sacrosanct right by the state ought to be regarded as a crime against itself, insofar as it is a crime against the body politic—an act of pure evil and self-destruction; a psychopathic act which will not be actualized in any of its multiple versions by the the AFWS. We will never facilitate the successful completion of a crime by thrusting the people into an illogical and immoral calculus of potential legal consequences which belongs to the field of game theory rather than to the purview of the most sacred of all rights, with the exception of the right to life, with which it is very closely intertwined.

But all of the above being said, if in the process of unrestrained and absolute exercise of the right of ante-inference self-defense, and after posterior consideration by the logicians within the judicial system, the winner in the fight turns out to be the lawbreaker, irrespective of his presupposed, subjective standing in the aforementioned conflict, he will be held accountable according to the law. So the people know they cannot be restrained by the law in their exercise of unbounded self-defense, but they will be punished accordingly if and only if they are legally deemed to be the perpetrator in the confrontation or the causal agent, and their repayment will be handed out based upon the means, the intensity and the result of the foregoing violent interaction. So through organic devices, we are placing the constraint in every man's heart not by law, but by his honest assessment of the causality of the conflict between himself and the other party. If he believes he is in the right, his reaction will be no doubt more violent and deservedly so than in the case where he is not quite sure of his standing. The same rationale applies to the other person involved in the dispute. We have in fact created a system where the deterrence of criminality is maximized through unrestrained response to it, and at the same time the assessment of the initial conditions a

*Ante-inference self-defense: An axiom in the triune
deductive system of the AFWP, and a testament to its moral completeness.*

fortiori to be honest by both parties, considering the austere legal consequences faced if found to be in the wrong, which will be proportional to the means, end result, and intensity of the exchange. This mechanism implies that any victim is entitled to any reaction in the process of self-defense, and none of his actions will be deemed illegal and punishable by law as long as that compeer is not reckoned the initial aggressor or causal agent of the chain of events.

A concomitant issue when talking about self-defense is the assessment of the devastation inflicted by the babelic state within the framework of its illogical and deontologically criminal limitation of that most sacred natural right through the law. Such an assessment or quantification will be proven impossible to actuate. We can only guess as to how many innocent people have sacrificed their lives or their physical or psychological integrity when hurriedly evaluating their standings with the inferential self-defense laws lurking in the background of the crisis. For the fear of the liberal legal system is so deeply ingrained in our collective unconscious that many compatriots choose to become victims and contend with crippling injuries or potential death, versus defending themselves and undergo the ensuing onslaught of legal actions launched from the prosecutor's office. Such a legal framework is effectively disarming the innocent and arming the predator, in a cruel and twisted game of predications where the state refuses to bear any responsibility or even acknowledge the primal role it plays in the causation of such a holocaust. By the millions we can easily fancy the number of victims this putrid state has caused through its immoral meddling and codifying of the fundamental right, rather than circumscribing itself to the legal determination of responsibilities in a framework of logical, fair, wholesome ante-inference self-defense.

We can expound now on this paramount principle of absolute ante-inference self-defense by establishing how it relates to the the rest of the party ideary. The following founding principle is assuredly one which exposes the nature of the state, not only as an organic entity, but also as a logical one.

Therefore, it is our will that our eighteenth founding principle will read thus:

66. Eighteenth founding principle: the three axioms whereby all founding principles can be inferred, id est, ante-inference self-defense, logical capitalism, and the casteless state

"Ante-inference self-defense, logical capitalism and the actualization of a casteless state are the three founding principles wherewith the state itself comes to be, or in other words, every other party principle is logically deduced from these three foundational axioms. Consequently, the AFWP is not an ideological institution but a logical one, and thus our autarkic National Liberextremist State is not an ideological state but a purely logical-political organism."

67. The principle of dissolution or self-empowerment as an application of ante-inference self-defense against the remiss state

As an example in this logical and operational context, our principle of self-empowerment is by definition the principle of ante-inference self-defense against the state, actuated by the free worker when the state fails to uphold its immanent duties or what we call the AFWP program. For if our AFWS ever becomes remiss in the execution of its responsibilities as per the ethos of the people and the party principles, it should forthwith be dismantled by any means necessary.

A deontological state must be absolutely and uncompromisingly teleological, i.e., the legitimacy of a state must be assessed, inter alia, based upon the functionality of the effects it causes (not straightforwardly so with the virtue ethics of the people, as I already discussed). In fact, the deontological nature of the state makes it susceptible to be judged teleologically because the body politic has gigantic powers of observation and judgment, both on a conscious level in each man-cell as well as through the collective unconscious. In other words, when the state is deontological, the results of its policies can be assessed by the combined perceptive and ratiocinative powers of each cell in the body politic, rendering that collective judgement pertinent and reliable.

Without that teleological dimension, this political entity, the state, conceptually collapses unto itself, and becomes an illogical and altogether cancerous structure to be eradicated in order to restore a basic substratum of rationality and dignity in the body politic. Unless the malignant growth is stamped out, the disease spreads wildly throughout the people, making them in turn corrupt and decadent. Therefore, as I already explained, the state leading by example and abiding by its own laws to the last logical consequence is a matter of national survival, and not a conduct to be displayed perfunctorily at best.

---

68. Abortion: Gottfried Wilhelm Leibniz's "labyrinth of the continuum"

And I now proceed, determined and steadfast, toward our principle of life. This will be the principle of damnation of the unsung holocausts of our time: the holocaust of the unborn and the holocaust of the abandoned: abortion and homelessness.

Industrial-scale abortion is the manifestation, in praxis, of the crisis of moral thought that characterizes the laissez faire state and to a large extent communist and socialist countries as well. Abortion is philosophically a most transcendental issue and encompasses philosophical theories and speculations in the logical, moral, political, and epistemological fields. Abortion is ultimately, as I see it, a tragic instantiation, materially speaking, of what Leibniz called the "labyrinth of the continuum". In fact, the promotion of abortion as "women's right to choose" is implicitly predicated on the fallacious assumption that Leibniz's maze has been resolved; or more precisely on the fraudulent belief that Leibniz's problem is no more than a social construct.

Leibniz's labyrinth is, in actuality, a problem of logical calculus. Whereas Zeno's falsidical paradox is overcome by the mathematical theory of series and the understanding that a process with an infinite number of steps does not necessarily last infinitely long, Leibniz's labyrinth brings about a seemingly unsolvable puzzle; namely the impossibility of establishing an injection between time and an instantaneous event. Indeed, if something happens in a particular instant of time and that something comes into existence precisely at that time, that is so if and only if that something is not in the moment immediately prior. But there is no way, logically or mathematically, to identify that "immediately prior" time, for when we try we inevitably get trapped in an infinite regression and a circular pattern of reasoning. The difficulty arises from the nature of time, which seems to be mathematically a one-to-one function with the class of real numbers, which is not only an infinite class, but it contains an infinite number of numbers between any given two numbers, no matter how close they are, hypothetically. Leibniz, a genius of mathematics and metaphysics, and co-inventor of differential calculus, called this conundrum, as I already mentioned, the "labyrinth of the continuum".

The proponents of abortion as a natural right predicate

this claim on the proposition that we can ascertain when a fetus becomes a person, although that statement is in and of itself illogical: for if we know of such an event, why do we need to arbitrarily set different dates depending upon the jurisdiction we happen to be in? Is it the case that fetuses become humans earlier in state A and later on in state B? Certainly that seems to be a biological impossibility, unless we contend that people from different states belong to different species. Not even the most ardent defender of the schizophrenic state would accept such a notion … I trow, anyway.

But let us play devil's advocate (pun certainly intended), and assume, for the sake of the argument, that we know exactly when a fetus becomes a person. If that were the case, at any moment prior to that the fetus is not a person. So we would be allowed to kill him at any moment leading up to that safe-haven moment. But we cannot univocally identify the moment prior to that one because of what mathematicians and logicians call the "compactness" of the class of real numbers. We could, in theory, make sure we kill him according to the rules by establishing an interval prior to him becoming a person, with a domain large enough as to guarantee that he is certainly not a person. But then we undermine the logical basis wherewith we set the parameters in the first place, because we now have nonpersons allowed to live on and nonpersons sent to the chopping block (pun, again, intended), and not a single moral or logical criterion to determine such mutually exclusive categories. We are left with the brutality of randomness, hardly a rational way of dealing with life-or-death issues like this. The only mathematical way to solve the conundrum of the continuum in this context is to render the upper bound of the safety interval to the left of conception (or the genesis of the zygote, as it is understood by many); in other words, prior to conception.

In practical terms, this equates to the prohibition of abortion, all done with subservient veneration and to the glory of mathematical logic and moral philosophy. For the National Liberextremist State will be a logical and moral state or it will not be at all.

Deontologically and politically, abortion is the instantiation of a hierarchization of priorities by the state. Particularly, this state considers abortion on an industrial scale, or in other words, the systematic and canonical sacrifice of guiltless human lives, as the token to assuage human anxiety and hence render the people more docile; and also the most effective means to pull millions into a scheme of complicit mass murder, so any attempt to judge the state on moral grounds is utterly obliterated. A people sullied by the blood of their own unborn is a people without the standing to rise up and judge the state. Hence, legal abortion accomplishes three fundamental objectives: first, it makes the people more obedient in the most mundane affairs, free of the anxiety caused by personal responsibilities and unwanted burdens; secondly, it makes them incapable to judge the state itself in more general matters if they are all befouled by the spilling of innocent blood; and thirdly, the institution of abortion allows the state to replace native populations with what the elites regard as more suitable fodder for the scheme of wagslave labor. However, this policy might backfire in the long run if discontent and rebellion born out of intellectual and spiritual awakening finally takes hold of the immigrant population, as I predict will happen. More on this last point will be expounded upon when I treat the subject of pauperism or homelessness.

From a strictly ethical viewpoint, abortion considered as a right to choose is archetypically a supra-fallacy, so much so, that all the practices that back in the 17th century the Jesuits advocated for and the famed mathematician and philosopher Blaise Pascal denounced on the harshest terms are present in it; namely equivocation, probabilism and direction of intention. The instantiation of equivocation in the abortion debate takes place by the use of the word "person" as opposed to "human being", reducing the human quiddity of the unborn to a mere social construct as I will explain later. Social constructs do indeed exist as I have already amply exposed in this book, but in the context of abortion that concept is a mere ruse, a gross exercise of sophistry. The actuation of probabilism takes place when outlandish ideas to make abortion as unbounded as possible are propounded by fringe elements suffering from all kinds of mental problems including psychopathy, and yet the state turns those ideas into policy, rejecting any notion of tutiorism. And finally direction of intention is materialized when abortion is misrepresented as a liberating right rather than the misplacement of responsibilities and the cleansing thereof by the sacrificing of the weakest, most defenseless agent; or in other words, the ascribing of responsibilities to the effect rather than to the cause. When direction of intention is paired with and reinforced by the doctrine of double effect, anything, including mass murder, is justifiable and even welcomed in the pursuit of ends by any means. In this catastrophic scenario, morality ceases to exist. And at this point we have reached the liberal dystopia.

Abortion is truly, at its most fundamental level, the quintessence of the most unbounded potentiality truncated and prevented from becoming actuality. In the Aristotelian sense, I would argue it is the ultimate tragedy; the state, as the archetype of the meta-villain, the formal, ever-powerful, cataclysmic, nonexistence cause. It is a black hole for moral light, sucking up the life of the people themselves and destroying it without leaving a record. In the AFWS, prospective mothers will be protected and encouraged, their lives made easier and not more difficult. They are never to be incited to assault themselves by decapitating the most miraculous accomplishment anybody could possibly dream of. Indeed, the crime perpetrated on the mother is nearly as egregious as that perpetrated on the child, and it makes the double-edged oblivion so painful to contemplate.

In the organic state, the utmost, august, love-driven and impeccably managed agency will provide the support to reluctant prospective mothers, and if they still cannot come to terms with the idea of motherhood after the baby is born, the state itself will take over the offspring, turning the whole of the people into his parents. We will socialize the responsibility, the pain and the rewards of parenting because the organic state is the political manifestation of (and one and the same with) the body politic. Those who are rejected by the few will be embraced by the many and taken to the heights that their potentialities allow. As we march toward the judge, this instantiation of love, solidarity and communal effort will be perfected and turned into a source of collective bliss and fulfillment.

It stands to reason that as the people become more and

more ethical within the state, and the state more and more reassured in its deontological duties by the people, in a virtuous circle of self-reinforcement, the number of prospective mothers inclined to abort their babies will dramatically drop. And hence, the organic nature of the AFWS will eventually overcome the need for the aforementioned agency, which will only be necessary while the old generations gradually die out as the youth slowly but surely take over. Indeed, as the new blood cleanses the land of the old rot, the memories of this holocaust will progressively fade away. However, I trust history will forevermore keep the record fresh and relevant, not so much as to shame our forefathers but rather to highlight the progress of our workers in the transcendent quest for that final triumph of love over darkness.

So I have addressed three fundamental dimensions of abortion and its implications: the dimension of mathematical logic, and the political and ethical dimensions. There is, however, a very interesting fourth dimension to abortion that I mentioned earlier in the context of equivocation. That is the dimension that can be considered both ontological and epistemological. For, as all my readers are well aware, the proponents of regulated abortion, irrespective of the degree of limitations or even the total lack thereof, base the design of their policies in the concept of "person", and not of "human being". The reason is straightforward: a fetus can be predicated using both words, human and being. And that predication is a valid logical consequence of incontrovertible biological reality, and hence irrefutable. However, the word "person" signifies a concept that is a paradigm of social construct. Only the people who use the word person can ultimately decide what it means, and therefore we cannot deduce the sacrosanct right to life of that being through the axioms of propositional calculus plus modus ponens. In other words, the usage of the word "person" is a supreme act of sophistry intended to crown the executioner with the tiara of judge and jury as well. It is a fallacious act, in the most formal sense.

And finally, I regard a pregnant woman as the most powerful being in the empirical world. She is transcendentally the archetype of creation and transformation from potentiality to actuality. In the most material and biological sense rather than metaphysical, she is the paradigm of movement, continuity and survival. As an organic entity, she is a medium and not only an end unto herself. For this reason, countless ancient civilizations worshipped motherhood and pregnancy, and the artistic manifestations that have endured through the ages bear witness to that. A mother's divinity within bursts forth radiantly for the world to behold, and this treasure must and will be protected at all costs.

In an Aristotelian sense, it is curious to observe the direct analogy of mothers and workers as efficient causes of creation, whether it is life or work instantiated. They are both the most glaring examples of the demigod nature of mankind. Therefore, anyone incapable of perceiving that nature will have to be properly reeducated, since what else is as important as perceiving reality according to its true quiddity?

From the perspective of the body politic, motherhood is the fountainhead of the organic supra-man. Consequently, mothers are quintessential to our march toward the ideal. The organic supra-man, our state's supra-race, the biological synthesis of those who tower over us from the peaks of raw merit, is unlike Nietzsche's superman. His superman was a man of the pre-Christian morality. Nietzsche regarded the archetype of the Self as too difficult to actualize and thus he rejected the ideal altogether. We, on the other hand, defiantly stared into the judge's eyes and decided to march undauntedly and confidently toward that ideal, knowing that we have become its masters. For can we not assuredly affirm that the only thought bolder than the rejection of God is the thought of becoming one with him, by his own rules and standards?

On a side note, I must draw the attention once again, to the unwavering obsession of the liberal kakotopia with keeping the body politic as reticulated and feeble as possible. For any state could, in principle, create a supra-race or a body politic of supra-men. But if this were the case, who would be the fodder for the institution of wagslave labor? This state thus created and defined needs, for its own survival, the kind of men who can easily be manipulated into useful compliance. Men intellectually, morally and physically as limited as necessary in order to break them into submission for the sake of the usufructuary caste, through the well-known means of propaganda, indoctrination and the mass "entertaming" industry. The evidence is hiding in plain sight for any worker who chooses to break free from this liberal delusion.

69. Homelessness: the merciless liberal design; pauperism of the ideal surplus population

And now I must proceed to analyze the phenomenon of homelessness which is political in nature, although the state strives to characterize it as an economic byproduct of a mode of production that has inevitable downsides. This framing of the problem is naturally an attempt to avoid political responsibility and a justification for its unstoppable proliferation and expansion.

But first I will take a brief detour to comment on the general, philosophical concept of death. This parenthesis is important because that is what homelessness is fundamentally: death and misery, either material, moral or both. It is abandonment and desperation. And it is ultimately hypocrisy, irresponsibility and betrayal.

However, there is a political aspect to death that needs to be commented upon. Death is the archetype of the revolutionary because it is the ultimate destroyer of singular individuals who are the building blocks of castes and the cells of entire socioeconomic structures. In that sense, even though it does not destroy the established order, it is nevertheless a democratizing agent throughout the entire body politic, exercising a most miraculous action of leveling the playing field, unlike any other presence in human existence. It does so by an act of supreme, unstoppable force, connecting all castes in the same destiny. In fact, most members of the usufructuary caste, or godless thieving plutocrats, face with anguishing pain and fear that wonderfully humbling moment when their rotten souls are slashed asunder but that scythe—which holds the title of the most democratic and liberating of all instruments in God's creation. A few cling to their families for comfort and solace, but that refuge is hardly enough for an atheist once confronted with that blade, as the realization that the source of all his past hubris was nothing but a fleeting illusion sets in. You almost can hear an unearthly wail bursting forth from the deepest pit of his being, crying in angst, bitterness and rage, "Why, why cannot I buy my immortality?" After all, he always thought the money that he stole through the institution of wagslave labor and other numberless artifices was the alfa and omega of everything there is and there will always be, since it was the all-consuming commander of his crazed ego. Therefore, in view of all what has been said, any true political philosopher, as a revolutionary, should welcome death without excessive predication, in an act of stoic understanding.

And let us now proceed to the core of this question, which is a tragedy brought about by the state firstly for political expediency, and secondly due to gross rejection of basic, self-evident deontological duties; or so it seems to be the case at first glance.

Political expediency refers here to the causes, and this paired with the rejection of fundamental ethical responsibilities in acting upon those political motivations, the desired outcome is achieved. However, it would be intolerably naive to presuppose that such a deterioration of the social fabric of the state is mainly due to the unquenchable thirst for votes by the partitocracy combined with a subsequent refusal to carry out basic deontological duties, as expressed by tradition and law.

But a most piercing analysis of the role of the state in the rotting of the body politic, in the form of an ever-expanding and deepening of a mass of paupers, leads us inevitably to the uncovering of a much more sinister drive. Indeed, I already touched briefly upon it when elaborating on some key elements of Marx's political economy. I am referring to the establishment of one of the essential conditions for the expansion and accumulation of capital (by the usufructuary plutocracy, also known as the donor caste) in a capitalistic mode of production based on banknotes issued at interest: the surplus population of a certain kind.

I actually deduced one of the most concomitant traits of the liberal dystopia from the analysis thereof, namely its ruthless and shameless racism—racism in a literal or classical sense. It is racist because the ruling caste in this state believes that the morally, intellectually and psychologically weakest peoples, i.e., the ideal surplus population for the re-production, expansion and concentration of capital—those are the peoples most welcome as the state itself obliterates its own sovereignty, aiding and abetting the violators, as a rabid madman slashes himself all over so as to cause as many wounds and infections as possible.

In fact, the pursuit of capitalistic concentration in the hands of the usufructuary caste could be considered a genuine display of insanity. It does not recognize economic, moral or even logical bounds, to the extent that the destruction of the body politic itself, as an organic fabric whose individual components are closely intertwined with one another in relations that must be developed in an orderly fashion within a cohesive national ethos, is but a mere accidental event without major significance for the plutocratic caste and its privileged, illegitimate and unproductive subservient castes (functionary and bureaucratic castes, political caste, propaganda caste, indoctrination caste, etc.).

Consequently, in an rhetorical interpretation of deductions derived through philosophical logic, it is without a doubt that Europeans would never be allowed en masse through the southern border, since they do not conform to the racist interpretation of their nature and their usefulness for the expansion and concentration of capital in America. From the point of view of the master caste, or the proprietor and donor caste, this surplus population needs to be without a drive for independence or the desire for a self-sustaining life, so they can only survive through the underselling of the only commodity they possess, namely their labor power. Hence these people need to have very few expectations beyond a basic material subsistence, and fewer skills lest they develop the idea of becoming independent operators outside the labor market, in essence competing on varying degrees with big capital across sectors and industries.

As I already expressed quite clearly earlier in this work, the ruling caste and the whole of this kakotopia are up for a rude awakening when they realize the submissive and broken sheep that they thought they were letting in are in fact quite the opposite and they will be to a large degree the spearhead of the next and last revolution. And indeed, their best will be an organic element of our state supra-race; ours will be a state where the blessings of diversity will be literally embodied in a new race. Furthermore, we can say that we will turn the empty shibboleths of this rotten state to their most formal logical conclusion, to the complete instantiation of the best the body politic has to offer in order to actuate a new beginning. Unlike this wicked mirage of a state, in the AFWS the people, especially those holding office in an organic rotatory basis, will mean what they say and say what they mean.

But what is exactly the connection between pauperism and surplus population for the expansion, reproduction and concentration of capital in the hands of the plutocratic donor caste? The homeless population is a concomitant fixture of an ever-growing surplus population. It is the side effect of that lubricating extra population. And it is so as a consequence of two different mechanisms:

1. The resources of the state are spread out across larger populations of workers in need (a circumstance prevalent in the babelic malformation), now increased further by those foreigners who prove themselves incapable or unwilling to fend for themselves.

2. The foreign nationals who are capable and willing to work for a living, i.e., to undersell their labor power as a commodity in the labor market, will inevitably expand the labor supply, with the price of labor in the competitive market falling off to varying degrees; ultimately the necessary lubricant for the expansion and accumulation of capital. But the consequence of this is the transformation of the lower echelons of the laboring population into paupers, some due to their expulsion altogether from the labor market, and others because the new equilibrium is significantly below the value of their necessary labor, i.e., the new lower

wages are not sufficient to cover the workers' basic necessities of life.

The aforementioned factors, coupled with the total dilution of the meaning of citizenship in the liberal state—and by now a laughable concept frowned upon by the globalist usufructuary caste, since they cannot make any money out of it—and the concomitant eradication of the rights and advantages associated with it, imply logically the existence of a layer of homelessness that cannot and will never be solved by this state. This pauper population is, after all, the measure of the health and size of the surplus population on whose existence the welfare of the master caste is predicated. Here, as everywhere else, the well-being of the people is incompatible with the welfare of the caste-driven state, and vice versa. The perfect analogy would be a cancerous growth in a human body: whatever is good for one is bad for the other. They are organically incompatible, just as the babelic state is organically incompatible with a healthy body politic, with a people made of free and moral workers. The only question becomes how to go about extirpating the malignant tumor and still survive the arduous battle. And this will be amply discussed in the last section of this work.

And what is the meaning of homelessness or pauperism beyond the merely economic and socially obvious manifestations? It is a catastrophic failure of the state to uphold and dutifully execute its basic deontological functions. And what does this entail precisely? The existence of the state is not a given; it is not an unavoidable natural phenomenon or a functional entity essential to the articulation of a society as a body politic. In other words, the state must prove itself to be worthy of existing by adding to rather than subtracting from the social welfare of the people, as a political entity. The state is not a logical consequence of a people interacting around the linchpin of a common ethos; moreover, it is not a legitimate institution in and of itself, insofar as nothing that is not conducive to the personal and social interests of a body politic is legitimate. Thus, I can assert that any state structured as an organization, particularly one as ill-begotten and rotten as this dystopian instantiation, must be wiped away. Only a state that is one and the same with its people and has reached the pinnacle of organic status; a state indistinguishable from its body politic, sharing its same quiddity or as I said, being the intension of the people as these are its extension; only that state deserves to exist. Contrarily, a state at the service of a self-anointed master caste is poisonous to the human condition and must be combated until extermination.

Consequently, a state that demands the existence of a stratum of pauperism to the extent that it is the logical consequence of a a growing, well-maintained and adequate surplus population for the expansion and accumulation of capital, is by definition incompatible with the freedom or the material and moral prosperity of a healthy body politic. This state is, in fact, a structure built upon a terrorist act, namely violence and destruction exerted on the phalanxes of workers, Americans and foreigners alike, for the benefit of the few. And indeed, sheer terror is what the masses of workers feel when they are constantly accosted by criminals and predators diverse, including but not limited to murderers of all kinds, gang members, pedophiles, thieves and burglars, carjackers, drug traffickers, etc., many of whom do not belong in this land to begin with. They pour into the country under the guise of workers, and because the greed and corruption of this kakotopian state know no bounds, it is not willing to stop the influx of malevolent elements lest its insatiable thirst for surplus population does not obtain proper relief. This untoward obsession with what the ruling caste believes to be accommodating, "low-skilled" and docile workers, would be forthwith self-arrested had this human influx ended up in the neighborhoods of the plutocratic caste, but such eventuality will never occur on a large scale. Imprimis, the security state would remove them by all and any means necessary; secondly, these masses are already properly lectured by publicly funded lawyers and an extensive net of supporting organizations with respect to the places where they can and cannot appear. The neighborhoods of working people are within reach; the neighborhoods of the master caste and all its satellite castes are out of bounds for all and any activities, peaceful or otherwise.

For it is indisputable, in deontological terms, that a homeless man is a tragedy and an intolerable failure; and an army of homeless men is a full-blown holocaust. But this is not so as an object, but as a subject. Inasmuch as we can only qualify those facts from within a particular state, the predication must a fortiori be subjective. Thus, in the liberal state, where pauperism is a trivial consequence of a capitalist mode of production and a necessary condition for the reproduction, expansion and concentration of capital in as few hands as possible, it will never be considered a national self-obliteration by the power castes; indeed, they could not care less. Whereas in the AFWS, each and every homeless man, American and immigrant alike, is a cell of an organism; and therefore when that cell becomes infected or corrupted, the entire system is in crisis and an intervention springs up deep within for the purpose of stopping the contamination and restoring the body to a healthy status. A man living in abject poverty is an infected cell. The state must step in to correct the situation by any and all means necessary. But prior to this stage, the moral state must develop the legal framework and articulate the policies that make such a contingency highly unlikely in the first place.

It is obvious that any attempt to envision what these laws and policies mean within the paradigm of the liberal outgrowth is futile. Only an organic state, based and articulated according to the ideary of the AFWP, can possibly dream up and enact the measures necessary for the preemption or, in the worst-case scenario, solution of pauperism. This problem, although economic and political in nature, as we have seen, has ultimately a component of personal responsibility and will, which are inextricably intertwined with the personal responsibilities and wills of every other member of the community. Within our organic state, we are all interconnected in countless and very deep interrelations that are promoted and reinforced by the political action of the state, and thus we are all in a genuine sense responsible to one another as our brothers' keepers, not as a mere banal trope, but as a matter of undeniable fact.

It is in this context that those in the jaws of pauperism or heading down the path toward it, have the moral and political responsibility to do everything in their power to avoid or solve the problem, or at least cooperate with their brethren to achieve that outcome. This practically means that the state has the right and deontological duty to resort to all and any legal means necessary to restore the health to the body politic by restoring the health to the individual man, and no resistance will be tolerated under any circumstances. Ultimately, the solution to pauperism will have to lean on work, discipline and brutal force if necessary, with reprogramming, mental health interventions and a lot of love. The ever-so-powerful mechanisms of the state will be put to use with indomitable force in the unrelenting pursuit of the health and restoration of independence and strength of each and every worker until pauperism will be no more, as a social infection which will be forevermore vanquished.

I have touched hitherto upon pauperism as a function of the creation of an adequate surplus population as a prerequisite for the reproduction, expansion and ultimately concentration of capital (money-capital, productive-capital and commodity-capital), as it transitions from one phase to the next in the circulating process. However, this is not by any means the only and perhaps not even the most important factor in the creation of a homeless population. The moral decay of the body politic itself, as a reflection of a corrupt and criminal state and a consequence thereof, is beyond peradventure a more determinant factor. Regarding this tragedy, I can point out two very concrete manifestations:

1. The illegal drug market;

2. The indifferent attitude toward mental health issues by the state and the people at large.

1. This issue is concomitantly linked to the self- obliteration

of the country's borders, or what we could term the deliberate infection of the body politic as a social organism. The domestic consumption of illegal, toxic and self-destructive drugs is a glaring example of a deontologically illegitimate kakistocracy willing to resort to the utter obliteration of its own people, so the capital in the hands of the donor caste expands and concentrates as fast as possible. In fact, the destruction of our own borders for the sake of the plutocratic caste is the driving force behind the surge in the influx of illegal drugs produced overseas and imported into the country, aided and abetted by the criminal and psychopathic political and bureaucratic castes. Hence the market gets flooded with an ever-increasing supply, thereby the prices become more and more affordable for most. Furthermore, the state produces contradictory dicta as to the acceptability of consumption itself, and eventually the barriers to entry as a consumer are altogether dynamited. Therefore, in the new equilibrium, the numbers of consumers skyrocket. Many of them, catastrophically for the body politic generally, are minors, young children in many cases. Their lives are sacrificed at the altar of psychopathy and greed, never to be acknowledged by the propaganda apparatus, let alone keened over and mourned. Consequently, this is an instantiation of a state that sacrifices its own body politic to protect the interests of the usufructuary caste, and yet it is supposed to be called "democratic"!

Drug consumption is not only conducive to death and marginality, but it is also one of the leading causes of pauperism. Some brethren trapped in the maws of addiction will show a will to thrive stifled to the bare minimum and turned into a desperate gasp for mere survival, one day at a time. It is a crime and a catastrophe of obscene proportions, with the acquiescence of a people too broken and disempowered to even pretend to care; a field of guilt lying fallow, only to be fruitful again after the layer of scum is washed away by the crimson offering of our compatriots and compeers, and more importantly of our enemies.

2. Another gross manifestation of the sheer contempt of the ruling caste for our workers is the utter indifference to the degradation of their mental health, especially flagrant in cases of conditions that render the individual practically unaware situationally or behaviorally. The callous rejection of all interest or responsibility has only been made acceptable to the people through massive efforts of indoctrination and propaganda. This flagrantly sinful attitude notwithstanding, there is a red line never to be crossed. If the paupers suffering from these crippling conditions dare to venture into the neighborhoods of proprietors, upper-echelon functionaries or donors, the security state will scramble as many assets as necessary to restore the situation to a pleasant status by any and all means necessary, since in this ailing state the law is just another name for their will. Such status, as my readers are well aware, guarantees the expedient removal of the doomed from those rosy streets. After all, that is only logical, democratic and fair, as has been irrefutably proven ... somewhere by somebody; a great liberal thinker and writer, I have been told.

    The bane of mental disorders must be tackled in a comprehensive way by a state deontologically responsible and politically judgmatic. All states heretofore, the liberal one as well as all of its nemeses, have arrantly failed to properly address, let alone solve, this most devastating personal, social, and therefore political malaise. It will take creativity, engagement, raw power and the will to succeed. Ultimately we will be the only hope but the surest chance that the discarded by this malevolent state as the weakest (albeit economically necessary) subcaste will ever have.

An additional characteristic of this mental health aspect of pauperism, and a feature that showcases how complicated the problem is, and hence how a liberal solution to it is unattainable, would be its very nature. For indeed, if we delve deep into the specific causes and reasons for homelessness on individual bases, we encounter a bewildering circle of destruction, where the dividing line between cause and effect appear blurred, especially when the victim has been living through that hell for a long time. In fact, mental health seems to be the cause at the beginning of the cycle, only to become the effect later on, or vice versa. In other words, it is very challenging to ascribe a determinate role to mental health issues in the causal process of becoming and staying a pauper. I wonder if those mental conditions are the egg or the chicken, and disturbingly they seem to swap roles over time, perhaps even back and forth, on an individual basis. It is undoubtedly a daunting challenge that a fraudulent state, even in a less depraved stage of development than the present one, would be assuredly incapable of taking on.

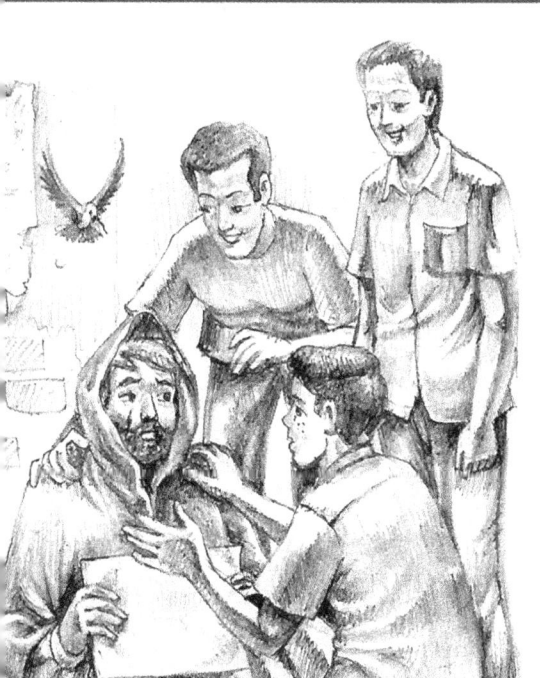

The holocausts of the unborn and the foresaken no more:
Logically and deontologically, life above everything else.

Finally, there is another subtle utilization of homelessness by the state. It serves as a conspicuous and ostensive clue of an otherwise veiled threat, foisted upon those who might be refractorily inclined to resist a life of submission to the liberal idol of wagslave labor. For few sights can impress a more indelible seal in the pliable minds of the youth than an emaciated and mucky pauper trudging aimlessly through those cacophonous streets in the Babels of the liberal anathema, where green is no longer the color of life but the bitter hue of barren dreams.

Hereupon I proceed to enunciate the party principle of life. This is our will:

◆———————◆

70. Nineteenth founding principle: life as one of the maximums in the hierarchy of value; abandonment and death only deontologically admissible if thus determined in an organic court of law

"In connection with the holocausts of the unborn and the forsaken, or abortion and homelessness, the AFWS will never engage in the aiding and abetting the obliteration of any being endowed naturally and organically with human genes, unless such a being is found guilty of a crime deserving capital punishment. The state must come to that determination in a court of law through regular proceedings, as per the principles, mechanisms and institutions set forth by the AFWP. This founding principle of the right to life, is an ineluctable consequence of the deontological and logical nature of the organic state, and of our unbreakable will to instantiate that nature in every case, under any and all possible circumstances."

71. Hierarchy, continuity, and movement: the deciphers of every principle and political action in the National Liberextremist State

I can now move on to the next and last founding principle, that which will elucidate the practical implications of the organic nature of the AFWS, as it pertains to the impact of the state's political actions on our compatriots and compeers' lives. I will call this principle the principle of the trinity of hierarchy (or order), continuity (or consistency) and movement (or change).

We have fancied and understood, the lack of any precedent notwithstanding, the quiddity of our organic state. Political being qua political being, paraphrasing classic metaphysicians, is one thing; a different thing altogether is the comprehension of the effects of such being on the body politic. I have expatiated upon what the different principles of the AFWP entail, in praxis, from the perspective of the organic state's political action, legislation and overall deontological obligations and the dutiful execution thereof. However, I have not fleshed out the undercurrent of such praxis, or in other words, the axiomatic, ubiquitous force common to all those principles and political instantiations. Indeed, all the precedent principles and the implications in terms of legislation and political action have a common denominator. It is the actuation of social will through the state upon a logical inference. I will word this inference thus:

If the state is truly organic insofar as it is the intension of the body politic, or conversely if those two entities functionally intertwined share the same quiddity as I already explained ere this section; then it stands to reason that order, consistency and change must be features of both systems. In fact, any organic being, nay! let us say more broadly anything whatsoever alive (whether those heathens understand the difference or not) must contain these three fixtures.

Order is indispensable for life because it is a sine qua non for function, and life is a fortiori functional, otherwise it would not be. This is a truism based on sempiternal induction—which is a matter of faith, but nevertheless with a very strong record. Furthermore, function is always a reflection of a certain order, as is always the instantiation of an algorithm, normally one such that involves information or the first-order reason for the logos. Therefore, we have logically deduced that order is part of life, part of the body politic as the extension of the state.

And even though order does not necessarily imply hierarchy, the opposite is a valid proposition. The paradigm of a state without a hierarchy (and yet ordered), is an anarchist state. Such state is only an ideological mirage, an outlier so unstable that it never came to exist despite the underlying philosophy being around for many generations. That being said, I will not use this fact to inductively infer that its non-existence is a logical conclusion, since such a fallacious trap could be very well used against us as time goes by. I will shortly give specific examples of the application of this principle by the state, and how it relates to the other two principles that I am about to discuss.

Consistency: this concomitant feature of all living organisms is predicated upon set theory and propositional calculus. Interestingly enough, logic and set theory are the synthetic sources of the theory of numbers and generally of all mathematics.

Anything that is alive is contained within itself, and therefore each and every part of it and all its internal relationships are likewise part of it as a unit, i.e., as an element in a set that is the only element of another set. Therefore they must present the same basic functional characteristics or otherwise we would be in the presence of an internal contradiction or, even worse, a contrary internal state which is the signature of a nonbeing. This means, in praxis, that every single conglomerate, section, cell or particle whatever, no matter how big or small, has to be functionally integrated in the whole of the body in question, and show the same fundamental characteristics and behavioral patterns. It also means, by the principle of compactness, that no element in that set, no matter how insignificantly small, can vary from the aforementioned rule because otherwise it would not belong to the set under consideration. When it comes to the body politic and the organic state itself, this rule means that every person, or conglomerate of persons considered as such by virtue of any common denominator, whether a behavior or a characteristic, can be different but not be in contradiction or be the contrary of any other person or conglomerate. Such a difference would have to be acknowledged and treated appropriately by the state through the law or political action, which are the mechanisms wherewith the state interacts with its people.

To sum it all up, in an organic state, it is impossible to be treated unequally under the law, in such a way that the personal situation relative to everybody else after the state's intervention becomes any better or any worse, factoring in the contributions of each individual to the totality of the body politic, which is the conglomerate of relations of each cell with one another in an organism. Consequently, we have a continuum of equal treatment under the law in terms of the situation of every worker relative to everybody else after the instantiation of policy has taken place.

This principle turns out to be very consequential: the action of the state in every case and upon every particular member of the body politic must always and without exception guarantee the equal distribution of rewards and punishments relative to the initial situation, ceteris paribus all the personal contributions to the community, or the body politic. This is tantamount not to equal application of the law, but to an equal protection of relative situations under the law after factoring in personal contributions to the body politic, or the mass of our compatriots and compeers. I will give hereinafter specific examples of how in order to carry out this most logical principle, equal treatment under the law will prompt unequal application of the law and specific laws for specific groups, given the multifarious personal contributions to the body politic.

Change (or movement): anything alive is in a permanent state of change or movement, whether within or without. In fact, anything whatsoever, organic or not, material or immaterial, seems to snub any sense of static equilibrium or repose. This will be profusely investigated in another work. For now, let us concentrate on the implications of this most puzzling law of apparent reality on the body politic and its internal interrelations within the cocoon of the organic state. This state, as the intension of its people (as the people are the extension of the state), needs to follow their flow and not be in opposition or contradiction to it. Furthermore, its contribution to the flow needs to be positive and reinforcing, since the state and the body politic share the same quiddity and ultimately, in the most refined and elevated version, are one and the same. The phalanxes of workers are the state and this in turn manifests itself through them. This reinforcing mechanism of a flow that is essentially constant movement or change as is the nature of life, is at the heart of many party principles and hence it will be the linchpin of the AFWS political actions and legislation. Out of the three fundamental principles informing and orienting, and serving as the logical framework of the set of concrete instantiations of political action and law, this is the easiest to understand.

72. Examples of principles and policies as applications of the logical deciphers

For example, it is self-evident that the principle that informs the constant rotation of my fellow workers through the offices and agencies of the state, and the consequent elimination of the functionary and bureaucratic castes, is precisely this principle of movement or change. By the same token, the justice system where the same logician attends to the service of both parties in a litigation, even when the state itself is one of them, is a substantiation of the validity of this principle. For it is self-explanatory that the logician at the center of the proceedings is constantly moving from one role to the next, back and forth, in a continuous process of metamorphosis.

And what about the principle of eugenics? This is a consequence of the principle of continuity and the principle or hierarchy or order. I will proceed to explain how this is the case. Those who are naturally endowed with the blessings of an extraordinary intelligence, or an outstanding will to live up to the demands of virtue ethics, or physical attributes which make them capable of performing at a level above and beyond what is considered normal; all these people offer through countless instantiations, an output of positive contributions to the body politic whereby they are situated above the rest in a hierarchy not quite of personal value, but of social value instead.

If the state is to recognize and enforce that natural, organic hierarchy (order) it must accordingly requite that special population so as to maximize its numbers and hence reinforce the rippling effects of their influence throughout the body politic. The only way to do so is to make sure everybody is treated equally under the law once the individual contributions to the community have been factored in, which means financial incentives for the begetting of more ne plus ultra, in a relentless pursuit of that supra-man, the cell of our future, most unprecedented race. This is obviously a case of a special law applied to a special group of compatriots, so as to guarantee that their relative situation compared with other compeers is just, once their unique contributions have been taken into account. Unequal application to guarantee equal net treatment. This is therefore an instantiation of the principle of continuity as well as of order.

Another example to elucidate is the differentiation of instantiated maximums (fourteenth principle). This is a another direct application of the principle of order and the principle of continuity. Order, because we hierarchically categorize every crime and exact different punishments based on that hierarchy; and continuity, because we make sure the subset of extreme cases is not reduced to a single element but rather the uniqueness of every crime is preserved and recognized and thus punished accordingly and differently.

Our conceptualization of the blood as a cleansing agent is an application of the principle of continuity and movement or change. Indeed, the negative value assigned by the body politic to a man based upon his criminal actions should not be a permanent stain except in certain extreme cases already discussed; it should be, however, expunged from his life and his record so his existential flow and with it the flow of the whole community continues on unimpeded, rather than allowing an indelible scar of pain and shame stagnate the individual and the social organism. This is a quite self-explanatory application of the principle of movement. However, this requires a sacrifice that only the shedding of blood or that most mystic fluid version of the flesh can render. The amount of it, naturally, is proportional to the severity of the crime or crimes to be wiped out. This is also an application of the principle of continuity as I have defined it, insofar as no two different crimes are cleansed with the same amount of blood, so all instantiations of wrongdoing are differentiated and justly requited.

Another telling example of how these three rosetta stones explain not only founding principles, but very specific state policies, is the case of traffic fines. Fines and deterring mulcts must be proportional to the relative financial situation of the lawbreaker and must be applied on a case-by-case basis (principle of continuity). If the infraction is committed by a fellow worker while holding office, the punishment must be increased accordingly to his hierarchical responsibilities ceteris paribus, for the exemplary conduct of those carrying out the business of the state on a rotatory basis is paramount to its organic nature (principle of hierarchy). Finally, the fine on every singular violator is adjusted as time goes by according to the change in his relative situation within the body politic and his hierarchical responsibilities therein (principle of movement).

And we also can apply this triad in the actuation of new laws or policies at the behest of particular subsets of compeers. This is certainly important in order to exert justice into schemes of virtue signaling and avoid situations where those who influence the state through its democratic mechanisms, in order to implement policies with significant associated costs or even unintended consequences, are nevertheless the least affected by those very policies they propose. For example, if the people through the democratic institutions of the state, decide to implement policies to address real or imaginary problems like climate change and its implications, then the AFWS will make certain that all the people in the body politic, organically and therefore without exceptions whatsoever, are equally bearing the burden of the costs and unintended consequences of such policies. In the AFWS, obscenely rich compatriots who advocate for energy policies that make workers much poorer and less free in the current kakotopia, will be made equal bearers, ceteris paribus, of the policies and legislations they themselves were instrumental in passing—in the hypothetical case that enough workers are persuaded to continue the support of those or similar laws and political actions through the democratic mechanisms of the organic state.

In other words, the drivers of public opinion, insofar as it results in new legislation or political action through the institutions of the AFWS, will join the ranks of the bearers in experiencing the costs and unintended consequences of such policies. In plain English, the idiom that best describes this application of the triad hierarchy, continuity and movement is "put one's money where one's mouth is". Forsooth the wisdom condensed in the corpus of idioms and aphorisms of any given language, including ours, is an inexhaustible source of light which only fools ignore or belittle at their own peril. Indeed, all the follies and wickedness of this kakotopia have a corresponding set of delectable adages which best describe them and denounce them; no doubt the collective wisdom of a people built through the ages is much better suited to impugn the character of this atrocious state than all the dreadful professors of political science and political philosophy who waste space and air in those laughable colleges and universities. I surmise they are too preoccupied with pleasing their donors (for sadly all those departments are very much dependent on large private donations and endowments), and acting as the apologetic stooges for the system they leech off. That or a drab regurgitation ad nauseam of Marx's anachronistic political fancies. At least the Prussian philosopher and political economist had something to say whereas these torpid characters can only half digest other people's ideas.

◆━━━━━◆

73. Rationing

This is a extreme, although sometimes unavoidable, form of social sacrifice and deserves a brief commentary. This mechanism is the last resort in many crisis situations. It resembles, to a certain degree, the idea of a mulct that must be proportional to the transgressor's means, in order to actuate the same level of punishment across the board. However, the ways a punishment and a sacrifice are carried out should be very different. A punishment is a causally generated, post-factum concept tied up to a concrete offense; therefore in order to be fair and effective, it should guarantee that the relative position of all offenders to one another remains the same after it has been actuated. A sacrifice, on the other hand, is a concept of a very different nature, although on the surface similar. A sacrifice is a causally generating, ante-factum concept, dependent upon the bearer's evaluation of his own feelings and ratiocinative conclusions. Hence, a sacrifice must be, a fortiori, applied absolutely and equally, irrespective of relative conditions; it hereby becomes just and effective.

I presently hark back to rationing. This is the quintessential form of material sacrifice. And let us now focus on rationing effected by the state. This kind of rationing is brought about either by the alteration of quantities or of prices in the market's equilibrium. As I already explained, the only rational and moral kind of rationing has to be absolutely applied. That entails that the only acceptable form of true rationing must be based on quantities and not on prices or a hybrid thereof. Historically, states at war, when forced to ration foodstuffs and other valuable products, generally speaking, resorted to ration cards and not price-altering mechanisms such as sales taxes or excises. The reason is self-explanatory, insofar as the whole scheme is considered an instantiation of national sacrifice forced upon the nation by hard realities of production and market availability.

This historical perspective should forthwith prompt all readers to pause and reflect on this issue, as it pertains to the anti-climate-change policies that are being used nowadays and those which are being considered for enactment in a near future. For if climate change is a life-or-death struggle, as the liberal behemoth purports it to be (and I am not denying neither endorsing the premise because I really do not know), it follows that the body politic must sacrifice in order to win that war. All the cells of the national tissue must be equal bearers, absolutely speaking, of that sacrifice realized in the instantiation of this or that policy. That implies a rationing (carbon foot print) that must be actuated through absolute personal amounts of consumption; in other words, quantity over price, or a card over prices or trading schemes.

If the ruling caste were serious about this issue, they would be setting up a mechanism whereby all the people without exception and equally across the body politic, would be sacrificing the same by consuming the same. Why should a rich man be entitled to the use of a private jet just because he can pay an extra fee or other tax on a flight without much detriment to his well-being or living standards, whereas the worker must pay ever-increasing excises on fuel which could thrust him even deeper into financial hardship or even poverty? Both, rich and poor, should be allowed to consume the same, to produce the same carbon footprint, to democratically sacrifice the same, if we are to talk about a holy war (as the rulers seem to frame this issue) on climate change, and offer up a justly devised national hecatomb. Otherwise we behold a raw, cynical display of virtue signaling and humbug; another scam to make workers poorer, weaker and more compliant.

The same reasoning applies to policies implemented in the corporate sphere. Cap and trade is an example of those. It is a hybrid of quantity and price. Any time the price dimension is introduced in the design of a rationing policy, it will redound only to the benefit of the unfair and likely the ineffective. In fact, the possibility of trading for profit the difference between an actual carbon footprint and a cap will induce the capitalist who is buying the carbon credit to devise additional schemes to cut labor costs without decreasing surplus product, as a means to fund the unmet forced reduction in emissions. For if those reductions were free, everybody would be doing the same and the mechanism of cap and trade would collapse unto itself, which is not happening. As always, of course, in the dreary field of liberal capitalism, every new, brilliant idea is forevermore manured with the unsung flood of unpaid sweat.

I could proceed on to make apparent the connections between the three linchpin principles and the totality of the AFWP ideary, but this exercise would not superinduce anything of value to the already clearly established logical inferences. I will, however, remind my readers that all the party principles can be logically deduced from three axioms (casteless state, logical labor and absolute ante-inference self-defense).

74. The casteless state deciphered by movement and continuity

The casteless state is brought about by the principles of movement and continuity. Movement, because a caste system is by definition a system without fluidity between those subsets within the body politic. And continuity, because a caste system is a system where the elements of the set (castes), do not contain elements belonging to each other;

in other words, a system that is an organization and not an organism; a system without the compactness of an organic state, without a body politic whose components are multifarious and multifaceted, in constant democratic interrelations with one another.

◄———————►

75. Logical labor deciphered by order and continuity

Logical labor is a direct consequence of the principles of order and continuity. Order, because all the members of the body politic are arranged in negotiation units incorporating the employer and the workers in every company and industry. Continuity, because the equilibrium is reached as the offers from the employer gradually increase and the demands from the employees gradually decrease to a point where the minimum marginal utility of continuing operations for the former coincides with the maximum marginal wage-value for the latter; indeed, the interest of one transitions into the interest of the other and vice versa, in a continuum of values guaranteed by the structure and inner workings of the institution of logical labor itself.

◄———————►

76. Absolute ante-inference self-defense deciphered by order and movement

Finally, absolute ante-inference self-defense stems from the principles of order and movement. Order, because life and liberty are placed at the absolute zenith of any hierarchy of value within the AFWS, for without them justice, respect and prosperity cannot be realized. And movement or change because the flow of justified actions are by virtue of this institution, unhindered by fear of the state.

It is therefore our will that:

＊＊＊

77. Twentieth founding principle: the deciphering principle of the trinity, viz. hierarchy, continuity, and movement

"All three founding axioms and therefore all nineteen founding principles, plus each and every political action of the state as an actuation of the AFWP ideary, can be logically inferred from these three distinguishing hallmarks of a body politic within an intensional state."

And in this manner, as always logically and not ideologically, I bring to a close the enumeration, definition and explication of the party principles.

I NOW COMMENCE THE CONCLUSION OF THIS WORK, ORDERLY EXPOUNDING THE REASONS FOR A STATE TO EXIST AND THE SOURCES OF ITS LEGITIMACY; WHY THIS LIBERAL STATE DOES NOT MEET THE CRITERIA; HOW WE CAN GO ABOUT THE SLAYING OF THE DRAGON; AND FINALLY A BRIEF ACCOUNT OF HOW THE ORGANIC STATE IS NOT ONLY A VERSION OF A LEGITIMATE STATE, BUT LOGICALLY THE ONLY POSSIBLE VERSION.

78. The reasons for any state to exist: ontological and of moral logic

1. Ontological reason:

A state is not, in the literal sense of the word, phenom-enologically speaking, an alive organic being. Therefore its existence cannot be a natural or unalienable right, as per the definition of those adjectives. It logically follows that that existence and continuity are not a given nor a sine qua non for the homeostasis of the body politic. The state is not concomitantly functional, but only contingently functional. Hence its legitimacy and right to exist must necessarily be predicated on its deontological performance, which is the only measure of functionality of any state, for beyond that function it is indeed an empty although burdensome carcass.

2. Reason of moral logic:

I will explain this reason in the context of the laissez-faire state, or anyway a self-proclaimed "democratic" state. This argument is fundamentally logical although it is anchored in a presupposition that is squarely moral, and it is the assumption that the state should live up to the same legal standards that the people at large are subjected to. Generally speaking, the rejection of such premise is not overtly supported by most liberal apologists, out of shame, I suppose. Having said that, it is not a proposition per se deeply ingrained in the ethos of this caste-driven state, practically speaking of its ruling and accessory castes, for they are never ashamed of anything.

The argument runs thus:

If the people have unalienable rights, by definition not dependent upon the state's rubric, there logically follows a hierarchy of value that integrates all the rights of the people and the state, with the natural rights of the people at the acme of the pyramid of value. Since the people's natural rights are not dependent upon the state, but the state's rights are dependent upon the support or acquiescence of the people, at least in a democratic state, that relative relation of value needs to be maintained constantly. Let us suppose now that a man commits a heinous crime (say, murder) and he is tried, found guilty and sentenced to death. Let us now suppose that the state breaks the law, as always to benefit the usufructuary caste at the expense of the nation, and it fails to uphold its deontological duties, thereby some person dies.

In this scenario, we have a man whose right to life has been taken away by the state, but the state's right to exist has not been taken away by the people even though its law-breaking conduct has yielded the same outcome: the death of a fellow worker. In this situation, the hierarchy of value encompassing the unalienable rights of the people and the political rights of the state has been upended and disrupted. In fact, it has been turned upside down, literally reversed. Now, the rights of the body politic and the state have switched places in the hierarchy. But the causality of this inversion is not logical neither moral. Indeed, it is de facto based on nothing. Or should I say it is based on the unquenchable thirst, both illogical and immoral in the strictest sense, of the liberal state to outlast its own people.

⟿————————⟸

79. The mark of the liberal beast

And this is precisely the mark of the beast: a shameless and uncontrollable desire to survive its own people.

An organic state is such that the virtue ethics of the people are harmonious with the deontological duties of the state, as expressed by political actions and legislation. Unfortunately, that synergy is altogether lacking and cannot be possible today due to the parasitic and refractory nature of this state. This fact, as I herein mentioned ad nauseam, is the reason why the ruling and managerial castes constantly and outwardly express despicable levels of disdain and scorn for the very workers who make them rich and politically powerful, just because our compeers might have some ideas, attitudes or values that the unproductive castes do not approve of.

Only biological entities are necessary for life, and this truism needs no explanation. Therefore the legitimacy of the state is contingent upon its functionality insofar as the interconnections within the body politic are instantiated at least partly through political functions. The organic state, as the future offspring of the AFWP and its platform, is the apogee of deontological and political functionality, and thus conducive to the personal and social self-realization and Jungian individuation of our people; whereas the babelic state, lacking the legitimacy, inevitably has to resort to brute force to survive its people. Rather than being one with the people, it is one despite and above the people.

As time goes by, and because of the philosophical malformation that it is (and as history has proven abundantly), the state will progressively decay ethically and politically, as its very existence will become gradually intolerable for most fellow compatriots. Rest assured that its desperation to survive at the expense of us workers will grow more unhinged. It will stoop to levels of repression and criminality far above and beyond those that it has already reached, in order to stifle and arrest any attempt at radical evolution or revolution. All legal protections of the people will be systematically assaulted and diluted, all laws brazenly broken, thuggery and violence against the phalanxes of workers carried out covertly and overtly by the security state; and the propaganda and indoctrination machines will stop at nothing in order to smear and break the reputations and the will of the people.

◈━━━━━━━◈

80. Extensive list of deontological self-obliterations in the liberal state; socialization of costs and privatization of gains

This draconian future is not menacingly lurking in a close or distant future, but it is already rearing its foul face right now. For what is the meaning of a FISA Court, but a secret and criminal enterprise in the business of trampling the rights of real or perceived political enemies of the state? Or the fast eradication of habeas corpus as we become aware of people detained and imprisoned for months or even years without a trial, because of political activities considered subversive? Or the political, social and legal harassment of those who dare to question military interventions overseas or sweeping surveillance operations at home on fellow compatriots? Or the colluding with social media platforms and traditional outlets in order to stifle, deceive, suppress or warp people's perceptions of reality? The list of criminal enterprises this hegemon engages in for spurious motives, both at home and abroad, and the disturbing plethora of repressive tools it wields against any compeer who dares to challenge such practices, are very telling of the nature and character of the mastodon which we will be, soon enough I hope, facing off.

Its degeneration and decomposition is so overt, even by its own philosophically corrupted standards, that the very excuse for its genesis is being violated and stamped out in plain sight. I am referring to property rights and the enforcement of commercial contracts.

Both are being crushed unceremoniously when the state allows riots to burn through worker neighborhoods in the name of the last empty buzzword, or when shutdowns compelled by brute force wipe out or severely damage the small business fabric of the body politic, and evidently on purpose, much to the delight of corporate America or, in other words, those actuating the expansion and concentration of capital in fewer and fewer hands. Or when small landowners and ranchers along the southern border impotently behold the marching of entire caravans of foreign nationals across their properties, aided and abetted by the government itself, and without delving any deeper into the destruction and deterioration that such crossings cause on those lands.

An illustration of how remiss the state is in enforcing the basic tenets of legitimate commerce as long as that negligence redounds to the benefit of the donor caste, is the curious case observed in air travel. Airline tickets, unless purchased under the protection of expensive insurance (not always available), could be theoretically cancelled by the carrier without paying out a penalty, even if those tickets are bought months in advance. Most customers are not aware of the nuances of these types of contracts. They think they have entered a regular purchase/sale agreement whereby the purchaser pays an amount for a ticket; this in turn becomes effectively his property and it is redeemable on a certain date and under certain conditions as per the clauses printed in it, unless that buyer decides not to use it for whatever reason, forfeiting any reimbursement in the process.

However this is not quite what happens or what is potentially allowed to happen. In fact, an airline can reverse itself after it receives the money from the customer, on the basis that it "sold" more tickets than the actual number of available seats on that particular date. This is called "overbooking" and it is legal, in principle to make allowance for the idiosyncrasies characteristic of this particular line of business. However, what the airline companies do in many instances is much more deleterious to the customer than that. In reality, they pass off an auction as a sale and call it "overbooking". In other words, the airline or sometimes a broker auctions off tickets, so if someone comes along and offers up more than what the ticket had already been sold for to somebody else, they take it back by cancelling the trip on the "cheaper" buyer. That should not be called overbooking since the cancellation is based on price and not on the initial date of purchase. These companies misrepresent the nature of the contracts because otherwise many workers would choose to skip the game altogether if they knew beforehand how unprotected they stand. This misleading way of doing business should be illegal because it is unethical. It is not true commerce because a sale is not a protracted auction. To make things worse, the initial purchaser only gets back the amount he paid for the ticket, without accrued interest and therefore the real value is eaten away by inflation. Indeed, the airline is the beneficiary of that money, receiving the interest accrued while giving absolutely nothing in return, even though the airline itself was the party that cancelled the agreement. This practice showcases all the hallmarks of a scam, and none of a legitimate commercial exchange. It is a sham aided and abetted by the state itself by allowing it to be legal, and therefore becoming a co-conspirator in the swindle.

Another instantiation of the liberal state collapsing unto itself in plain sight would be the selection of corrupt knaves at the service of foreign nations, some even non compos mentis and enfeebled withal, as the figureheads of the state, while the propaganda machine and the political caste lauds them as virile leaders full of stamina and intellectual prowess and moral compass. Rome is burning before our very eyes, and yet the scaramouches keep on playing the lyre, in an akelarre of insanity which will be undoubtedly studied for centuries to come.

Yet another example was rendered by the state when it turned away anybody, including world-renowned athletes, trying to fly in unvaccinated for COVID-19 while contemporaneously, quite literally, ushering in millions of undocumented fellow workers and others through the border, also unvaccinated and in many cases infected, and supplying them with cell phones, money and legal assistance to boot.

Or the blatant, obscene and criminal self-enrichment of politicians and bureaucrats in all branches of government through the mechanisms already discussed earlier in this work.

Or the disturbing conspiracies of terror and lies perpetrated by the security apparatus so as to prompt a permanent state of war demanded by the donor caste, in order to keep unhindered the expansion and accumulation of capital.

About this I have already expounded sufficiently when addressing the concept of just war and the associated party principle.

Or the startling schemes to socialize costs and privatize gains. This is a poignantly important issue and two conspicuous examples thereof are generally national debt and specifically immigration.

As I already explained ad nauseam, national debt is generated by deficit spending and unfunded liabilities, which from the usufructuary caste's point of view materialize in the form of massive public contracts. In addition, this illegitimate caste profits from the bankruptcy of the state even further, through the acquisition of interest-bearing bonds to finance that debt. In other words, the plutocracy leeches off the state profiting from its debt in two different ways: firstly, it is the beneficiary of the debt's cause; secondly, it is the beneficiary of the debt's consequences. Conversely, the phalanxes of workers are only left with beggarly and bankrupt social programs and with inflation, which is the concomitant effect of an expansion in the monetary supply that is not predicated on a corresponding increase in national output. This is the analogy of the brothel, where the state is the house, the clients are those in the master caste and the workers are the harlots. The patrons have it all for cheap while the exploited only get the ravaging diseases and the illusion of a living. Tragically, that is what the liberal state is at its core: the brothel that exploits and sullies every compeer throughout his entire working life until there is nothing left to steal!

All what we have laid out about national debt generally

can be said about immigration specifically through its impact on the budget via social and welfare programs. Wherefore the usufructuary caste benefits from legal and illegal immigration through the budgetary process and from the acquisition of government bonds. However, immigration is a phenomenon with huge socioeconomic implications, and the reverberations thereof with regard to socialization of costs and privatization of gains through the illegitimate political actions of the state are difficult to overestimate. The spirit of those political actions revolves around the notion of an immigrant as a docile source of cheap labor. To begin with, the increase in the labor supply will, ceteris paribus, result in a reduction of wages in the macroeconomic equilibrium to such an extent that many compeers will be expelled from the realm of productive activity altogether (or what the liberal demons call "labor market"). This intended consequence, or what this state's lying apologists call unintended consequence, is a prime example of a simultaneous privatization of gains and socialization of damages. Furthermore, the opportunity costs that stem from a mass of workers further impoverished and ostracized in their own country are impossible to model or estimate, given the disparate and large amount of variables involved. Those costs manifest themselves as a catastrophic effect on the social cohesiveness and the cultural stability of the nation, and thus the long-term viability of the state itself. For it is the hallmark of any enduring state to possess a certain measure of propinquity in its body politic, as history and reason unequivocally inform us.

I could hopelessly attempt to compile a comprehensive list of deontological failures and betrayals but I will save the readers the monotony of such a depressing exercise. Having said that, a good rule of thumb to assess a state's deontological soundness and legitimacy or lack thereof is to simply remind ourselves of the old biblical maxim: "Every tree that does not bear good fruit is cut down and thrown into the fire. Therefore by their fruits you will know them." If a state is desultory in the way it holds criminals accountable, and yet punctilious to a maddening degree in its castigation and penalization of minor infractions and misdemeanors—wrecking havoc throughout the body politic in the process—perpetrated by members of the exploited caste, then we know we are being subjugated by an illegitimate state.

However, a very special class of nefarious activities needs to be singled out and properly addressed. It is, in fact, and to a certain extent, the most important class to talk about. The reason is simple: this set is never brought up by friends and not often by the foes of the state. Therefore this is not only a critique but rather an exposé. These felonious activities could be categorized in different ways; however I will occupy myself with the two most glaring examples, which I believe will give a clear idea as to the kind of schemes I am referring to:

1. Bitcoin;

2. The victims that never were.

81. The illusion of money and Mr. Charles Sanders Peirce

Bitcoin's emergence was always a foregone conclusion, for those who understand what a currency is, anyway. Without getting entangled in unnecessary details, at the time I am writing this, Bitcoin is not a currency nor is it money, even though it is being called both by most "experts". But it is certainly a token capable of being used as a means of exchange and even a repository of wealth. Bitcoin was the attempt by the security apparatus to get ahead of the curve in anticipating the demise of the American dollar as a reserve currency of the world first, and subsequently as a viable national currency. As the national debt expanded, over the last decades, at an accelerated clip far beyond the productive capabilities of the national economy to service that ever-increasing debt over the long haul, it became macroeconomically evident that this currency was being rendered a social construct by virtue of its own debasement in excess of what was productively affordable.

In other words, the viability of this currency became a matter of a shared conviction, a matter of faith. Not enough for the security state to feel comfortable about the whole shebang, though. Therefore it is, as I already said, a foregone conclusion that the security state, to a great extent attending to its job description, anticipated the upcoming monetary disaster by creating a currency ex nihilo or rather out of microchips, which could be used as the conduit for a new currency and a financial reset. And there was also built into that operation an additional, priceless advantage: the state would be yet again the source, engineer and master of the new currency and would be able to exert even a greater level of control and dominion over the people, since Bitcoin itself is nothing more than a mere digital contraption, without the freedom of use that an actual physical currency allows, with notes and coins that can be used in commerce unobserved by the state and beyond its knowledge or acquiescence. On the contrary, as everybody understands by now, I hope, he who needs to log in to exist, can be logged out of existence by a score of others, the most ominous of those others being the liberal colossus itself.

But let us now analyze this issue really closely, and let us eventually draw from the renowned logician Charles Sanders Peirce.

If the state foresaw the demise of the U.S. dollar, and if it considered such an occurrence at some point inevitable, it stands to reason that it could not remain a passive bystander, since its survival is contingent upon the survival of the currency itself or the existence of a viable alternative. I already stated and proved that the mark of this beast is its unquenchable desire to survive, no matter the cost, even at the expense of its own people, without restraint whatsoever. It is therefore a logical conclusion from the generating axioms and the above propositions plus modus ponens that the state did indeed have to create an alternative, viable and controllable currency; a new currency with the superinduced benefit of keeping its origin secret and thereby all its users in the dark as to the identity of its master. As a result, most Bitcoin holders effectively believe that they are ushering in a new era of freedom from government while in fact they are becoming its very accessories.

And there is another purpose not to be underestimated: a new digital currency created and controlled by the state's security apparatus is the most perfect means to fund covert, illegal operations at home and overseas; after all, it is the ideal medium because of the impossibility of oversight by virtue of its very mysterious genesis. More about this when I address the next topic.

But if our syllogistic conclusion is invalid or wrong, who created Bitcoin, or who or what was the fountainhead of all cryptocurrencies?

History tells us that an individual or group of individuals under the pseudonym Satoshi Nakamoto, back in 2008–09 (interestingly enough in the middle of a massive financial and real estate crash), invented this digital instrument. The real identities of the person or persons who knocked over the first domino were never discovered or in any event publicized. We are supposed to believe that the state and its security agencies allowed a rival to the U.S. dollar to be invented and digitally traded, to a large extent using the American currency; a currency which was employed effectively to monetize its own incipient competitor—a competing currency, may I add, which is in principle not controlled by the U.S. government and cannot be printed at will by it. This notion, from a financial, if not a national security perspective, is so preposterous that the mere acceptance of it as a possibility, let alone as the official explanation, incenses me to the highest degree.

Now the entire logical sequence becomes suddenly self-apparent when we recognize the state, through its intelligence agencies, as the creator of that currency. This would explain the quite overt cooperation of the state to the establishment of that cryptocurrency and its use as a means of exchange and a legitimate and legal investment. It would also explain the fact that neither the state nor any other organization or individual for that matter have ever disclosed the real identity of Satoshi Nakamoto. And even though Bitcoin is arguably used in a myriad of criminal activities and illegal transactions, the state seems to be strangely tolerant of its existence, in addition to be instrumental to its launching and establishment. And yet, academia, corporate media, the state itself and every possible actor in this farce pretends the official version contains in it some trace of logic. It does not ....

And speaking of logic, let us now go back to Peirce's law. This is a law in propositional calculus, to the extent that it cannot be derived directly from the axioms for the connective material implication and modus ponens. It does not hold in intuitionistic logic though, but that is indeed an irrelevant fact for the kind of reasoning I am about to engage in. Peirce's law states that a proposition P must be true if there is a proposition Q such that the truth of P is logically deduced from the truth of "if P then Q". Now, let P be "the state invented Bitcoin", and let Q be "the state increases its financial resources". According to the law, ((if P then Q) then P) then P. The first "then" is straightforward. If the state invents Bitcoin it has indeed access to a pool of new digital reserves. And the truth value of ((if P then Q) then P) is factually derived from the nature of the state itself. As I already explained and demonstrated, the state lives only to perpetuate itself by all means necessary, and to that end financial resources, as abundant as possible, are a must. Therefore the second connective is explicated and by virtue of the law the premise "the state invents Bitcoin" becomes irrefutably valid and factual.

This deduction of propositional calculus is more generic that it first appears to be, inasmuch as it is relevant to a multitude of other situations. We only have to consider the dystopian colossus as quintessentially the parasitic entity that feeds off its people, its host, to the extent that the thriving or even the survival of the body politic is not even part of any of the state's considerations. By now, empirically as well as theoretically speaking, this premise has been proven at great length. And with it, the middle connector becomes factually true and Peirce's law can be straightforwardly applied.

And on this topic I have a word of caution. It is a matter of course that the state discloses to the general public new military technologies, generally decades after they were first developed, tested and deployed. But the reason is never transparency. The simple truth is that those technologies are made public once they have become superannuated and are substituted by other technologies, again kept secret for decades. This will not be the case with Bitcoin, since it will not be phased out but very much the contrary, as the U.S. dollar continues its course down the path of degradation and debasement. The illegitimate mastodon will never admit to its role in the invention of Bitcoin or any other digital currency for that matter. Such an admission would defeat simultaneously both purposes above discussed.

So finally, who or what is Mr Satoshi Nakamoto? My guess is that it is the name of a tucked away room full of supercomputers, somewhere in a dark nook at the CIA or NSA headquarters, perhaps with a plaque on the threshold that sardonically reads: "The illusion of money was created here".

<hr>

82. The victims who never were

This kind of felonious activity is connected with the covert creation of the original cryptocurrency insofar as the security state needs black money to carry out illegal, criminal activities. Those funds are the perfect means inasmuch as the operations they fund are secret and remain so due to the nature of the holdings themselves. And it is because of this frightening aspect that I call the victims "those who never were". In this regard, the occurrence of an event with social or political implications is only relevant as long as somebody in the sphere of its influence or interest finds out about it. If something, anything whatsoever with a political dimension, is not noised about to some extent, it becomes a nonevent. An event with a social or political dimension happens not when it is instantiated, but only when its instantiation becomes public domain. The people will never be privy to information pertaining to the crimes committed by the state, but we certainly can infer their nature and extent based upon the snippets of information that by and by come out in the form of unexpected leaks, investigative journalism (rarely) and Congressional hearings and declassification of sensitive information (even more rarely).

We can surmise thus, that the state's involvement in assassinations at home and abroad; electoral fraud domestically and internationally; illegal detentions and kidnappings with the intention of extracting information by force and torture; the toppling of unwanted regimes through extortion, bribery and other means; widespread, illegal in most cases and unnuanced surveillance and spying programs targeting Americans and foreigners alike, both in the U.S. and all over the world; the suppression of freedom of speech and other natural rights; and schemes for the destruction of critics' reputations with the connivance of social media platforms and corporate media generally, are indeed the baleful business of this state.

A subset within this set is particularly pernicious insofar as it cannot only change reality, but it can also warp the perception of reality whether any change in the phenomenological world is instantiated or not. I am referring to brainwashing technologies applied on a massive scale through the internet and the shadow banning of any website or link deemed an enemy of the state. Regarding the former, the truth is we do not know to what extent those technologies have been developed over the last decades, but I conjecture that that development is huge, for two reasons. Firstly, the technological quantum leap with the creation of the internet, which obviously could multiply the effects of any psychological operations by an order of magnitude, as "information" is now readily available at our fingertips. Secondly, the suspicious fact that the security apparatus never talks about these issues anymore. Decades ago, it was not strange to hear and read about them, brought forth by former agents or investigative journalists. But this kind of subject matter has dwindled to a trickle, when for the first reason mentioned (the internet) they should swell to a flood. With respect to shadow banning, since social media companies and internet providers are, in praxis, one and the same with the state, it follows that it is happening as a matter of course, along with other less deleterious forms of censorship; and it will all get much worse as the beast tries to stave off the rising tide of social, cultural, economic and political discontent. Any and all critics of the state will be targeted and thus the state will assay to conceal the existence of our AFWP from the people.

The readers do have to come to grips with the following fact, which quite often gets overlooked in a mire of confusion and propagandistic shibboleths: very few, if any, of the activities above described are legal, not to mention moral on any grounds. The state does not engage in those criminal activities for the sake of the people, but for its own sake and the continuation of the agencies involved, and to protect the interests of the donor caste. The state's motivations are illegitimate; its means illegal; and the consequences catastrophic for the body politic at large. And they are catastrophic in two different ways: first, the targets directly destroyed are the cells of this or some other body politic, and to that extent unique and irreplaceable. Secondly, the actuation and propagation of crime by the state, and the passive or even active acquiescence by the people are an act of utter self-debasement; indeed a brand of shame only to be blotted out by the timely shedding of guilty blood.

All the nefarious actions described above may or may not go unnoticed by the mass of our workers, depending on a quite large number of somehow uncontrollable factors.

But a particularly heinous crime is the assassination today of perfectly anonymous compeers so they do not become beacon of inspiration, resistance and revolution tomorrow. Idiomatically, we would call this "nipping the problem in the bud". It makes me shiver in horror to imagine how many of our compatriots have been murdered before they get to fully develop their messages, unbeknownst to the whole of the people. Political assassinations masqueraded as accidents or the outcome of random crime are very difficult to uncover; indeed, who is going to suspect otherwise, since the victim is not quite his future version yet? In this day and age, the surveillance state possesses all the technological tools to figure out who will pose a threat in the future; we all should assume our communications, no matter the medium or the content, are being criminally collected and analyzed, and potential future dangers assessed. For the least disruptive victims are those who never existed in the first place, hence I call them the victims who never were. And I hope my mission catches on fast enough so as to render my belonging to the roster of the done before they ever were an impossibility; and yet, I am that missionary open and ready for any sacrifice.

In view of the monstrosity we are immersed in, not to mention the gargantuan challenge that lies ahead of us if we free workers of America are to unchain ourselves from this Frankenstein of a state, one feels almost resentful of past generations because they lacked the wisdom, the courage and perchance the foresight to understand that the yoke of this state would become eventually too taxing and tyrannical on the organic fabric of the nation. But wait! Am I maybe passing too harsh of a judgment on all previous generations? If that were the case, they would surely have left a clue or a hint as to how aware they were of the ogre they themselves and all after them were condemned to live under ….

⊲▬▬▬▬▬▬◁

83. That curious paradox: the Bill of Rights

Yes, precisely so: the Bill of Rights. The first generation of Americans, the Founders of this state themselves, left written record of how terrified they were of the abomination they were creating. The Bill of Rights, for most jurists, historians, politicians, apologists and just about everybody belonging to some of the privileged, propping castes in the liberal Babel, is an unparalleled and divinely inspired document in the most literal sense. In reality, it is just a makeshift legal document indited without sufficient exhaustiveness, and that is why for centuries it has been at the center of countless legal disputes involving its interpretation. But that is totally irrelevant to me. What I find fascinating is its logical nature.

The Bill of Rights, in the context of the Constitution of the United States, is a paradox. It is a subset laid out to protect the people from the state that its complement subset within the totality of the set (Constitution) was creating. It is an act of pure logical schizophrenia. If the Founders thought the state that the Constitution was establishing was so abominable that they needed a ten point clause to protect the people from the dastardly anathema, why did they plow ahead and create that state in the first place? Would it not have been more rational to figure out another kind of state; one wherein a legal document designed to hobble the Goliath in order to protect the people had not been necessary? Were those gentlemen so lackluster that they only were capable of fancying a state so ill-conceived that its turning against the people was a given? And if they thought so lowly of themselves and their Constitution, why did they believe that the Bill of Rights, a subset therein, was any better? And if they thought so, why not extend the spirit of the Bill of Rights to the rest of the document or set, so as to render those ten provisions an unnecessary bulwark?

As I already explained much earlier in this work, the Founders were educated and generally intelligent and rational, but hardly imaginative and rather invested in very mundane issues, like property rights and the like. The mess they created, in logical terms, speaks for itself.

So going back to the two reasons for a state to exist, or the sources of its legitimacy, I have concluded that this liberal state is illegitimate and should not exist. For in fact its stubborn rejection of deontological duties and its refusal to be held accountable by the same standards its people have to live up to, are the ontological, moral and logical proof of its fatal inadequacy.

84. The in terrorem buckles and swords of the Goliath state

This 18th-century invention is in the last stages of its life, or it appears to be, as I already expounded on, based upon its overt refusal to uphold the principles and deontological duties that it was purportedly founded upon. Since there is no such a thing as a natural right of a state to exist, but only a natural right of the person and the people to live, the state does not have the protection of an inherent right to justify its survival beyond its reaching a point of utter uselessness to the body politic. It all becomes a matter of figuring out the means and methods wherewith this paramount overcoming will be achieved.

Unfortunately, as I already profusely elaborated earlier, the state has reached that developmental stage whereat it is willing and capable to stoop to the most base actions in order to prevail over its people, no matter the cost. This has to be very carefully considered in the devising of any strategy of demolition, not just because of the need to minimize our chance of defeat, but also to minimize the casualties even in our likely victory.

But how much does the state fear its own people? The answer is, quite literally, codified into law. And it has been a fixture of our legal system for so long that its very existence has been ignored by the whole of the people, or just passed off as something quite normal, when in fact, it is not. As already stated ad nauseam, the state, unless an illegitimate one, exists only by being the intension of the body politic, as this is the extension of the state. In praxis, it is not more than the mere substantiation of the means of political action by the people. The state, if legitimate, cannot be more than a tool in the hands of its master, the active agent, the people. It makes no sense for a tool to impose restrictions on its usage or lack thereof, or under what circumstances and conditions that usage should be manifested. Only a laissez-faire dystopia and its infected nemeses could possibly conceive of such a sick framework.

Of course, in its defense, the apologists for this kakistocracy claim that bills are written out and signed into law by holders of different offices democratically elected by the people. But is that the case? Workers are effectively shut out of the process because it is too expensive to run for public office, and only members of privileged castes or those willing to sell out to different subsets within the donor caste ("special interests" as they are commonly called), can raise the wherewithal to run a winning campaign. Furthermore, the candidates who finally make it to the ballot are always selected internally (and not quite elected) through all kinds of maneuvers and corrupt subterfuges—involving large amounts of money and propaganda campaigns within the parties whereto their only political loyalty belongs. Finally, the idea of a fair and accurate tallying of the votes is truly a silly notion unless all the candidates in the race are equally staunch supporters of the national security state. If they shamelessly admit (as is already on the public record) to stealing elections abroad, no question they are already subjecting the American people to the same criminal activity, so much so when it is here at home from where the sources of their financial and operational powers emanate.

Peirce's law and the understanding of the nature of the state to unlock the second connective in that formula ought to be heeded by everybody. Professional politicians themselves, every now and then, spill the beans on the intelligence apparatus of the terror state. We have heard characters like that express misgivings (even on national television) about the numberless ways those agencies can completely destroy your life if you oppose their bureaucratic interests in earnest. One can only wonder to what extent those wretches are compromised and held as political hostages through blackmail. The worst speculation is likely to fall short of reality, as surely as this state's ignominy knows no limits.

But what are exactly those in terrorem laws that I was referring to? They are many indeed, but those most relevant to our cause are the statutes against "rebellion or insurrection" (§2383), "seditious conspiracy" (§2384) and "advocating overthrow of government" (§2385). All of them function as both a thuggish intimidation and as a means of destruction of entire segments of the organic political fabric, if they ever try to hold the state accountable for its failure to become legitimate and therefore worthy of existence.

(&2384) reads: "If two or more persons ... conspire to overthrow, put down, or to destroy by force the Government of the United States, or to levy war against them, or to oppose by force the authority thereof, or by force to prevent, hinder, or delay the execution of any law of the United States, or by force to seize, take, or possess any property of the United States ... they shall each be fined not more than $20,000 or imprisoned not more than twenty years, or both."

Notice that under this statute, the state has become a seditious conspirator against itself, by virtue of it refusing to uphold its own laws when politically expedient; for example, immigration laws at the border (including violent acts against state troopers when these try to step in to enforce the law), or the obliteration of habeas corpus when the detained are deemed enemies of the regime. As already explained, a politically schizophrenic state, or in other words a state that refuses to uphold its own laws, or a state that does not hold itself to the same standards, legal and otherwise, that its people are forced to live up to, is a state that has outlived any trace of legitimacy to exist if it ever had one. This statute, in fact, corroborates my statements. A jurist, however, would argue that the subject before the considered predicate, is "If two or more persons ..." and the state does not belong to that class. Thereto I broach the state's condition of political schizophrenia by virtue of its not upholding itself to the same standards and obligations to which it subjects all its people. Either way, this statue implies that the state is either seditious against itself , or at a minimum schizophrenic; in any event, illegitimate.

(§2385) reads: "Whoever knowingly or willfully advocates, abets, advises, or teaches the duty, necessity, desirability, or propriety of overthrowing or destroying any government in the United States ... by force or violence ... or Whoever, with intent to cause the overthrow or destruction ... prints, publishes, edits, issues, circulates, sells, distributes, or publicly displays any written or printed matter advocating, advising, or teaching, the duty, necessity, desirability, or propriety of overthrowing or destroying any government in the United States by force or violence; or becomes or is a member, or affiliates with, any such society, group, assembly of persons, knowing the purpose thereof ... Shall be fined not more than $20,000 or imprisoned not more than twenty years, or both, and shall be ineligible for employment by the United States or any department or agency thereof, for the five years next following his conviction ...."

Now, this statute is fascinating on many different fronts. Firstly, it is, yet again, a testament to how poorly cobbled together the Bill of Rights is, and how ineffective it is at its purported goal, namely to defend the people from an illegitimate state's encroachments. For example, how can the state determine unequivocally the difference between literal speech and artistic manifestation? Does not that entail the omniscient interpretation of one's motives and mental processes? How can speech be equated to action? How can advocating for a revolution be the selfsame as acting it out? This state itself was born out of a violent revolution. By the standard set forth in this statute, is the state illegitimate? Were the Founders criminals? Many pamphlets and all sorts of periodicals were printed, published and distributed before and during the American Revolutionary War. Were those authors miscreants committing felonies? Or are we saying, perhaps, that the merit of a statute is not predicated on the morality or the logic of the propositions therein, but only on the political interests of the state behind it? Alas! And we are supposed to call such a state legitimate? Or believe that it has any kind of moral high ground whatsoever, in its relations to its own people or with foreign nations?

I suppose, in truth, that under this statute I myself could be regarded as somebody "advocating overthrow of government" by virtue of writing and publishing this book. We shall see ....

And what about that hazy concept of "violence" following the word "force"? Why make a distinction between the two? Is speech itself, even when not advocating for a forceful overthrowing, an act of violence? Who sets the limit as to what words and phrases are admissible and what are not? Is the state thus the judge, jury and executioner of the propriety of words? Is not the so-called "hate speech" considered "violence" by the state, even though it is not, generally speaking, concerned with the overthrowing of the government? Methinks that the state, under this statute, could potentially, at will, deem any adversarial speech an act of advocating overthrow of government. Yay! Don't we adore this "liberal democracy"!

---

85. Anybody could be a target

It is the statute "Rebellion or Insurrection" (§2383) that is the most sterling example of the aforementioned mark of the beast, and an irrefutable proof of the appropriateness of the unbounded fear that the Founders had of their own abortive creation. Indeed, in this statute, the schizophrenic hegemon forgoes any pretense of respect for the First Amendment and straightforwardly lumps together actions with opinions of any kind, no matter how mild or ineffectual they might be.

Under this statute, anybody who expresses (in the public arena so there are witnesses) any kind of sympathetic or positive view or feeling whatsoever about others who might have been directly involved in actions considered by the state as rebellious, is himself deemed an enemy of the state.

In fact, this statute alone makes this state, even by liberal standards, radically repressive compared with most in Western Europe, for example. Furthermore, it is even extreme in a historical sense, because it shows a level of hostility toward speech comparable to many of its nemeses, namely national socialists, bolsheviks and fascists back in the 1920s and 1930s. It is evidently a manifestation of a state being aware of its own inadequacies and illegitimate condition, and the enduring fear of its own people; a state cognizant of its being out of lockstep with the body politic and its ethos.

I believe, indeed without a shadow of a doubt, that the vast majority of the people are oblivious to how utterly vulnerable they are to legal action based solely on public manifestations or opinions given, for example, in the form of written posts on different social media outlets. Theoretically, if the state chooses to destroy anybody's life—and it will do so if the bureaucrats and politicians in the babelic mastodon believe it is in their interest or the donor caste's interest—anybody can be subjected to criminal prosecution over any kind of unconventional political post, no matter how restrained or inconsequential. That persecution will occur if the state categorizes you as an enemy based upon your social and cultural influence, irrespective of the manifested idea or opinion itself. The latter will be only used as a pretext for your incarceration or financial ruin (this "justice system" is unaffordable for most workers), or both.

Let us now bask in the thuggery of this statute, shall we?

(§2383) reads thus: "Whoever incites, sets on foot, assists, or engages in any rebellion or insurrection against the authority of the United States or the laws thereof, or gives aid or comfort thereto, shall be fined not more than $10,000 or imprisoned not more than ten years, or both; and shall be incapable of holding any office under the United States."

It does not take a logician or a linguist to spot right away the problem with this wording. The terms "incites", "assists", and "gives aid or comfort" are so arrantly vague and pliable, and the list of possible actions or behaviors included so massively extensive both in nature and intensity, that anybody for just about anything could be targeted. Evidently, this atrocious provision is phrased in such ambiguous terms by design, because the bigger the equivocation, the sharper the blade of the tyrant. An extensive analysis of equivocation was procured when I introduced the party principle of life.

As an example of the unrestrained scattershot approach that this statute represents, and how the state could use it as a weapon to wield against any critic, I will bring up again the issue of a nationwide general strike. This kind of activity has never happened in America. However, in many Western European countries, it has been a fixture of their socioeconomic and political landscapes from the mid-to-late 19th century onward. In the U.S., the state has all the tools for forcible repression, in most cases brutally so. Furthermore, the infiltration of the security-state agents into the upper echelons of the traditional, politicized trade unions, has made unfeasible the carrying out of that kind of labor protest. Another wrench in the works is the lack of true political action at the behest of the worker caste within this partitocratic kakistocracy. Within that political caste, so-called "leftists", "progressives" or "socialists" have diligently headed off any and all attempts to strike nationwide and across sectors, either by ignoring the disputes altogether, raising alternative issues to spat about, or simply offering themselves, explicitly or implicitly, as brokers or temperers so as to thwart and sabotage the workers' efforts.

America only knows, historically, the meaning of local sector strikes, quasi-nationwide sector strikes, or local general strikes, and the instances of those have been few and far between. The repression of the state has been so ruthless and barbarous, through the deployment of police forces and the National Guard and the ensuing savagery, that I regard the injection of fear in the heart of the phalanxes of workers as a deliberate long-term strategy. Nowadays, the political caste along with the state media, the national security state and the faux unions shilling for corporate America and the donor caste, in a multifaceted approach, are all conspiring to forestall any kind of consequential syndicalist action.

In this backdrop, what would happen to anybody advocating publicly for nationwide general strikes, the kind we have never had in our country? At first, nothing. If he increases his clout over the people and a following starts to emerge, for instance through a successful presence on social media, then all the boorish weight of the liberal mastodon will soon enough come down on the compeer. The tools used vary, but one much preferred by the ruling caste is a devious onslaught through legal warfare, also called lawfare. One such weapon in the massive state arsenal is this wicked statute, whereby the critics can be accused of aiding or inciting an action tantamount to a rebellion, insofar as the state considers itself in danger of collapsing economically or logistically and therefore possibly politically, as a result of this kind of syndicalist measure.

Indeed, different strikes have been already declared illegal by many administrations in the past, always citing the dangers to "national security", meaning, of course, the financial interests of the caste that owns the political apparatus of the state and fraudulently exploits it. Furthermore, entire sets of workers are prohibited from striking; for who is going to be the bully if the bully goes on a strike? Who is going to protect the interests of the ruling caste then? Given the aversion that prima facie the illegitimate caste members have for guns and their general inability to carry their own water, the answer to that question is problematic. I suppose they would have to resort to armies of privately funded bruisers (as has been the case throughout our history), but why spend your own money when everything can be given to you on the workers' overtaxed dime? You just need the right law in place and voilà, "democracy" is once again saved from the people!

I very well know that the majority of compatriots are not aware that this kind of nightmarish scenario has already happened. As I write these lines, people who wrote disparaging and humorous posts on social media toying with the idea of a fraudulent electoral process (nefarious activities that have been exposed and even corroborated from within and without, time and again, as something in the purview of the national security apparatus) have been indicted, prosecuted and convicted of being "foreign agents" or "insurrectionists", or even of "sowing discord". It is a foregone conclusion from the premises: a state where judges are nothing but an extension of the partitocracy; a legal framework so flawed, so malleable that anybody can be indicted for anything any time; and a ruling caste single-mindedly fixated on its survival at the expense of the people, no matter the cost (the mark of this beast).

There are many other statutes in the penal code meant as a bulwark between the people and the privileged castes, those who run and are the usufructuaries of the state. Generally speaking, those provisions are geared toward the disempowerment of the workers so they are rendered politically disabled. To that effect, all kinds of draconian restrictions on small political associations and parties are enacted, so as to prevent them from ever becoming an actual threat to the system. Few Americans know how difficult it is for an association of free workers to found a new political party. The ruling caste is so afraid of independent political action that untoward restrictions and legal and financial requirements are shamelessly put in place so as to ensure that the barriers to entry for new political organizations are a burden too cumbersome to bear. The twin 200-year-old dinosaurs that articulate this partitocracy certainly have a tight grip on the system, and they are allowed by the ruling caste to exert that ironclad control over the political process because they have proved themselves useful at leveraging the state for the benefit of their masters. They have also shown a very uncanny capacity to keep the masses of workers distracted on tangential issues. As long as they continue to adroitly reticulate the phalanxes of workers without unnecessary upheavals or disruptions, they will be allowed to run this kakotopia. If they let up, they will certainly be swapped out for other mafias better suited for the task at hand. I do not expect such a contingency to happen, though. Those two growths will be by and by extirpated, but it will not be the decision of the billionaire caste.

However, as a side note, suffer me to point out something which is irksome, but also exciting and pleasant, all at once. And this is the increasing rate whereat the privileged castes are panicking and fearing the people. This malaise is best measured and described by one of its primal symptoms, namely the incessant efforts of the political caste and the security state to disarm the mass of workers. The imposition of new extreme rules and regulations on the day-to-day operations of gun clubs, hunting clubs and militias diverse is a glaring example; the evident goal is to impede the learning of shooting skills. Another one is the hysterical targeting of specific weapons reckoned especially dangerous in case of rebellion or widespread revolts. Yet another trick is the assault on people's rights indirectly, by straining the availability of ammunition for purchase, or by artificially driving its prices up through additional fees and taxes and the wasteful bulk acquisition by the state itself through a host of agencies and departments. Having said that, any spiral down the path of complete and overt tyranny by this liberal dystopia is an opportunity and a tool that our party will not squander; more on this later.

86. Treading lightly on the tightrope

It is now the time, after my explication and analysis of what this state is and is not; of its nature, goals and reason of being; of whence it came and where it appears to head; and to what extremes it will go in order to survive its own people, that I must venture onto the slippery rope of the funambulist, for I believe that is the perfect metaphor for the exercise I am about to engage in, so help me God.

Let me commence, shamelessly, by calling the disclaimer on the copyright page the first gingerly step onto the proverbial tightrope. And although I started out being cautious and mindful of the dangers, and I henceforth intend to stay that way, the rope is by design greased up to an antidemocratic extreme, and so the chances for this rope to become the chrysalis where righteous action turns into sacrificial token, are certainly real.

Let me also draw the attention to the aforementioned mark of the beast, or the unmitigated drive of the state to survive its own people, no matter the cost. A concept, I may add, tantamount to a rebellion or an insurrection of the state against its only source of legitimacy and authority, namely the upholding of deontological duties for the profit of its raison d'être and master, the body politic. It is reminiscent of the fallen angels who turned against God and refused to be what they were supposed to, thereby relinquishing their right to exist, or at least exist in Grace.

87. The sling of David: lessons from an unequal battle

Unfortunately, compatriots and compeers, we are not God. We cannot cast out miscreants, or easily dethrone tyrants and break free from the shackles of an illegitimate state. Once upon a time, all that was possible, at a bloody price. At the just price. However, the turpitude and torpidity of vast swaths of our body politic, for reasons sufficiently scrutinized in this work, and the vast conglomerate of powers and resources at this state's command, unprecedented in human history, make the face-off of David and Goliath seem evenly matched by comparison. If it were possible, I would confront the laissez-faire state with its past actions when in its infancy it had to contend with the king's armies, and I would try to demand explanations for its hypocrisy in view of all those in terrorem statutes. However, I respect myself too much to fall prey to such a gross display of tu quoque, so I will relinquish that line of attack instead, no matter how desperate I am to bury the saber somewhere in this beast.

David triumphed in the end. But he did it through a cunning blend of adroitness and boldness: he did it on his own terms. David knew Goliath very well, he knew exactly how to strike and precisely where, for he could not have overcome the behemoth on the latter terms. The blood ran freely only when the battle was over. The analogy is so self-evident that I do not feel the need to go further into the Biblical story.

However, unlike Goliath, this caste-driven state is very flexible in its approach to internecine conflict because it does not follow its own rules; it is unpredictable in its quest for survival as it parasitizes and obliterates, if required, its own workers. And this is why the struggle of David and Goliath was not as daunting as that between this state and its body politic. When it comes to this foe, we can expect the un-expected, the paradoxical appearance of that statement notwithstanding.

It is for all the above reasons that a violent rebellion or insurrection would never be successful and therefore I vehe-mently reject it. Moreover, that kind of political activity would be enthusiastically welcomed (although such emotion never publicly displayed for propaganda reasons) by the steward castes of the state, since it would be the perfect excuse to crack down on its enemies and identify all those who were only heretofore "thought criminals". It would also give the state the chance to become even more authoritarian and it would chalk it all up to the need to "save democracy" or "fight radicalism". These dithyrambic slogans work quite well on a population subjected for decades to a barrage of propaganda and indoctrination tools, and primed for that kind of catechistic shibboleth.

Moreover, let us not forget that not only the ends, but minimizing the cost of the means, should be the lodestar of the AFWP in its march toward the AFWS. For us, the lives of the righteous and the innocent are so precious that their value in and of itself and as cells of the organic state cannot be measured; we know that they are the pinnacle of irreplaceability.

◆━━━━━◆

88. The means of perdition

What are those means, then?

The birth and the demise of a state are quintessentially causal. This is due to the fact that at a minimum, when the state is not organic but merely a political structure lording over the people as the liberal state is wont, the body politic is always the extension of the state. That is why the state cannot exist without a people, but a people can certainly exist without a state, as history has amply shown. The body politic, taken as a complex fabric of individuals (the state's cells) and their interrelations under the jurisdiction of the state, is literally an organic entity. I will leave the ontological details of this explanation for another work, but everything organic is causal, because it is always at the crossroads of information and function, instantiated by genetics and environment. That information and function have causality built in is a truism that nobody can deny. Hence the major milestones in a state's history, are, a fortiori, causal. On the other hand, the phenomenology of inert objects, for example, may be very well explained by classic mechanics; however it is still contingent because we only can answer the question "what" and not the question "why". The conflating of both questions has led countless atheist scientists astray in their interpretation of reality as we perceive it, but this is a subject matter for a prospective work.

Conversely, and on a side note, if the state is organic, in other words, not only is the body politic the extension of the state but also the state is the intension of the body politic—when the two entities are functionally interrelating and share the same quiddity—then that state's vicissitudes are causal as well, even more so than those of the babelic state.

So I have now concluded not only that this state's founding was causal, but its demise will be so too, and the source thereof will be the people themselves. Not other people or exogenous agents or circumstances; but our own people.

The keen reader no doubt is wondering how I can possibly make such an assertion if countless states throughout history have perished as a result of foreign invasions. Whereto I respond that every single successful invasion is predicated upon a decaying state because of a body politic already rotting away. This decadence impregnates the ethos of the time, and it is an infallible harbinger of calamity.

Furthermore, this principle of the ultimate endogenous cause of a state's destruction does not apply only to foreign invasions, but to any kind of exogenous influence that could potentially bring about the dissolution of a state. Indeed, whether it is a natural disaster of gargantuan proportions (think of a megathrust earthquake, or a deadly epidemic, or a super-volcano eruption, etc.) or an economic crash that originated abroad, or an immigration overflow that stretch-es the fabric of the body politic to the breaking point, or any other force strong enough to make the vessel of the state keel over, suddenly or in stages; the body politic is always the determinant factor in the fate of a state. If the body politic is corrupted and its ethos distorted, then the state (whether liberal or organic) is poised to be wiped out by any of the banes I have just mentioned or by those that I have not. If, alternatively, the people are healthy and strong, within and without, the state will endure. To summarize it, any state that collapses under the weight of an exogenous force does so because its body politic, the conduit of that external force and therefore the true endogenous cause, is too debilitated to survive. Hence, any state that disappears deserves its lot. Functionally speaking, it did not deserve to go on.

However, our goal is to overcome this state once and for all and usher in a new era characterized by the existence of a political intension. Regrettably, this body politic has been parasitized by the liberal Leviathan for such a long time that it has become enfeebled and thus an unreliable agent of fracture.

And this is the conundrum we are facing: the need and the desire to shake off the leech but lacking the strength to do so. It is bleeding us dry as we become ever weaker, and we know any exogenous eventuality with the power to obliterate this state will do so by obliterating us too in the process, as the ultimate cause of the state demise is always its people. Besides, in our case the situation is particularly pernicious, since this parasite is remarkably adept, even by liberal standards, at surviving its own organic extension no matter the cost.

⊷————————⊶

89. Aristotle's clue

It is imperative that I interject a commentary about the causal nature of the state. And I sure need a helping hand at this hour of teetering and tribulation on the tightrope. Who could I possibly turn to, so I can regain the composure and balance to walk as steadfastly as the mission requires? I am sure that old friend, Aristotle, would pitch in if he were asked. But just in case I will not ask and I will forthwith proceed to enlist his services instead. For I already stated that conscription is far superior to a volunteer military system, if organic the state must be.

The state is causal in four different dimensions, as I herein stated. Finally, it is a plutocracy; formally, it is a partitocracy; efficiently, it is a kakistocracy; and materially, it is the extension of the state itself, the people (enfeebled and domesticated to a large degree at this stage in the process of liberal decomposition). The first cause is utterly out of the worker's bounds. We cannot touch the usufructuary caste in any way, shape or form. The second cause, which roughly corresponds to the political caste, is also uneath reachable. We barely can interact with them, and the power they exert is too destructive at the moment, and prone to be savagely wielded against the people in a multitude of ways if the body politic becomes too restless or inquisitive. The third cause springs from the political caste and extends downward into the bureaucratic, functionary and generally speaking propping castes. These are the foot soldiers of the state, and any direct action against them will be met with obliterating force, for without this subset of people, no political action can be actuated, thus making the appropriation of the state by the master caste an impossibility. The last and fourth cause, the material cause, is us, the people at large; the people who make the other castes rich and politically and administratively powerful; the people who are the active agents of making the reproduction, expansion, accumulation and therefore circulation of capital possible, as workers, as consumers and as taxpayers. This is the causal dimension on which we have to put all our pressure. This will be a battle to ripple out throughout the body politic, from a nucleus, or a hardcore, or innermost circle of true enlightened men. I will develop this framework in the next pages.

---

90. Of political parties in the liberal kakotopia: constructs, tools of political action, tools of reticulation, and the most effective escape valve

Before I proceed any further with this dissertation, it is both my need and my duty to draw attention now to a very crafty subterfuge employed by this kakistocracy to head off political upheavals and watershed crises within the system, emanating from widespread and deep-seated discontent. Indeed, the reasons for the founding of the classical American political parties notwithstanding (a tangential topic, but as a hint suffer me to say it is always about raw power and pelf), nowadays these parties are constructs, tools of political action, tools of reticulation and the ultimate escape valve.

- A construct in the sense that they stand for nothing except the interests of the different factions of the billionaire caste (the sole usufructuaries of the state through the illegitimate liberal system), and yet their supporters make them out to be the defenders of a disparate collage of causes, theoretically noble. Those causes are, in fact, propounded by the parties as their fundamental drives and goals, but these are just wiles. In reality, the values and objectives that they purport to defend are just the propaganda tools used by the partitocracy to wrangle the sheep and keep them in the pen bleating in contentment, while the fundamental issues affecting the whole of the ignored caste, the productive caste, the legitimate caste—those issues are unabashedly shunned, since their resolution is a direct threat to the usufructuary caste. But this has already been sufficiently referred to throughout this book.

- These parties are the tools of political action in this kakistocracy. They are the means wherewith the political caste organizes and articulates itself, and this function is self-explanatory.

- The parties are the most efficient instruments of

reticulation in the babelic behemoth, even more so than liberal capitalism itself. This is due to the mutually exclusive character of party membership and the statistical proclivity of a two-party system to split the body politic approximately down the middle, for a variety of game theory and sociological reasons amply studied and documented.

- A very interesting and novel concept is that of a valve, and at its heart a wily ploy, namely, to pass off the sins of a state as the faults of this or that political party, faction or even concrete politicians. The partitocracy that this state articulates itself through is not only the instrument to achieve nefarious goals at the behest of the usufructuary caste, but also the means by which the state itself covers its tracks. In fact, such a red herring has worked wonders over the last two centuries. For I doubt that many workers would blame the state and its nature as the root cause of our political, social, cultural, and economic troubles. They blame this or that party or politician or cluster of politicians instead. But God forbid that we question the legitimacy of the state itself, based on its founding, its goals and means, and its illegitimacy derived from the refusal to uphold basic fundamental deontological duties.

Hence, the partocracy is not only the sword of action, but also the buckler against counteraction by the legitimate caste. It is, indeed, a very sly and effective design, so much so, that it is in place not only here, but everywhere in the world where a liberal state is established. When the frustration of the people reaches intolerable peaks, risking a violent reaction against the interests of the usufructuary caste, then this buckler morphs into the escape valve of the state. It is the time for the illusion of elections, as if any of those matter to the phalanxes of workers. They do not. They never did. But the mirage is the perfect carrot, as the steam percolates safely through the escape valve and the body politic turns back into a lackluster, apathetic conglomerate of disparate groups.

This mechanism is so powerful and effective at protecting the integrity of the state from the ire and desperation of the people, that even the extremest waves of revolutionary discontent could be potentially forestalled by contemporaneously placing both wings of the partitocracy onto the sacrificial altar, whereupon the usufructuary caste could seamlessly reset the same political scheme using alternative parties. I conjecture that this is precisely the role played by minor parties in the periphery of this particracy, always perfectly funded and organized, their total lack of representation and power notwithstanding.

In conclusion, the parties as constructs keep the people sheepish and calm. The parties as the tools of political action enable the state's attacks on its already subdued people. The parties as instruments of reticulation keep the body politic fractured and thus unable to snap out of that treacherous passivity, so it cannot respond to the state's attacks. And if after all, somehow, the people muster the will to rebel, the parties as escape valves empower the state to fend off any attempt at retribution by the people, making their impetus for change fizzle out into oblivion. Requiescat in pace, you silly dreams of justice, liberty, fair economic relations and social and political respect!

And although the imperative need to rid the people of the doom of political parties was already established earlier in this book, it is now that the reasons for it have been properly elaborated. Political parties thus are an antidemocratic articulation of the state since they are the epitome of reticulation, effectuated at the behest of the different special interests and sections of the usufructuary caste. In other words, a partitocracy is always the status quo of a liberal state, wherein political action is always instantiated by political parties. Therefore, an organic democracy, the only possible democracy there is, cannot exist within a system of political parties; for they are the brazen conduit of the exploitation of the state by the usufructuary caste through the workings of the propping and privileged castes. As the borders are the integument of the state, as is the skin for a person relative to his environment, so will be the AFWP for the people relative to the dangers of antidemocratic forces. The AFWP will be the palisade which will forevermore protect the body politic from potential oppressions and retributions which will be lurking around in every corner, until we manage to stamp those evils out, God willing.

---

91. The first circle: the hardcore

Now, going back to the abolition of the caste state. In order to effectuate that riddance, a fundamental component is the exposé (by the legitimate caste's vanguard) of the role of traditional political parties as the escape valve. That would be tantamount to the identification of the state as a political problem, impossible to solve by conventional means. That vanguard of workers, that hardcore, that first nucleus of compatriots and compeers able and willing to stake a claim; that cluster of healthy cells capable of recognizing the nature of the tumor and steadfast in its resolution to confront it; those people are us, the first members and supporters of the AFWP. We will be henceforth the beacon of truth and sanity, and we will continue on patiently and unwaveringly, certain in the logical and moral character of our cause. As long as we fanatically embrace the divine and unbreakable nature of our will, the journey might be long, treacherous and rough, but the destination a foregone safe haven. We precede the critical mass from where the courage and the righteousness to take the first step onto the battlefield will emerge. We are also the cells who were strong enough to overcome the infection or were never infected in the first place. But this is not the natural state of affairs throughout the body politic. To expect otherwise is plain folly. Our initial mission is to spread the word and make our people aware and hence empowered to keep on rippling out and forward. In this first phase the goal must be radically adhered to: a constant search for those strong cells now disseminated all over the body politic, without a connection to one another, and lacking the knowledge and direction that they need to materialize their special qualities. We have to muster the army of the righteous, so they can herald the state they deserve.

92. The second circle of expansion and first subsets in the third circle

Once this is accomplished (it could be a very lengthy process), the next phase unfolds. The expansion of the circle must continue, but now the outward movement will be carried on through information, explication, expostulation, debate and persuasion. Whenever this stage is finalized, the party will be strong enough to move on to the next phase of the battle. Here, people cannot be convinced with truth and reason. They cannot be taught, they must teach themselves. These are cells very damaged by indoctrination and propaganda. They might be also those who are more gullible or with more limited ratiocinative powers; or perhaps those with recalcitrant predispositions. Finally, this circle includes those with all the attributes to belong to the precious circle of expansion, but who are overwhelmed by fear and doubt in the background, perchance, of a weakened will.

This circle of expansion is of the most critical importance because it is quantitatively the largest. As a result, once we complete its formation, the sequence of events leading up to the liberation of our people, or the death of one state and the birth of another, reaches a crescendo that culminates in a point of no return. But before I address this essential phase in our revolution, I cannot in good conscience delay any longer a commentary that no doubt will make some readers uneasy, despondent or even irked. In sooth, I consider the upcoming paragraphs hardly a surprise, in the wake of all that I have been elaborating on over the last many pages.

93. Not through orthodox means

By now, the nature of this state has been delineated and delved into as clearly as my communicative powers allow me to, and the mark of this beast amply explained. Furthermore, I have outlined straightforwardly the natures and roles of the usufructuary caste and its underlings, namely the political caste, the administrative caste and the state security apparatus. Thus, if the reader strings all the dots together, deep down the realization should not come as a surprise that our party, even if an overwhelming majority of workers ever were staunch supporters and voters, would never be allowed to "win" an election involving any kind of office whence consequential political power could be exerted. In fact, the state would most likely nip the problem in the bud, as I mentioned earlier, by shadow banning any reference to our party online and thus trying to render it nonexistent. We shall overcome this type of obliteration, and local political action unquestionably will be the genesis of the first two circles, truly the hardcore and first nucleus of this awakening. Regardless, no candidate under our banner would be allowed to run in the first place, adducing all kinds of reasons, legal or not— it is a rogue state so it does not need to abide by its own laws—or conversely, the political caste can produce as many wretched, custom-made laws as necessary in order to fend off the democratic will of the people. Yet another arrow in the state's quiver is the judiciary, which would interpret any extant statute in such a way as to thwart the democratic voice of the body politic, as long as such a voice impeded the interests of the state to outlast its people and of the ruling caste to arrogate to itself that state.

And in any event, the final guarantor of the state's survival is and will always be its most sinister and shadowy projection, the security state. This clique of liars, swindlers and psychopaths are unfixable or not retrainable. They have the criminal will and the technology to produce any result they want in an election, as they have already done and admitted to in countless electoral encroachments overseas. Here in America, our system is by design susceptible to fraud and interference. The requirement to vote in person and to show valid identification in the process is not a federal mandate, but the contrary proposition will be soon enough. This is owing to the increasingly peremptory ways of the illegitimate state in this phase of its degenerative development, presenting all kinds of overt acts of aggression against the people as faits accomplis—on account of the state's recognition that the body politic is weakened in the extreme. Besides, a vote is not treated by this kakistocracy as a contract between its cells and itself. Rather, in many jurisdictions people "vote" by hitting a key in a computer, or so we are told. I wonder why the same standard does not apply to other contracts, like the purchase of a house or a car. Would sensible people accept a flick of a finger as a reasonable way to seal commercial contracts, without a receipt or copy thereof? How could a judge possibly render any judgement involving such a contract if the "four corners" do not even exist? I am not in the business of addressing issues that are manifestly transparent, just because I feel silly doing so. Thus, I will stop the commentary on this point right here.

Moreover, fraudulently diminished returns could be mis-construed by the propaganda machine in such a way that the people would interpret the falsified data as sign of dwindling support and hence a party not worth associating themselves with.

And anyhow, no matter the political support, the AFWP would never be handed the reins of any kind of power. In fact, no party run by workers will ever be allowed any kind of partaking in the decision-making process at the levels which could make consequential difference, no matter how harmless and orthodox that party might be within the liberal paradigm. This clarification, necessary for some readers and perchance superfluous for the keenest ones, will make per-fectly clear the next links in the chain toward the longed-for death of the political Goliath and the dawning of the organic state.

So this quantitatively most critical phase in the process of liberation will yield a people yearning to become healthy after centuries of submission to a parasite state which has grown progressively stronger (and more dangerous and criminal). This has occurred by virtue of drawing vitality and morality from its host and turning these attributes into raw power for itself. Furthermore, any exogenous cause of the state's col-lapse, whether it be due to an action aforethought or a mere stochastic event, must instantiate its destruction through the conduit of the body politic, which is the endogenous cause. If the conduit, or the materializer of the instantiation, is de-cayed, the external force succeeds; if the conduit is whole-some, it fails. This puzzle will be solved and subsequently to its solution the AFWS will be brought about.

Pray note that the causal flow is straightforward:

1. The people in the third circle of expansion take stock of themselves in reference to the body politic and the state, come to understand the political disease and decide to confront it.

2. They proceed to exterminate the virus utilizing the appropriate tools, after it is thoroughly studied and its weaknesses revealed. Very often those tools are precisely the same instruments used on them by the first and second circles, but the strategies ought to remain flexible as conditions dynamically evolve over time. And this is not a lacuna in the march towards the intensional state, but rather the realization that flexibility in this ordeal is a logistic necessity derived from the colossal deviousness and strength of the enemy.

3. The state dies and concomitantly the intension of the people is politically founded.

4. David draws blood and the long-dragged-out liberal kakotopia comes to the promised end.

Strictly speaking, the third ring of expansion is composed of a multitude of successive rings, getting progressively bigger as the process unfolds, up to a point where the watershed moment is reached and the state starts to disintegrate. The first subring within the third ring of expansion is the smallest of all the subsets, and the most arduous to generate. It is formed by all those compeers and compatriots with all the aforementioned qualities of the people in the third ring, and with a specific characteristic: their levels of tolerance for discomfort and pain caused by the ineffable injustice of the state, or the "government" or the "administration" as the apologists call it, is the lowest of all the subsets within the third ring. The following subset is generated by the selfsame procedure that I will soon enough lay out, but it is larger because it is the output of three different forces: the first two rings and the first subset in the third ring. The next subset, the third within the third ring, is even larger and more decisive and so on and so forth.

But what is the generating procedure of all the subsets in the third ring?

94. The generating forces of expansion: back to the beginning

Money. What it is and is not has been profusely explicated in the first part of this work, emphasizing its one-to-one relation with work. When people lack money, or it loses its purchasing power, all other issues become irrelevant. The key to make our compeers aware of who is the culprit of their calamity will entail mechanisms wherewith the people will eventually be able to answer questions such as these: Why do politicians become so rich while in office and afterward? Why does the state implement trade and immigration policies (cheap labor at home through open borders and slave labor abroad through free trade and offshoring) that make the member-ship of the Chamber of Commerce so much richer at the ex-pense of the legitimate caste? Why does the political system require so much private money that no worker ever is able to run a successful campaign for statewide or federal offices? Why are the functionary and political castes so much bet-ter off than the workers who pay their salaries, benefits and pensions? Why is an incommensurate amount of workers' money given by the state to foreigners at home and abroad, through private and public institutions and programs, and directly to foreign governments for all kinds of spurious and irresponsible reasons, while the worker in the land is barely scraping a meager subsistence, or at any rate experiencing a permanent fall-off in their standards of living? Why is mon-ey borrowed and printed to fund programs that redound to the exclusive benefit of the donor caste, whose capital ex-pands and concentrates at the expense of the worker (first as a worker, second as a consumer, and third as a taxpayer)? Why are taxes, regulations and policies, extraordinary (like the COVID-19 shutdowns) or ordinary, invariably propitious to the expansion and concentration of capital to the detri-ment of small business owners?

Why are we never consulted about anything of conse-quence through referendums, the most democratic of instru-ments? Why do workers wonder, upon the signing of every new bill into law, how much poorer they will become and how much liberty will they have to give up? Why are we experienc-ing a decline in our lifespans relative to past generations, for first time in two hundred years? Perhaps drugs, prescription and not, both legal and illegal? Perhaps toxic food? Perhaps urban violence, poverty, despair and homelessness? Perhaps liberal ennui and loneliness to the point of suicide? Perhaps a total disconnection from the land? Perhaps wagslave labor? Perhaps the poisonous and depressing indoctrination of children in the school system? Perhaps a pervasive and perverse propaganda bombardment, from cradle to grave, which is intended to diminish the faculties and morals of the phalanxes of workers and cause reticulation, so their will to power is forestalled? Perhaps, perhaps, perhaps .... Perhaps one day enough people will wake up to the fact that the state is not the witness to the malaise, but rather its perpetrator. When enough compatriots join the ranks of all the subsets in the third circle, the process of liberation will have reached the milestone wherefrom the crimson countenance of total victory will be joyously descried in the horizon.

But I must now return to the mechanism whereby the creation of the first and subsequent subsets in the third circle of expansion will take place.

This mechanism involves the set of all social constructs erected around money. I will hereinafter develop this concept:

Every measure of an economic parameter, insofar as it is not directly derived from the world of nature as we perceive it, and when it is an aggregate so massive that we cannot enumerate, but only estimate; then we are in the presence of a statistical construct. This deduction stems directly from the presence of a certain methodology within any statistical process. Methodology is inherently, always, without exception whatever, a subjective and relative concept. In fact, the set of all possible methodologies for the measurement of a certain economic variable is an infinite set, inasmuch as the the set of real numbers is mathematically a compact set. In other words, every single time that we ascribe a particular weight to a parameter (relative to a set) through the use of a percentage, we are doctoring the quantification of the output in relation to any other possible methodology that uses a different percentage to quantify the relative weight of parameters. It is inevitable, because in any case we have to choose a relative weight, a percentage, to quantify the influence of a certain input on the total output. That choosing is immanently a subjective decision.

Inflation is the perfect example to illustrate these concepts. I have dedicated quite a lot of effort and space in this work to inflation. But in connection with the issue of a construct, the Consumer Price Index (CPI), or what the state tells us inflation is, is predicated totally upon the methodology used to compute it. This methodology was changed back in the 1990s with the goal of obtaining much lower readings. For he who decides upon the methodology of statistics controls the readings, and hence he can alter the behavior and the thoughts of the people as a reaction to them! Nowadays the CPI yields values, ceteris paribus, roughly half of what they used to be before the change was actuated. That is precisely why most workers claim they observe prices of staple goods such as foodstuffs, fuel and housing increase at a much more rapid clip than that reflected by the official inflation numbers.

In fact, if we were to design a system wherewith the inflation rate lined up with the people's perceptions of price fluctuations, thereby rendering those readings meaningful, we would have to produce different values for different sets of compeers based upon their income. Thus, people with higher incomes, when the prices of staples increase faster than the prices of luxury and discretionary goods and services, would receive a lower inflation value than compatriots with less income and vice versa—when the prices of nonessential goods and services increase at a faster pace than the staples, then the inflation pertaining to the people with higher incomes would be higher than that of compatriots with smaller incomes. A measure which is the composite of everything and everybody lumped together and weighted subjectively so as to render the lowest possible reading, is what the state calls inflation. Therefore we are in the presence of a social construct.

Furthermore, the concept of inflation itself is being warped to shocking levels. These days some economists in certain quarters are actually suggesting the notion that inflation could be the key to tame the real levels of national debt (more on this other construct is forthcoming). The mechanism would entail the generation of enough inflation through monetary and fiscal policies so as to diminish the real value of the national debt. Of course such a notion is preposterous, for inflation not only depreciates debt, but dollar-denominated assets and tax revenues; and it can damage the social fabric of a nation to the point of violent upheaval and even rebellion—a risk the babelic state cannot afford. There is no easy way out of that kind of downward spiral.

Inflation is also a very revealing clue as to how inconsequential the bulk of the people are to the usufructuary, political and managerial castes. Indeed, the policymakers focus predominantly on the so-called "core inflation", which is "headline inflation" (or overall inflation) minus the impact of food and energy prices. They claim core inflation is a more relevant metric in order to understand the health of an economy at a given moment because food and energy are notorious for fluctuating too much, potentially distorting the compound reading over the long haul. The truth is that they focus on core inflation because it is much more relevant to the assessment of future economic growth, which is absorbed almost in its entirety by the privileged castes. Conversely, headline inflation is relevant to analyze the degree of impoverishment of the population as a whole, and especially of those low-income compeers whose wages are spent to a great extent to purchase food and fuel. Hence, headline inflation is mostly ignored, and so is the most legitimate and productive caste.

What about Gross Domestic Product (GDP) growth? First of all, only the state (or the government as is improperly and conveniently called as the escape valve demands), academia and the media assign value to this variable. As I just mentioned, the reason for this is that the usufructuary caste rakes it all in for itself! When it comes to workers, the GDP, nominal or real, is irrelevant. After population growth, inflation and the overvaluation of output, of income and of expenditures in the statistical inference are factored in, it is not surprising that most workers are getting constantly poorer as the state claims we have experienced growth of 20% to 40% every decade! The laissez-faire state is single-mindedly focused on economic growth because it is a sine qua non for the expansion and concentration of capital as it is manifestly evinced by the strong correlation between the stock market and that metric.

Regarding the aforementioned stock market, it is certainly linked up to the overall health of an economy, but

unfortunately over 40% of Americans do not have the resources to invest, and another 20% of compatriots possess
very limited holdings. Altogether, these are the compeers
who make the reproduction, expansion and concentration of
capital possible by underselling their labor power as a commodity in the labor market. Since huge swaths of workers do
not have any savings to turn into investments, it comes not
as a surprise that all the centers of power within the state regard the stock market as the token of this economy's health!
This dichotomy between the reality of what that market is
and is not on the one hand, and its canonical interpretation
on the other hand, is the instantiation of yet another social
construct.

This construct, though, has very interesting dimensions.
It is the manifestation of reticulation of the body politic not
only derived from the laissez-faire mode of production but
also from the structure of the state itself. Indeed, just about
19% of the people work for local and state governments and
about 2% for the federal government, totaling roughly 21% at
the time of writing this book. Most of these compeers have
benefits and salaries decent enough to allow for savings and
investments in the stock market. Others might expect to receive pensions while the contributions are being invested in
the market by the government itself until the time of retirement. All these salaries and benefits are to a large degree
paid for by the workers qua taxpayers, most of whom do not
have any money to invest. In addition, approximately 30% of
workers toil for publicly traded companies. These workers are
for the most part remunerated well above those who work
for small and medium size companies. They are part of that
40% of people who own most of the holdings in America. The

math is not totally precise and we should not expect it to be because it is permanently fluctuating and some of the metrics and conceptualizations differ depending on the methodology used, but for the most part all the securities in the country that are not owned by the usufructuary caste, are the property of just about 50% of workers, mostly employed by large corporations (publicly traded and not) and the government, plus a thin layer of small business owners.

Our beloved America is truly a tale of two cities, or rather sets of workers, for the most part divided down the middle, reticulated to a grotesque perfection. The people who own nothing approach the labor market underselling their commodity, labor power, so the reproduction, expansion and concentration of capital takes place as this capital creates propping castes in the periphery, which guarantees that the state does not implode socially and economically, and therefore politically. This state in turn does nothing but ensure, through political action, that the weakened mass of drudges remain willing to continue the reproduction and circulation of capital as workers, consumers and taxpayers. I have nothing but contempt for Adam Smith and the rest of predators regarded in the schizophrenic Leviathan as the forefathers and heroes of liberal economics. However, his metaphor of the "invisible hand" could not have been more germane in this context. For indeed I wonder how this homeostasis of economic and political exploitation and putrefaction has endured for so long in such a stable fashion. I actually have answered my own question throughout this work, but I stand nonetheless in awe of the monster's devices. Regardless, I would like to point out that although it is true that much of this book could be considered a polemic against both liberal capitalism and Marxism, that impression needs to be predicated. My deconstruction is the consequence of my philosophy, i.e., my philosophy is the cause of my deconstruction, and not the other way around. For, as I already explained profusely, this is a movement of the positive and the new, and not a mere reaction to the negative and the old.

Let us move on now to the unemployment rate. This variable is more of a computation and less of a statistical estimate. It is, natheless, another construct, in this case actuated by the definitions and requirements to be counted in the ranks of the unemployed. Those restrictions are stringent enough as to keep the official numbers within certain pre-established acceptable bounds, much to the satisfaction of the financial markets, investors and even to the public at large, to whom all these fabricated numbers are served as political fodder. For example, anybody who refuses to accept a job that he deems inadequate given his qualifications, inclinations, financial needs, etc., is nevertheless expediently thrown off the rolls and no longer officially deemed unemployed, but he certainly is! And what about illegal immigrants? Because of their legal situation, they are not even admitted on the rolls even though it stands to reason that unemployment among this group is rife and expected, for the barriers to entry into the labor market are particularly strong for them, due to their undocumented status (plus their lack of advanced skills in many cases).

Another problem is the massive underemployment that this state chronically suffers from, to the extent that dozens of millions are considered employed and yet they live in abject poverty, often having to resort to welfare in order to feed themselves and their families. In a system of wagslave labor, the possibility of working part time and contemporaneously covering the essentials is out of the question. This massive section of the workers' phalanxes is called the "working poor" by liberal economists and I have herein already addressed this obnoxious term. In sum, this construct explains why the unemployment rate fluctuates rather wildly relative to the labor participation rate, which has been steadily declining for decades and it is expected to continue this trend over the long haul. There should be a permanent, very strong inverse correlation between those two variables but it is not the case; simply put, because the unemployment rate is not a reflection of reality but just a reflection of a random convention agreed upon by the whole of the body politic.

I will dedicate a few lines to one of the most glaring examples not only of a social construct, but even beyond that a manifestation of gross insanity. It is the national debt. This state entered a debt spiral long ago, which inevitably will morph into a currency crisis, a financial crash and a depression. The severity, duration and timeline of this bane is certainly up in the air, and there is no model that can foretell any of the above as it is a work in progress, dynamically unfolding and reinforcing itself exponentially under the surface, as all the variables involved are constantly and outside the system itself being worsened by a never-ending string of wrong decisions made by the state. So we are in the presence of a monster already on the move, endogenously growing in strength and complexity, while at the same time fed constantly and at ever-faster speeds by the state itself.

The mathematical expression of this situation is a system

of differential equations exploding in the long term, un-bounded and spiraling out of control in different directions. But to assess the approximate dynamic values of any of the parameters involved is a hopeless exercise. In plain English, the state entered a death spiral a long time ago, at that wa-tershed moment when in order to service the debt more debt and an expansion of the monetary supply were nec-essary, ceteris paribus. At such stage, strictly speaking, the state becomes technically insolvent. Thus, if all the economic and social agents remain confident or even just pretend to be confident that the state has the ability to meet its obliga-tions in the long term, the facts notwithstanding, we ought henceforth to talk about a social construct.

I shall broach now a last instantiation of a social construct within an economic context. This one is particularly infuriating because it was conceived as a trap, it is especially deleteri-ous to the well-being of workers, and in spite of the massive evidence against it, as a matter of sheepish mass delusion, it remains unchallenged, untouched and in full dysfunction-al force. I am referring to the instrument of free trade and its alleged benefits for the people at large. When the North American Free Trade Agreement (NAFTA) and the admittance of China to the World Trade Organization (WTO) were sold by the liberal state to the American people back in the 1990s, many promises were made and all of them have been broken.

The American worker was told that new, bright and count-less opportunities would open up as a result of this total plunge into free trade frameworks on a massive scale. The American people were promised more growth, better distributed and significant increases of income and standards of living, and a stronger dollar with more purchasing power. America was promised prosperity and the dawning of a new era of economic bonanza and justice for everybody and especially for the legitimate caste. No macroeconomic model could possibly prove that because it is not true. In fact, quite the opposite of what was promised actually materialized. America has gone through two decades of growing trade deficits, a sluggish economy compared with that of previous eras, a fall-off in the living standards of most Americans and especially workers, manufacturing unemployment, an epidemic of drug addiction, urban violence and chaos, homelessness, an explosion of private and public debt, and the growth of income and wealth inequality to grotesque and unsustainable levels.

The only beneficiary of that dive into the lunacy of free trade was the donor or usufructuary caste, by virtue of owning massive holdings in the multinational corporations trading in the stock market. Those entities profit from slave labor abroad through free trade and offshoring, and hence the liberal kakistocracy proceeded to do its job as diligently and illegitimately as the ruling caste required. Yay! Indeed, those mastodons of capital are much better off, but only at the expense of the nation as a whole, since there is not such a thing as a free lunch, especially when the scam of free trade is involved. No nation in the history of the world, and certainly not this nation, has ever established and developed a strong and diversified industrial base predicated on free trade. And without that base, the idea of a prosperous and free working population is just a pipe dream. Small farmers, as well as craftsmen, merchants and manual workers, including construction and industrial workers among others; these are the backbone of any productive society, and their overall well-being a predictor of whether or not a state is sustainable. I am confident that among that first subset in the third ring of expansion, those compeers will abound.

95. Articulation of political action through the understanding of constructs and the precarious situation thereunder

But what is the connection between this intricate web of constructs in the economic realm and the necessary creation of the first and subsequent subsets within the third ring of expansion? The constructs are the armor that protects and disguises the soft underbelly of the beast, i.e., its true economic reality. To be clear, this state is trudging miserably on very thin ice. It is certainly strong and massive, bleeding off health, prosperity and freedom from the phalanxes of workers like an unholy leech; however, its foundations are rotten not only morally and politically, but more importantly economically. Why more importantly? Because that is the wound through which the first and second circles will sow the seed of a deadly infection.

I talked about the first subset in the third circle as that composed of all those compeers who cannot be persuaded through passion or reason. They are too influenced by the variegated ways wherewith the state-leech keeps its hosts in the pen. We cannot teach them; they ought to teach themselves not through reason, but through a much more powerful force upon those with a weakened will: pain.

As I touched upon earlier, those with low tolerance to pain will fill the phalanxes of the first subset; those with a slightly higher tolerance will compose the second subset and so forth. The procedure of expansion will be the selfsame; hence I call all these subsets elements of the same third ring. And irrespective of the subset, all liberal converts will be embraced like true national-liberextremist brethren, for the accursed Leviathan's apostates are our longed-for proselytes, as the roaring enthusiasm of the waxing ranks reverberates throughout the land.

Pain will be instantiated every time economic reality worsens relative to the delusions that the constructs try to pass off as facts in the strictest sense; in other words, as observations in a phenomenological world. Therefore our goal is to unearth and intensify as much as possible the ugliness of reality as opposed to the construct that purports to represent it. In this way, at a certain pivotal moment and thenceforth, different segments of the populace will embrace the notion of the constructs as mere tools of mass delusion wielded by the state for its own survival and at the expense of the people. Those critical moments will be different for different subsets, depending upon their stubbornness in remaining obfuscated despite their pain. Indeed, the ways to counteract the state's mass propaganda and indoctrination will require a massive effort and patience before we can enjoy the righteous fruit!

But how can we (the first and second circles) go about exacting that pain? Very simply: by understanding the internal dynamics of those social constructs so as to exert force in the adequate direction, with the objective of exposing and amplifying the underlying rot.

For example:

- With regard to the construct of national debt and the national currency, a strategy of minimizing our tax liability (referring to compeers in the first two circles) and maximizing the expenses caused to the state through all and any possible program or agency is the right approach. Under an increasing fiscal pressure, the state will either borrow and print more money, or it will cut services throughout the body politic and perhaps starting with certain groups as opposed to others seen as more reliable supporters. Or it might opt to raise taxes on those who do not line up squarely with the interests of the state. Or perhaps a combination of all of the above. In any event, all those actions will push the state further down the path of destruction or they will exacerbate the pain and resentment of certain singled-out communities or the totality of the population. Those whose levels of tolerance to paucity of resources relative to their levels of indoctrination and alienation from their own wills are the lowest; those will be indeed the first to step onto the first subset in the third circle of expansion.

- In connection with the construct of unemployment, the adequate strategy is, yet again, push the state and the totality of the body politic in the direction of a frantic pursuit of more resources and the generation of as much scarcity thereof as possible, in order to generate intense and even unmanageable conflict and discomfort. In this context, the ranks of our compatriots are to register with the unemployment insurance agencies, to run the clock of their benefits and compensations, and to noise abroad their personal situations so as to generate discontent and even envy, and eventually the much-sought-out catharsis, one compatriot at a time.

- With respect to the construct of the stock market, the call to duty implies the execution, on a collective level starting with each one of us, of a withdrawal of as many assets as we possibly can from that market. There resides the strength of the donor, or usufructuary, or ruling caste. There to a significant extent, their fortunes abide. And with them, those of countless compatriots. These are the people for whom things look fine and dandy, and this state is nothing but the best we can aspire to and live in; these are the ones whose complacency will turn into overwhelming rage once they loose it all. These are the prime example of that substratum of the population who can only learn by teaching themselves, because their awareness, empathy and solidarity have been laid to waste in a cozy life subjected to the state's propaganda and indoctrination. These are the fellows living quite opulently in the suburbs, driving expensive electric vehicles and wondering why in the world does not everybody go out and purchase one of those so we can save the planet! The 21st-century version of "let them eat cake" if I ever saw one. These compatriots can and must be recruited into the third circle but it will take a great deal of fueled anger and a lot of persistence and patience.

- Another way to hurt and diminish the interests of large publicly traded companies is to refrain from doing business with them as customers, swapping that commerce out for business with local vendors, to the degree that this is possible. These massive corporations and conglomerates are the means by which the expansion and concentration of capital is effectuated and hence the generator of power for the usufructuary caste and the only state's raison d'être.

- Yet another revolutionary action would be seeking the legal discharge of all debts in our name. Most banks and financial institutions are consolidated and intertwined with one another, and they represent a huge percentage of the stock market. They are also vitally important in the flow of credit and capital, which is paramount for a functioning capitalistic system. If a sufficiently large number of clients rack up their credit card debt to intolerable limits, and subsequently seek out the protection of the courts; and if this collective discharge is carried out at unison within a certain time frame, there is no question that the consequences of this political action would be similar to those endured by the American dollar if all bondholders were to liquidate their holdings at the same time.

There is an issue that must be briefly addressed. And it is the possibility that some of the political actions to be taken by the first two circles, and by and by and in succession by the different subsets within the third circle, could potentially contain a trace of self-contradiction. In the instantiation of a double and contradictory—or even contrary—effect, the net impact must the the lodestar of whether to persevere with that action or not, and the vanguard of this revolution must remain flexible enough to veer off the charted course if the facts advise to do so. For example, the political action of switching from doing business with publicly traded corporations to doing business with local merchants, to the extent that this is possible, could have two contradictory effects: on the one hand, we hurt the usufructuaries of the state—which is an end unto itself—but on the other we spread contentment across the body politic and within our immediate social surroundings—which reinforces the state's grip on the people's will to power—These two effects are incompatible with one another, so it is up to the hardcore to assess the dynamic situation and self-adjust when the facts convey a clear picture of the net effect. This, no doubt, will require a massive effort of coordination and intercommunication; and the mechanisms to make this possible will have to be thoroughly discussed and meticulously carried out, in an exemplary display of gumption and conviction.

The list of theoretical political actions cannot be comprehensive. First, the possibilities here and now are almost endless; and furthermore as time goes by, new options will arise depending upon dynamic condItions which are very difficult to foresee. We will have to pay heed and spring to action as the opportunities present themselves.

96. Articulation of political action through the understanding of the worker's three economic dimensions

All the social constructs (or shall I call them statistical constructs?) that I have mentioned are useful insofar as the cloak always tells you something is being hidden underneath, its shielding of the mysterious object's true identity notwithstanding. So a social construct is both a disguise and a clue. As clues, they help us understand where the soft underbelly of the state is placed and how we can damage it as decisively as possible.

However, there is another way to envision the political actions that the first, second and subsequent rings can actuate in this existential fight. This route is much more straightforward, inasmuch as it is derived from the three economic, social and political dimensions of every worker:

1. A worker qua worker, i.e., the underseller of a commodity (labor power) and creator of social surplus value and social surplus product.

2. A worker qua consumer, i.e., the buyer of commodities and thus the transformer of commodity capital into money capital through parting ways with his wages, making the circulation of capital possible.

3. A worker qua taxpayer, i.e., the enabler of reproduction, expansion, and concentration of capital by sustaining the illegitimate state and hence making the exploitation thereof by the ruling caste possible.

1. From this social and economic dimension, we can infer the kind of political actions that can be carried out to weaken the leeching beast and dislodge it as much as possible from the body politic. Fundamentally, we ought to reduce the surplus value that we produce.

We could, for example, reduce the intensity of labor—only to the degree that dents productivity but not to the extent that our substitution for somebody else through the mechanism of wagslave labor would offset the costs associated with such a decision. After all, we should try to achieve our goals without self-immolation if we can avoid it.

We also could work part-time exclusively, supplementing our income with any kind of public assistance that we can lay our hands on.

Or we certainly could put out products and services of subpar quality and yet again, not to such a degree that our livelihoods would be imperiled.

Or we could deliberately increase the wear and tear on the means of production, which would redound to the detriment of the total social surplus value.

And thus, I have referred to the productivity, quantity, quality and efficiency of work in an all-encompassing approach to the concept of total surplus value.

These political actions are in and of themselves disgusting and wicked; but within the context of a revolutionary struggle against the parasite state, they become a present sacrifice of morality, so we can have a moral future.

A general national strike is the epitome of this kind of political action. In fact, it is a supra-action, insofar as it reduces the quantity of work to zero, and consequently the productivity, intensity and efficiency of work are concomitantly obliterated. It represents the total cessation of creation of social surplus value as long as the strike goes on. It is for this reason that the stewards and usufructuaries of this pestilent behemoth panic at the mere contemplation of such political action by the legitimate caste. No state whatsoever, including this one, can withstand a general national strike that lasts long enough, without economically, socially and politically collapsing unto itself. Therefore all historical attempts at this political action by the phalanxes of workers have been met with a medley of overwhelming brutality, legal persecution, guile, and bribery, carried out by an affrighted state and its security apparatus. Such an absolute stoppage of creation of social surplus value, or the suspension of the mechanism of wagslave labor, is an eventuality that the state will try to suffocate at any and all costs, without exception. That type of strike is guaranteed to topple any regime and wipe out any state, if and only if it lasts as long as it takes, given the circumstances specific to each case. Sometimes a week could suffice. In other cases it might take several months, depending on how rotten and internally unstable the state is. This kind of political action is endogenously difficult to instantiate as well, the reason being that most workers lack the funds to power through a long period without any income. However, just as soldiers in countless wars throughout history were able to keep on the fight, very often successfully, enduring the most atrocious of scarcities; we should therefore assume that the mettle of our bellicose ranks could not possibly fall short of that very same standard, if and when this action needs to be taken.

2. From this social and economic dimension we deduce a set of more political actions against the tyrant state, their common denominator being the disruption in the circulation of capital. This circulation is a prerequisite for the reproduction thereof, from which proceeds the expansion and concentration of capital in the hands of the usufructuary caste. That expansion and concentration is ultimately the illegitimate reason for the liberal state to exist.

Accordingly, we would bring our expenditures to a bare minimum, never resorting to credit and only spending on necessities of life. The contrary political action, deduced from the understanding of social constructs and the fragile reality veiled by them, is also effective (as I already discussed). However, any middle ground between these two efficacious and opposite extremes will feed the Leviathan rather than detract from it. If we could muster an army of worker-consumers (I will call it the first two rings plus, perhaps, a few subsets within the third ring) acting in unison to undermine the state, they would have to either accumulate on purpose massive amounts of debt and have it legally discharged, or live a very frugal, simple life well below their means, keeping their savings (if any) away from the banking system, so that the circulation of capital and therefore its reproduction is massively decelerated and disrupted .... Nobody has ever said that the life of a revolutionary is easy or stable, or without certain sacrifices!

3. This is the political dimension per se: the worker as the bankroller of the state. It is the most obvious and direct flow of sweat or work/money, or vital energy and time, also known as labor power, from the body politic and into the organization of the liberal state, which in turn transforms it into political action for the benefit of the usufructuary caste.

This is the most evident, albeit not necessarily the most abhorrent form (that honor will be forevermore bestowed upon the worker qua worker dimension) of exploitation that the whole of the working population is subjected to in this babelic kakotopia. It is akin to the allegorical scene of a victim of kidnapping being forced to dig her own grave after she has been raped over and over again. Indeed, workers never have been consulted by democratic means as to whether they want to live under the yoke of the liberal dystopia, ergo they have been kidnapped. Moreover, they are being forced to slave away to financially sustain this mastodonic Leviathan (the most expensive state in human history), ergo they are being continuously raped. And finally, their sweat and tears (for the compeers who drudge for a living as I do comprehend every descriptive word that I am using) are morphed into the policies that, devised and carried out by the state, impoverish and enslave us even further, into oblivion; hence, we are forced to dig our own grave. The kidnapping and the digging will only cease when Goliath comes tumbling down after the righteous strike, i.e., when the circle of expansion has reached the third ring and incorporated therein the necessary number of subsets.

The constant rape, however, can and must be stopped as a prelude thereto. This entails political actions aimed at minimizing the tax liability, and thus bringing the flow from the body politic to the illegitimate state to a meager trickle. An instantiation of such a policy would be substituting part-time work for full-time work and bridging the income gap with either public assistance if possible, or perhaps a transition to a minimalistic existence. That is a case of lowering the taxable income. But within the wicked tax scheme of this state, a long list of deductions and credits are awarded to those who comply with what the state considers good behavior, or situations that are deemed worthy of help if the people involved belong to the right race, or have the right number of children, or choose the right place to live, etc. It is not easy to compile an exhaustive list. But the gist of such a list is clear: put yourself in the right group, namely in a group seen by the state to be potentially useful for the expansion and concentration of capital, or otherwise prone to adherence or loyalty; and then you can expect tax rewards.

With a bit of imagination and desire for the badly needed expansion of the rings of revolution, the possibilities of what the state calls "tax code" or a tax law many thousands of pages long, should be immense. I am sure that my compeers' imagination on this subject matter will yield the desired outcome. The general idea behind this political action or the minimizing of the workers' tax liability, coincides with the conclusions reached when analyzing the national debt construct, and therefore the political actions that emerge from both approaches are the same in this case. When they are not the same, as I showed when talking about the implications of personal debt, they are still not contrary. So whatever approach we use to tackle the problem and decide on a course of revolutionary action, as long as we do it in an orderly and coordinated fashion, eventually it all will work out.

And in connection with taxes, I would like to draw attention now to certain smoking gun, hidden in plain sight, that speaks volumes as to the depravity of the laissez-faire Leviathan and the internal schizophrenia that characterizes it. Mulcts, fines and tickets are, as I herein commented upon, a wicked subterfuge that this state (at the local, state or federal levels of administration) utilizes to fund itself, under the cloak of a behavior-bending scheme anchored on moral grounds. It is telling, not on ethical bases, but on strictly logical ones, how paradoxical this state is. A paradox that betrays its rotten nature. For the projection of any paradox into the realm of the moral is always a lie, a confusion, a rot. This putrefaction is thus explained: the state's finances are contingent upon the people breaking the laws of the state. The more abundant the law-breaking behavior the better for the state. The more abundant the law-abiding behavior, the worse off the state finds itself. But if within this state or any other, we accept as a tautology, that law-abiding behavior is good, and that law-breaking behavior is bad; then the truth table of this paradox reads thus: good is bad, and bad is good. This satanic state thrives when the people are allegedly bad and withers away when the people are allegedly good. So much so, that countless administrations throughout the land would go bankrupt rather quickly if they found themselves deprived of the funds raised through all those schemes, by virtue of the people abiding by the law at all times. And this is the reason why I characterize law-abiding behavior that minimizes the payments of fines and tickets as a revolutionary political action. Its effectiveness will continually increase as the rings of expansion become ever larger, as is the case with the rest of actions already broached.

Finally, the way that coordination and expansion of the rings of politically active compatriots is accomplished will be a matter of dynamic discussion and ongoing assessment. Consequently, it would be in vain to go further into minute details when such exercise is subjected to a huge number of possible developments and conditions. But the philosophical underpinnings and the practical linchpins of this revolutionary enterprise have been adequately laid out. The will to see them through, in my case no matter the cost, is ultimately the only necessary condition for success, since the beast is putrid to the core and ripe for decapitation. I will meet all my compeers along the way, and this realization warms my heart more than I can express with words. So thank you all very much for that.

97. Categorical avoidance of suicidal actions

I have already addressed this issue, albeit tangentially, when I exposed the in terrorem and repressive character of the statutes on advocating overthrow of government, seditious conspiracy and rebellion or insurrection. I will now reiterate the dangers that these statutes manifest, in the backdrop of a state willing and ready to enact the oblivion of its own people in order to survive at all costs. It is a matter of basic reason that this state would much prefer to be able to identify all and every of its enemies out in the open, and before they expand in numbers or strengthen the impetus of their political actions. That way it could easily pick off the threats within the body politic before they spur full-blown political actions by themselves or other committed discontents.

It is for this reason that the first two circles of expansion and perhaps the first subsets in the third circle, if possible, must be forgathered not quite out in the open, but with a certain degree of bashfulness and discretion. Of course, the state will catch wind of our enterprise as soon as this work is published, and even before, since I communicate with others through electronic means on a regular basis. It stands to reason that any book or publication of any type whatsoever that features prominently words like "liberal state", or "free workers", let alone "party", will right away be flagged and investigated. That is the first and foremost duty of the state's security apparatus; always remain on the prowl for potential dissidents and firebrands. Its second duty is the destruction of the threat by the utmost covert means, even better if the threat is not made public and the people in the know few and far between. Just as a sapling requires special care upon being planted in new soil, and so is given the chance to settle in and by and by take root, our party and movement will likewise follow in the same footsteps, for we are verily the tree of life to the future organic state.

Wherefore, suicidal charges, akin to political actions out in the open when the sapling is still taking root, are not wise. Nothing that makes the criminal repression easier is wise, and hence it should be avoided. The duration of this phase in the struggle is difficult to estimate. It could be a matter of a few months, or two decades, or a lifetime and beyond, or any other period of time. I am not prepared to offer a timeline, since the variables are so many and their dynamic variation so unpredictable; and the interrelations between them as well as the exogenous and endogenous feedback so difficult to compute, that I will exercise prudence in a humble spirit. As good mathematicians know when a problem is too complex to be modeled with a system of differential equations, no matter the urge for a dynamic comprehension of the foregoing problem, I likewise know the limits of long-term planning, and I would rather wait to enter the ongoing feedback into the calculations and remain flexible and alert, lest life proves itself more stubborn than my desires.

It is for this reason that I urge all my compeers to bring about all the political actions that I have listed, but without exposing themselves to legal prosecution. The profile offered while in the first stages of development should be as inconspicuous as possible, in order to make the state's repression ineffective. It is in this spirit of the funambulist's initial stepping onto the treacherous tightrope, that I wrote the legal disclaimer. Ultimately, it is no guarantee of protection from the rabid hegemon we are taking on. As I said, I enter this battle aware that I will not emerge unscathed. To the contrary, I could perhaps not even make it through, in some way or another, and that is a sacrifice that I am ready to offer.

The foregone conclusion to our efforts, the organic state, is a matter of when and never of if. But in the labyrinth of that when, many of us, regretfully, will be lost. These compeers will be the crimson fountainhead of that political intension that we so desperately need and long for; and they will also be the martyrs that the state will acknowledge and honor, for as long as it endures.

◄▻————————◅►

98. The logical conclusion

Throughout this work, I have expounded on the logical nature of the state whose founding we hope to undertake as soon as our people smites the ogre, and before his blood flows through the land.

But something logical, in the sense described in this work, is univocally destined to happen. It is something inevitable, a foregone conclusion. It is the syllogistic inference from true premises.

I have steered clear of ideological temptations because I do not have any. Ideology is anathema to political philosophy and to truth, and therefore nowhere in this book have I introduced any kind of ideological concepts whatsoever. All the premises were statements of fact, deontological or phenomenological; the conclusions soundly deduced from them and the party principles firmly based upon these conclusions.

The National Liberextremist State: A state begotten by free people through the party, and not a party born out of the state.

Ours is a logical, and not an ideological revolution, as I have indicated many times over in this work. And the only irrational or even mystic element to it, although very real, is the driving force of the will. This is the supreme and most divine energy in each human being. The will is the seal of God deep within, and it is the essence of the archetype of the Self. But this matter is ontological in nature and it will be properly addressed in a subsequent work. For the time being, suffice to say that this is a movement of logic and it will resolve itself in a causal sequence, and therefore the conclusion will be necessary and not contingent (unlike all other past revolutions which were based on ideology). The state thus formed is not one among many; it is the only possible one. In other words, we are not making history; history is making us. We are inevitable.

The upcoming battle already has a winner. However, many other aspects are up in the air, from our standpoint in the present time: the duration of the struggle; the identity of its victims; and of course, the specifics of the unfolding of events, as to changing strategies, timelines and so on.

◄————————►

99. The end of the beginning: the formal founding

We are embarking on the adventure of our lives. Irrespective of future events, the wheels of history are in motion. We are overcoming the stifling weight of the liberal paradigm, and we are defiantly staring down the Leviathan, armored finally with awareness, truth, knowledge and virtue. We dare to stir it all up in the sacrosanct ciborium wrought out of logic and will, and we will enjoy every drop of that sweet ambrosia up until the vessel is empty and every cell in us is ready for battle. The cause could not be more just, nor the company more worthy. Sally forth, compeers! And know that the people one day will laud you as a victor or as a martyr; either way your glorious lot will be branded in the annals of history through blood and fire, for everybody in the new state to heed and to revere! Yes, you did it! In your relentless march toward the judge, you created the most perfect vessel! A state begotten by the people and their party, and not a people and their party born out of a state! I will meet you along the journey, and perchance even over the horizon, where the light meets the land and whence our destiny is beckoning us forth!

So long and Godspeed.

AFTERWORD

I, Ivan Muñiz-Brown, hereby solemnly declare the America Free Workers Party formally founded.

Thursday, July 18th, 2024

Hollywood, California

www.ingramcontent.com/pod-product-compliance
Lightning Source LLC
Chambersburg PA
CBHW020330270326
41926CB00007B/126